Obie—
Thanks for introducing me to
computers all those years
ago at Hiram College!
— Howard '77

Digital Imaging

Theory and Applications

Howard E. Burdick

McGraw-Hill

New York   San Francisco   Washington, D.C.   Auckland   Bogotá
Caracas   Lisbon   London   Madrid   Mexico City   Milan
Montreal   New Delhi   San Juan   Singapore
Sydney   Tokyo   Toronto

Library of Congress Cataloging-in-Publication Data

Burdick, Howard E.
  Digital imaging : theory and applications / Howard E. Burdick.
      p.   cm.
  Includes index.
  ISBN 0-07-913059-3 (hardcover)
  1. Image processing—Digital techniques. I. Title.
TA1637.B87   1997
621.36'7—dc21   96-50397
                                                            CIP

McGraw-Hill

*A Division of The **McGraw·Hill** Companies*

1 2 3 4 5 6 7 8 9 0 DOC/DOC 9 0 1 0 9 8 7

P/N 008953-1
PART OF
ISBN 0-07-913059-3

The sponsoring editor for this book was Brad Schepp, the editing supervisor was David E. Fogarty, and the production supervisor was Suzanne W. B. Rapcavage. It was set in Century Schoolbook by Joanne Morbit of McGraw-Hill's Professional Book Group Hightstown composition unit.

Printed and bound by R.R. Donnelley & Sons Company.

 This book is printed on recycled, acid-free paper containing a minimum of 50% recycled, de-inked fiber.

McGraw-Hill books are available at special quantity discounts to use as premiums and sales promotions, or for use in corporate training programs. For more information, please write to the Director of Special Sales, McGraw-Hill, 11 West 19th Street, New York, NY 10011. Or contact your local bookstore.

Contents

Preface

Throughout my career I have had the luxury of being associated with a lot of intelligent engineers, artists, managers, and salespeople. Over the years I have had many discussions with them about the concepts and applications of digital imagery. In fact, it is because of these people that I wrote this book.

Something dawned on me a few years ago. It seemed like I was explaining the same things over and over again. "What is a look-up table?" "How does a high-pass filter work?" "Why does an image look fine on my computer screen but looks terrible when I print it out?" I would usually refer these inquiries to one of the many excellent books available on the subject of digital imagery; it was much easier and consumed less of my time. Very often, though, they would return in a day or two stating that the material I gave them contained only introductory information or, at the opposite end of the spectrum, were mathematically overwhelming.

Why was this? I began perusing the books, most of which I knew forward and backward after years of use, and tried to place myself in their shoes, as someone not well-versed in the subject. They were right! There were two distinct types of books: a few that were light subject overviews and many that were graduate-level image processing texts. Neither type satisfied their needs. The engineers needed answers to get a programming job done and did not have the time to digest a page or two of integrals and proofs. The digital artists needed to understand the processes on a deeper level so they could do more than just make pictures "look pretty."

This book is the result of that epiphany. I have tried to find the middle ground between the two extremes of existing digital image processing books. If you are a programmer, I trust you will find the thirty test programs useful. If you are artistically inclined, this book will help bridge the gap between technology and your art. And if you are a manager or are simply interested in the subject, I think you'll like the information about this wide and growing field of computer science.

Too often in the field of digital imagery there is reluctance, especially amongst technically oriented people, to ask questions. Whether it is pride or, more frequently, simply not knowing the right questions to ask, they stumble along, "reinventing the wheel" as they go and learn, usually the hard way, how image processing works. My goal is to answer some of those questions because, as the old saying goes, there are no stupid questions, just stupid answers.

To meet this goal I have written this book a bit differently than others on the subject. After the introduction, Chapter 2 jumps into the structure of digital images, in particular, relating how the real world that we see translates into the computer's world of bits and bytes. Chapter 3 discusses what too many books ignore but is probably the most important aspect of digital imagery: input and output devices. Chapters 4 through 7 are more what you would expect from a book on this subject: lots of explanation and implementation of various image processing algorithms. Chapter 8 deals with how digital images are stored in memory and on disk while Chapter 9 concentrates on how images are displayed on computer monitors. Chapter 10 is a survey of the wide variety of digital image processing application areas and, finally, Chapter 11 is a list of books, periodicals, and Internet sites for further reading and investigation.

Naturally, no one writes a book like this without help, and I have had a lot of it from a network of family, friends, and business associates. I would like to list everyone that has helped, but I know I would leave out someone. Every business, government, and educational contact that has supplied me with images or other information is listed in the last chapter, all of them have a presence on the World Wide Web. In addition, I wish to thank the people I have had the pleasure to work with throughout the years. A special thank you for the companies for which I have worked, namely Texas Instruments, Visual Information Technologies, and my current employer, Dream Quest Images, that have provided me with the opportunity to learn about this exciting subject.

And where would I be without Lois, my wife? She is my human anchor in a sea of technology. She has always been there with encouragement, insight, and sometimes a whip to keep my writing on schedule. And to top it off, she's a darn good editor! I can only wish others the kind of happiness, love, and good fortune Lois has given me for over twenty years.

Two other people I wish to thank are Mike Snell, my agent, and Brad Schepp, my editor. They were willing to take a chance on a first-time author.

I'd like to make one last offer to you, the reader. Feel free to contact me via email at the address listed below if you have questions or comments and visit my web site for more information on digital imagery.

HOWARD E. BURDICK
Simi Valley, California

hburdick@west.net
http://www.west.net/~hburdick

Digital Imaging

An Introduction to Digital Imaging

Color photographs adorn the pages of newspapers. Medical x rays and CAT scans probe inside human bodies. Spacecraft whiz by on movie screens. Every day we see images of all sorts and increasingly, whether we realize it or not, those images have been processed, shaped, or otherwise generated and altered by computers. The field of digital image processing is expanding at a tremendous rate, with no indication that this trend will change in the foreseeable future. In the last few years, what was a science reserved for a few specialists has now moved into many areas of daily life. Today this expansion is making itself known on that greatest of communication highways: the Internet. We can only imagine where this path will lead tomorrow, as digital image processing becomes as common in our communal culture as word processing and personal computers are today.

Unfortunately, not many understand the concepts and basic functions of this science. Digital image processing has, since its inception more than a quarter of a century ago, been the domain of those who could afford the powerful computers needed to work with the massive amounts of information that these pictures contain. This is changing as computer pictures are popping up all over, thanks to the speed of 100-plus megahertz microprocessors and cheap gigabyte disks and

CD-ROMs. A dentist can review digital x rays on a computer screen, or a weather forecaster can download the latest satellite pictures. Before they and others can fully appreciate and utilize what they see, however, they must gain a basic understanding of the data with which they work.

Who Should Read This Book?

This book is designed for programmers and software engineers involved in creating digital image processing applications. Its intent is to provide basic information about the subject without becoming mired in the complex mathematics inherent in the underlying theories. It also is useful for those who have little or no knowledge of the subject but are exposed to digital images during the course of their normal activities. Computer artists, earth scientists, and home hobbyists will find the overviews of digital imagery helpful.

Other readers may be more interested in understanding how various image processing techniques work and how to implement them. For them, the programming examples and technical information will be most useful.

All programming examples in this book are written in ANSI-C. It is not the intent of this book to provide complete application programs for various digital image processing markets. That is a task best left to those who are experts in their fields. What these programming examples do provide are concise, easy-to-read examples of the algorithms discussed. Well-tailored software to meet specific needs is best implemented after an operational sample has been digested.

History of Digital Image Processing

It was not too many years ago, in the early 1960s, that NASA's Ranger 7 spacecraft began sending fuzzy television pictures of the moon's surface back to earth. Those pictures needed to be enhanced so that scientists could extract details of potential landing sites for the upcoming Apollo manned missions. The Jet Propulsion Laboratory (JPL) in Pasadena, Calif., was given the task. Thus began the specialized computer field of digital image processing. As with many other technologies created by the space program, it was not long before people found other uses for this new science.

The military and intelligence aspects of pictures from space were obvious during the 1960s and 1970s, and the desire to obtain more images of higher quality grew insatiable. But there were other uses for pictures of the earth. Multispectral images, that is, pictures taken at frequencies other than the normal red/green/blue, gave crop and timber forecasters a new tool with which to work. Geophysicists at oil companies could search remote lands without leaving their offices. City planners could track urban sprawl and pollution.

More down-to-earth uses of digital image processing soon were found. In the middle 1970s, the medical field discovered its potential with a new device called the Computerized Axial Tomography (CAT) scanner. The Magnetic Resonance Imagery (MRI) scanner followed in the mid-1980s. The publishing industry followed suit, and today almost all aspects of prepress operations are computerized, with digital imagery playing a major role. Similarly, manufacturing was, and continues to be, revolutionized by robot machines that actually see. In the late 1980s, digital image processing found its way into the entertainment field and is now commonplace.

Today, a great growth of digital imagery is occurring as this science opens itself to a wider audience. Each year, as computers become faster and cheaper and as communication technology enables the practical dissemination of digital imagery, more and more people have access to it. Video teleconferencing is becoming a viable way in which to do business, and home computers can display and manipulate pictures. As will be discussed in the next section and in following chapters, digital image processing requires more raw computer power and storage space than almost any other discipline. This is also why this exciting science only recently has become accessible to more people. Luckily, this accessibility trend will continue, because in every application area in which digital imagery has found a foothold, it soon becomes irreplaceable.

Human beings are visual creatures. We gain most of our sense of the world around us through our eyes. Sight conveys a wealth of information to us in the blink of an eye; we don't even have to think about it. The old saying about one picture being worth a thousand words is no longer true. A digital image easily may contain 10 million bytes of data. The average word contains six or seven letters, and it takes one byte to hold a letter. Therefore, the updated saying for the 1990s should be, "One picture is worth a *million* words." Computers have opened many new frontiers for us over the last 40 years, and image processing promises to be one of the greatest.

Text versus Graphics versus Images

It might seem odd, but one of the greatest difficulties in the field of digital imaging is how to identify a digital image. In the broadest sense, everything that appears on a computer screen, whether it is black text on a white field, a bar graph showing next year's projected sales, or a scanned picture of Aunt Mabel at the Fourth of July picnic, is a digital image. A digital image is a discrete array, usually two-dimensional, of picture elements, or *pixels*, the intensities of which are represented by

0:	NUL	32:	SP	64:	@	96:	
1:	SOH	33:	!	65:	A	97:	a
2:	STX	34:	"	66:	B	98:	b
3:	ETX	35:	#	67:	C	99:	c
4:	EOT	36:	$	68:	D	100:	d
5:	ENQ	37:	%	69:	E	101:	e
6:	ACK	38:	&	70:	F	102:	f
7:	BEL	39:	'	71:	G	103:	g
8:	BS	40:	(	72:	H	104:	h
9:	HT	41:	)	73:	I	105:	i
10:	LF	42:	*	74:	J	106:	j
11:	VT	43:	+	75:	K	107:	k
12:	FF	44:	`	76:	L	108:	l
13:	CR	45:	-	77:	M	109:	m
14:	SO	46:	.	78:	N	110:	n
15:	SI	47:	/	79:	O	111:	o
16:	DLE	48:	0	80:	P	112:	p
17:	DC1	49:	1	81:	Q	113:	q
18:	DC2	50:	2	82:	R	114:	r
19:	DC3	51:	3	83:	S	115:	s
20:	DC4	52:	4	84:	T	116:	t
21:	NAK	53:	5	85:	U	117:	u
22:	SYN	54:	6	86:	V	118:	v
23:	ETB	55:	7	87:	W	119:	w
24:	CAN	56:	8	88:	X	120:	x
25:	EM	57:	9	89:	Y	121:	y
26:	SUB	58:	:	90:	Z	122:	z
27:	ESC	59:	;	91:	[	123:	{
28:	FS	60:	<	92:	\	124:		
29:	GS	61:	=	93:	]	125:	}
30:	RS	62:	>	94:	^	126:	~
31:	US	63:	?	95:	_	127:	DEL

Figure 1.1 ASCII code.

numbers. The structure and make-up of a digital image will be explained in the following chapter. Unfortunately, however, it's not this easy.

Objects that are manipulated by a computer can be broken into three categories: text, graphics, and images. All of these, of course, are composed of numbers or, more basically, strings of ones and zeros. Text is easy to identify. It is simply characters: the alphabet, numbers, punctuation marks, and a few special symbols such as %, +, and <\@>. Each character is assigned a unique number between 0 and 127, as listed in Fig. 1.1.

This number assignment is known as the American Standard Code for Information Interchange, or ASCII. It is the same on almost all computers across the country, and forms a common ground for computer communications. When a computer is given the number 50 as an ASCII code, it translates that number (which is 00110010 in binary notation or 32 in hexadecimal) into a series of pixels such as that shown in Fig. 1.2 to form the desired character 2. Of course, there can be many types of 2's: There can be large ones, small ones, maybe in italics or bold, but coded as ASCII 50, they are always recognized as the character 2.

Figure 1.2 qualifies as a digital image because it is an array of pixels, each of which has an intensity represented by a number. (Here those numbers are simply 0 or 1, which represent black or white.)

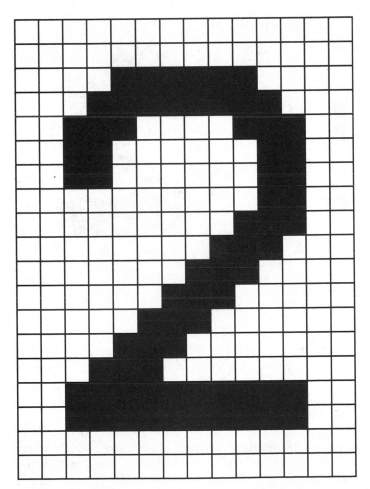

Figure 1.2 Character "2" pixel array.

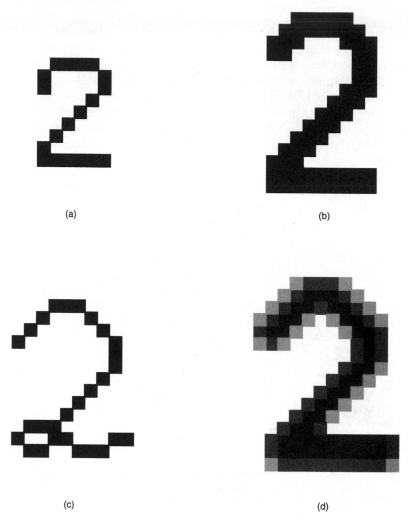

(a)

(b)

(c)

(d)

Figure 1.3 Various "2" pixel arrays.

Simply by changing the characteristics of the pixel array, the character 2 can take many forms, as shown in Fig. 1.3, but in all situations the ASCII number 50 is all that is needed to generate the character. In particular, notice the array of pixels in Fig. 1.3d, which differs from the rest because its pixel values are not simply 0 or 1 (black or white), but include shades of gray.

Not all entries in the ASCII table are used to generate printable or displayable characters. Special or *control* characters, as they are known, are used to provide text format or communication capabilities. For example, the number 10 (LF) tells the computer to generate a line feed: to move down one line before printing the next character.

Similarly, the number 13 (CR) indicates that a carriage return operation should be executed. Other numbers such as 6 (ACK) and 21 (NAK) are used for communication between computers.

Greater confusion arises when we move away from text and begin to look at graphics. Graphics is a huge area of computer science that is concerned with displaying mathematical formulae of some sort to the user. Unlike text, there is no set standard of numeric values that translate into known pixel arrays that represent characters. There are, however, several standards that govern the data structure and processing of graphical information, such as the Programmer's Hierarchical Interactive Graphics System, or *PHIGS*.

Figure 1.4 shows several simple graphical objects: a line, a circle, and a polygon. These objects can be held within the computer by just a few simple instructions: draw a line from point a to point b, draw a circle with its center at point c with a radius of r, draw a polygon with vertices w, x, y, and z and fill with a color. These elemental objects can be grouped to form structures such as the borders and icons that surround windows of a modern computer display. They can be very complex, such as dinosaurs that run across the movie screen, or the

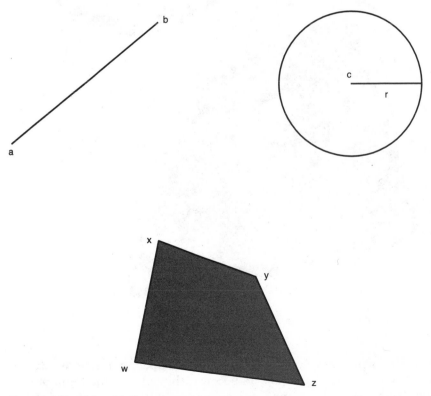

Figure 1.4 Graphics objects.

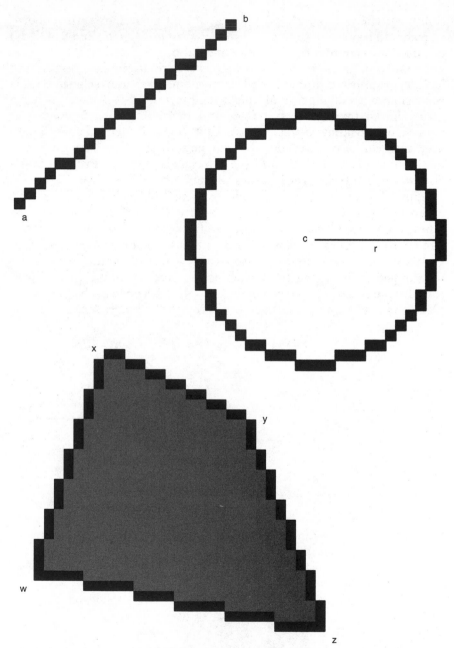

Figure 1.5 Graphics objects as pixel arrays.

simulated wind flow around an aircraft at supersonic speeds. But no matter how intricate the objects become, they all are made up of simpler structures such as lines, circles, and polygons.

The process of converting mathematical objects into something that a user can view on a computer display is called *scan conversion*, or *rendering*. During this process, the computer takes each formula in the data structure and, just as with ASCII code numbers, converts it to an array of pixels. Figure 1.5 shows the same simple objects of Fig. 1.4 drawn as arrays of pixels.

So text and graphical objects eventually become arrays of pixels of specific intensity values, which is the broad definition of digital images. But this is not what someone thinks of when they talk about digital images. What does come to mind is something more like a photograph. A narrower definition of a digital image, then, is *a set of data that never exists as anything other than an array of pixels*. It is unlike text, because text can be saved concisely as ASCII numbers that invoke predefined pixel patterns, or as graphics that can be stored as a series of commands to draw lines, circle, or polygons. A digital image must be saved as discrete, individual pixels in order to maintain its look and feel. A picture of a landscape has very subtle variations in color, sharpness, and depth, characteristics that are extremely difficult, if not impossible, to represent in a textual or graphical format.

This leads to a method of identifying whether something is a digital graphic or a digital image. If the object or objects that comprise a scene exist only within the computer as mathematical formulae, and not in the real world, it is graphics. If the scene exists outside of the computer and is brought, or *imported*, into the computer, it is imagery. The three-dimensional pie chart shown in Fig. 1.6a is graphics: it does not exist in the real world. The photograph shown in Fig. 1.6b is imagery: The fine detail of plants and architecture are a reproduction of reality. Sometimes it is difficult to tell what is real and what is not. A great amount of effort is spent trying to create computer-generated images that look real, an approach called *photorealism*, but that is still graphics. Similarly, real-world images of three-dimensional brain scans look as if they were generated by a computer, but that is still imagery.

That every pixel of a digital image must be defined and stored as a separate piece of data partially explains why digital imagery is only now becoming widespread. Only a few hundred bytes of data are required to maintain a full page of text. The same size display of graphical information may require only a few thousand bytes of data, but to fill the same area with a digital image requires several *million* bytes of information. Only in the past few years have computer disks and tapes become large enough and cheap enough to hold this much data. The speed of today's microprocessors has made it feasible to manage this much information efficiently and at a reasonable price. As a general rule-of-thumb, computer graphics require about 10 times the storage and processing capability required for text, and digital image processing requires 10 times that needed for graphics. Luckily,

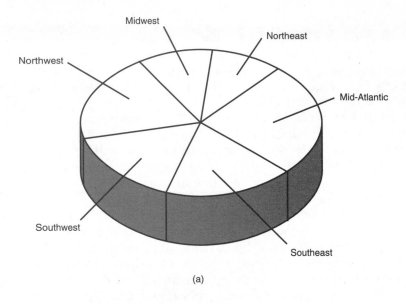

(a)

(b)

Figure 1.6 Graphics vs. imagery. *(Image courtesy of Eastman Kodak Co.)*

advances in computer technology will continue, and will make digital image processing even more practical in the future.

Source Code Examples

Throughout this book are many examples of computer source code that demonstrate the implementation of various digital image processing functions. All examples are written in ANSI C and are as clear and straightforward as possible. Each is written as a small, stand-alone program, with the assumption that you can fill in the necessary routines for reading and writing files and displaying the images for inspection. Whenever possible, sample images are printed to show a "before-and-after" effect of the process in question.

It should be noted that, with work by the programmer, the sample code shown here can be made to run more efficiently. Because these examples try to communicate the concepts of the operations in question, no short cuts have been taken to make the code run faster, which would detract from readability. This is especially true with the neighborhood operators. Besides, part of the fun of programming is making your own code run as fast as possible. These examples are presented as a guide, and you are encouraged to implement them as needed in your own applications, and to modify them in whatever way necessary to gain the greatest efficiency and functionality.

Image Structure

The world that we see is an image created in our minds. There are certain characteristics and a definite structure to our vision. Most of us see in wide-angle, and in vivid color. Our two eyes give us binocular vision that allows us to perceive three dimensions. We can see in bright sunlight or in nearly total darkness.

Analog Eyes and Digital Computers

Human vision is *analog*, a term defined to describe data that is represented by continuously variable physical quantities. This means that things blend smoothly for us: The blazing red horizon of a sunset merges seamlessly with the deep azure of the approaching night sky. Our ability to differentiate shades of hue and color saturation is almost limitless. We can see things that are very large, and at the same time things that are very small.

Computers can only begin to simulate the amazing nature and capabilities of what comes naturally to us. When a real-world image is captured by a computer, this infinite and continuous range of sizes, intensities, and colors must be truncated. The combination of physical characteristics that we so easily integrate in our mind's eye must be converted into numbers of limited scope before they can be used by the computer. The image becomes *digital,* and the physical characteristics are no longer *continuous*, but become *discrete*.

Whereas human vision can distinguish intensity or brightness levels on some arbitrary scale of, say, 1 through 100 (including all fractional numbers such as 1.5, 27.447, and 18.23), a digital image might only be able to differentiate levels of whole numbers like 1, 27, and 18. The same is true with color. The human eye can distinguish a nearly infinite number of different shades of red, but there might be only a few hundred (or at most, a few thousand) shades of red that a computer can distinguish. In other words, human vision has much greater *resolution* than the digital images of a computer.

If digital images are so inferior to what we see, then we could with some validity ask the question: Why should we even bother with them? The answer lies in what we can do with and to those images once they are in the computer. The world of human vision now can be converted to numbers and, because computers like to operate on numbers, there are nearly unlimited numbers of ways to manipulate the digital images, manipulation that we never could accomplish with our eyes.

All the colors of a digital image can be reversed to give us a negative of what we normally see. We can rotate the digital image at any given angle and we can scale it to any size. Multiple digital images can be combined to form a scene that does not exist in reality. Colors can be modified and changed to enhance or diminish the importance of objects in a scene. Like photography, digital images can freeze a point in time, something that our fleeting sense of vision cannot do.

Digital images also can see into areas that human vision cannot. Figure 2.1 is a diagram of the electromagnetic spectrum. From this we can see that the visible spectrum, energy wavelengths between about 400 to 700 nanometers to which our eyes are sensitive, consume only a tiny fraction of what is available. Certain sensors can generate digital images that allow us to "see" in the microwave, infrared, ultraviolet, or even x-ray regions of the spectrum. When regarded in this way, digital images can be thought of as extending the capabilities of human vision.

These capabilities can extend even beyond the electromagnetic spectrum. An ultrasound image of an unborn child lets us see with sound, and an MRI scan creates a digital image based on the responses of electrons, atoms, molecules, and nuclei to a magnetic field. So while digital imagery can never completely duplicate the intricacies of what our eyes see, it is a tool that allows us to extend our sense of sight into areas that were never before accessible.

Resolution: Spatial and Depth

The quality of data conversion from the analog world to digits for the computer is dictated by *resolution*. There are two types of resolution that govern digital imagery, *spatial resolution* and *depth resolution*.

Consider the picture shown in Fig. 2.2a. If this were a scene that we were viewing with our eyes, we would see all of its subtle shades of color. If our eyes were good enough, we also could see the fine detail in addition to the principal objects. This analog scene is continuous in detail (spatial resolution) and color (depth resolution.) But we have learned already that digital images have less information than reality.

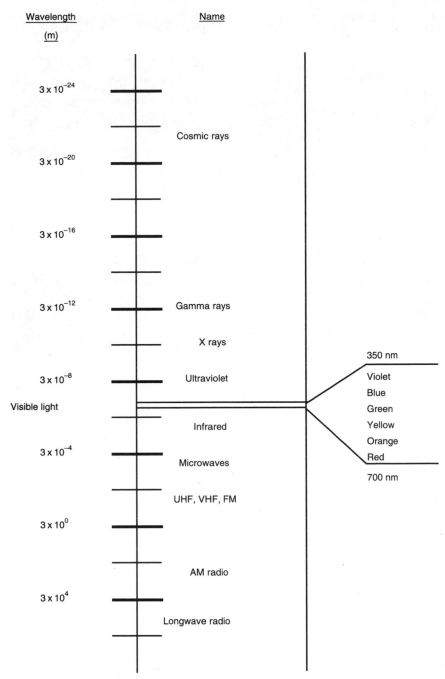

Figure 2.1 Electromagnetic spectrum.

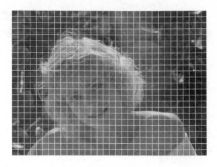

(a) Natural Image

(b) Grid Overlay

(c) 32x24 Spatial Resolution

(d) 64x48 Spatial Resolution

Figure 2.2 Spatial resolution. *(Image courtesy of Eastman Kodak Co.)*

How will this scene be degraded once it is *digitized* as it is brought into the computer? Let's investigate spatial resolution first.

Figure 2.2b is the same image with a grid overlaid upon it. It splits the image into 32 pieces in the horizontal dimension and 24 pieces in the vertical dimension. As can be seen, the detail of the image can still be seen between the lines of the grid, and many intensity values can be differentiated. What if we now impose the restriction that allows the entire area within each square to be represented by only a single intensity value? The resulting image is shown in Fig. 2.2c. The image still is somewhat recognizable, but all fine detail is lost. In other words, the digitized image in Fig. 2.2c. has *low spatial resolution*.

Spatial resolution is usually determined by the sensor used to digitize the image. The digital image in Fig. 2.2c has a spatial resolution of 32-by-24 pixels, which is usually written as 32×24. The horizontal dimension is usually referred to as x and the vertical dimension is y, with the origin, location (0,0), in the upper left corner. If each pixel needs 1 byte of computer storage space to hold its value, saving this digital image would require a total of 768 bytes (32 times 24 pixels, times 1 byte per pixel).

Now suppose that we captured the same scene with a different sensor, one that has higher spatial resolution, say 64×48 pixels, or twice the resolution of the first sensor. The resulting image is shown in Fig. 2.2d. It is obvious that this image can convey finer detail about the scene. It has a higher spatial resolution. But there is a cost involved. Even though the resolution of this image is only twice as high as the 32×24 pixel image, it requires 3072 bytes to store (64 times 48 times 1), or four times the amount of space required for the lower-resolution image. This is because digital images are *two-dimensional* data sets. If one room in your house were 10 feet by 10 feet in size, for example, the area of the room is 100 sq. ft. If another room were twice that size, or 20×20 feet, its area would be 400 sq. ft., not 200. The storage required for a digital image is a function of the product of the dimensions, not a simple sum.

In practical applications, a 64×48 pixel image is not usable. North American television transmissions, when digitized, are commonly converted to 640×480-pixel images; digital images to be projected in movie theaters are a minimum of 2048×1536 pixels in size. If you consider that these images are in color, meaning that each pixel requires 3 bytes (1 byte each for red, green, and blue), the storage requirements are 921,600 (almost a million) bytes for each television image. Each movie image, or *frame*, requires 9,437,184 bytes—more than 10 times as much. And if you further consider the fact that television displays 30 images per second and movie film runs at 24 frames per second, it becomes clear that only the recent advances in low-cost data storage have made digital imagery accessible to a wider number of people.

Some applications, such as space-based sensors that capture images of the Earth, have very high resolution. These can be on the order of tens of thousands of pixels in the x and y dimensions, requiring phenomenal amounts of storage space for each image.

The other resolution with which digital imagery is concerned is depth. This refers to the number of bits that each pixel requires to store its intensity value. A *bit*, short for *binary digit*, is the basis for all digital computers. Unlike the numbers we are accustomed to using, where each decimal digit can have a value from 0 up to 9, a binary digit can have only a value of 0 or 1. This is convenient for computers because the value of a bit can be represented by the absence (0) or presence (1) of an electrical current. It also is useful for digital images, because one or more bits can define the color intensity of a pixel.

Figure 2.3a illustrates how a single bit can represent a pixel value of black (0) or white (1). Figure 2.3b illustrates how two bits combined

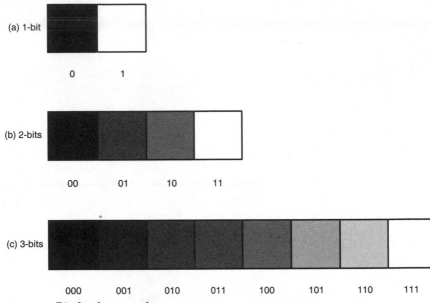

Figure 2.3 Bit-depth grayscales.

can represent a pixel value of black (00), dark gray (01), light gray (10), and white (11). Similarly, Fig. 2.3c shows how three bits can represent eight levels of intensity. Eight bits, or 1 byte, provide 256 levels of intensity. The number of intensity levels is represented by the formula 2^b, or 2 raised to the b power, where b is the number of bits. So 2 bits can provide 2^2, or $2 \times 2 = 4$ intensity levels, 3 bits provides 2^3, or $2 \times 2 \times 2 = 8$ levels, and eight bits can provide 2^8, or $2 \times 2 \times 2 \times 2 \times 2 \times 2 \times 2 \times 2 = 256$ levels.

The number of bits used to hold a pixel's value defines the *depth resolution* of a digital image. Figure 2.4a shows an image that has a depth resolution of 8 bits, or 256 intensity levels and the image looks quite natural. Now look at the image in Fig. 2.4b. This image has a depth resolution of 3 bits, or only 8 intensity levels, and is beginning to have a synthetic or unnatural look to it; its depth resolution is too low. Finally, Fig. 2.4c shows the same image with only 1-bit depth resolution. It has the stark, contrasty look that is the result of each pixel having only two possible values: black (0) or white (1).

So how is the depth resolution for various digital images determined? It depends on the content of the images and the application where they are used. The text on this printed page can be represented with a depth resolution of 1 bit, or with pixels of either black or white. Television can represent only about 7 bits of depth resolution, or 128 levels of intensity ($2^7 = 128$). Computer screens, if not used correctly, may reproduce something less than 256 levels of intensity each for red, green, and blue—sometimes as little as 64 levels, or only 6 bits, of intensity per color. For data storage reasons, these images usually are kept as 8-bit depth resolution, or 24 bits total for the red, green, and blue information.

High-end, full-color images, such as those for photographic film or detailed satellite imagery, require a minimum of 8 bits per color, with 10 bits or even 12 bits being preferable. This means that a total of 36 bits is needed for each pixel of a red-green-blue image. Most computers available today operate on images that have a depth resolution not greater than 8 bits per color. For that reason, all programming examples in this book will be limited to that, unless otherwise noted. You should be aware, however, that higher (and lower) resolutions do exist.

Program 1 illustrates how to change the depth resolution of an image, which is how the images in Figures 2.4b and 2.4c were created from the image in Fig. 2.4a. This program uses, as input, an image with 8-bit depth resolution and converts it to a lower depth resolution

(a) 8-bits (256 levels)

(b) 3-bits (8 levels)

(c) 1-bit (2 levels)

Figure 2.4 Depth resolution. *(Image courtesy of Eastman Kodak Co.)*

(this example creates a 3-bit image), but still maintains it as an 8-bit file, which is what most computer display systems require. You are encouraged to experiment with generating different output images, and to notice that little or no degradation is visible until the depth resolution drops below 6 bits per pixel. This is due to the fact, mentioned earlier, that many CRT displays have a depth resolution of only 6 bits, so any resolution higher than that has no added visual benefit.

In this, the first program to be presented, you should take note of several things, because all the other programs will be similar in form. First, there are many formats in which image data may be stored, a topic to be discussed in Chap. 7. Because of this, the sample programs all invoke a function called read_image to read an image, and another called write_image to write an image, but do not attempt to describe how this is done. It is assumed that you have the programming skills required to supply these functions. If not, the routines provided in Chap. 7 can be used to read and write the sample digital images. Since digital images are usually two-dimensional, the processing loops of all programs are two nested for loops: one for the x dimension and one for the y dimension. Finally, most programs are written for processing three-plane color images, but can be modified to process single-plane grayscale images. It is also assumed that you have the means to display or print the images that are generated.

One final consideration about spatial and depth resolutions is that they are not independent of one another. In other words, an image that has low spatial resolution and high depth resolution could, in its final output form, look similar in quality to one that has high spatial resolution but low depth resolution. This might sound confusing, but it can be explained with the example that follows.

Many newspaper photographers now use digital cameras to capture their pictures. These images generally have low spatial resolution, 640 × 480 pixels, but high depth resolution, 8 bits per color or 24 bits per pixel. Once an image has been enhanced, cropped, or otherwise manipulated, it is ready for printing on the newspaper page. This generates a dilemma. Most monochrome newspaper pictures are printed with only 1-bit depth resolution; for color pictures, there is 1 bit for each of the primary printing inks of cyan, yellow, magenta, and black. Either way, there's only a dot of ink that's on or off.

From the previous example, however, we know that if we reduce the depth resolution of a 24-bit color image to only 4 bits, the results will be unacceptable. Therefore processing methods such as halftoning, discussed in Chap. 3, are used to simulate depth resolutions greater than 1 bit. The lack of depth resolution can be traded off for higher spatial resolution. The original 640 × 480 image may be expanded in size to thousands of pixels across (15,000 is not uncommon) and—

```
/***********************************************************/
/*    program 1: modify depth resolution                   */
/***********************************************************/

#include "math.h"
#define  DEPTH   3
#define  XSIZE   640
#define  YSIZE   480

unsigned char *ir,*ig,*ib;
unsigned char *or,*og,*ob;

main()
  {
  long int x, y;
  float scale;

  /* allocate input and output memory buffers */
  ir = (unsigned char *) malloc (XSIZE*YSIZE);
  ig = (unsigned char *) malloc (XSIZE*YSIZE);
  ib = (unsigned char *) malloc (XSIZE*YSIZE);
  or = (unsigned char *) malloc (XSIZE*YSIZE);
  og = (unsigned char *) malloc (XSIZE*YSIZE);
  ob = (unsigned char *) malloc (XSIZE*YSIZE);

  /* read the input image (8-bit resolution) */
  read_image("input",ir,ig,ib);

  /* calculate the scale factor that will reduce 8-bit values
       (0-255, inclusive) to evenly spaced values of 0-255 for
       the requested depth resolution. */
  /* example: if DEPTH = 2, values are 0, 85, 171, and 255 */
  scale = 255.0 / (powf (2.0, (float)DEPTH) - 1.0);

  /* reduce depth resolution by generating new 8-bit pixel values
*/
  for (y = 0; y < YSIZE; y = y++)
    {
    for (x = 0; x < XSIZE; x = x++)
      {
      or[(y*XSIZE)+x] = (ir[(y*XSIZE)+x] >> (8 - DEPTH)) * scale;
      og[(y*XSIZE)+x] = (ig[(y*XSIZE)+x] >> (8 - DEPTH)) * scale;
      ob[(y*XSIZE)+x] = (ib[(y*XSIZE)+x] >> (8 - DEPTH)) * scale;
      }
    }

  /* write the output image */
  write_image("output",or,og,ob);

  /* free memory buffers */
  free (ir);
  free (ig);
  free (ib);
  free (or);
  free (og);
  free (ob);   }
```

Program 1 Change depth resolution.

miraculously—once the image is printed, even with only 4-bit depth resolution it maintains a high-quality look.

Color Spaces

Computer display terminals have three electron guns that illuminate phosphors on the front, or face, of the screen. (This subject will be discussed in Chap. 8.) What is important to note here is that those phosphors glow with the red, green, and blue primary colors of light. From these, all others shades are generated.

A combination of physical characteristics defines what the human vision system perceives as color. A *color space* is a mathematical representation of these characteristics that can be used easily within the computer. Digital imagery operates to a large extent within the red/green/blue color space, known simply as *RGB*, but there are others. The cyan/yellow/magenta space, known as *CYM*, is used in printing. Hue, saturation, and intensity, (or *HSI*) is the color space used by artists; intensity-chromaticity color spaces, *YUV* and *YIQ*, are used for television broadcast.

Each of these color spaces is described in this section. Though most work in digital imagery is performed in RGB, which is native to computer displays, many digital image processing applications require transformation to the other color spaces. Sample programs are provided to perform these transformations.

Red, green, blue (RGB)

All color spaces are three-dimensional orthogonal coordinate systems, meaning that there are three axes (in this case the red, green, and blue color intensities) that are perpendicular to one another. This is illustrated in the graph in Fig. 2.5. The red intensity starts at zero at the origin and increases along one of the axes. Similarly, green and blue intensities also start at the origin and increase as the distance along their axes increases. Because each color can have only a maximum intensity of 255 (for 8-bit depth), the resulting structure is the cube shown in Fig. 2.5.

This description provides us with a mathematical model from which we can define any color simply by giving its red, green, and blue values, or *coordinates*, within the cube. These coordinates are usually presented as the red, green, and blue intensity values enclosed within parentheses: (*red,green,blue*). This is referred to as an *ordered triplet*.

Figure 2.6 illustrates several colors mapped into their locations in the RGB cube, or color space. Black has no intensities in red, green, or blue, so it has the coordinates (0,0,0). At the opposite end, white has maximum intensities of each color, or (255,255,255). By no coincidence,

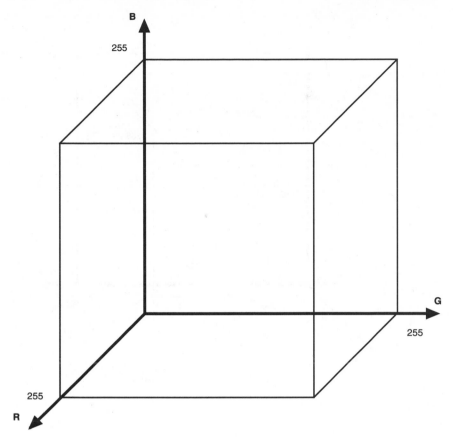

Figure 2.5 RGB color space.

black and white are located at opposite corners of the color space.

In Fig. 2.6, full-intensity red, having no green or blue components, also is positioned at a corner of the cube at location (255,0,0). Yellow, which is combination of red and green, is positioned at (255,255,0). Cyan and magenta, which are combinations of green-blue and red-blue, respectively, are at (0,255,255) and (255,0,255). Finally, note that gray is at the exact center of the cube at location (128,128,128). All other colors, from orange to brown to pink and everything between, can be described simply by locating their coordinates within this cube.

The RGB color space is called an *additive* space because, in nontechnical terms, its origin starts at black, and all other colors are derived by *adding* intensity values. This is why it is a natural choice for computer display screens where black, or no light intensity, is the starting point, and the increasing intensity of the red, green, and blue electron guns provides the colors.

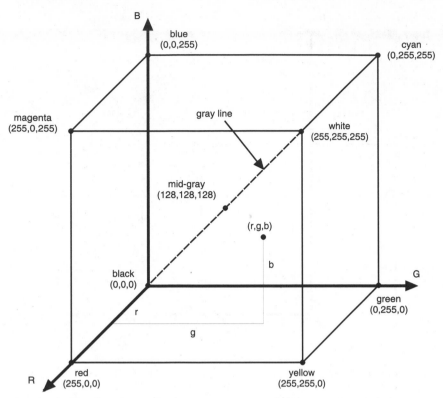

Figure 2.6 RGB color mappings.

Cyan, yellow, magenta (CYM)

The CYM color space is related to the RGB color space by being the exact inverse of it. Figure 2.7 illustrates the CYM color space. Note that the origin of the color cube is not black, but is white, and the primary axes of the coordinate system are not red, green, and blue but are cyan, yellow, and magenta. The color red in this space is a combination of yellow and magenta, whereas green is composed of yellow and cyan. Blue is made up of cyan and magenta. The following equations define how to convert from RGB into CYM color space and back again:

$$c = \max - r \qquad m = \max - g \qquad y = \max - b$$

$$r = \max - c \qquad g = \max - m \qquad b = \max - y$$

In these equations, max is the maximum intensity value which for an 8-bit depth resolution image is 255.

Program 2 shows how to convert an RGB image into a CYM image. Note that once an image has been converted, or transformed, into the CYM color space, it cannot be displayed correctly on a computer monitor, which requires images in the RGB color space. If this resultant image is displayed, using the red, green, and blue planes for the cyan, magenta, and yellow data, respectively, an inverted or negative color image will be seen.

The CYM color space is most often used in the printing industry, where images start with a white piece of paper (the origin) and ink is applied to generate colors. Over years of experience, many techniques have been developed to create the highest-quality printed images at the lowest possible cost. One of these methods is called *under color removal* and modifies the normal CYM color space into something called *CYMK*, where the K stands for black.

What this process does is acknowledge that any CYM color has some underlying gray component, which is equal amounts of cyan, yellow, and magenta ink. This gray component can be generated with cheaper black ink, and small amounts of more expensive colored inks can be

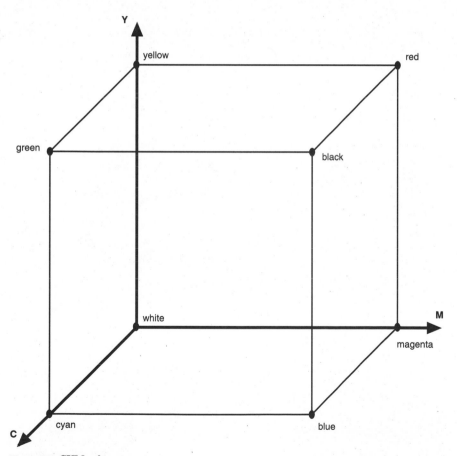

Figure 2.7 CYM color space.

```
/***************************************************************/
/*    program 2: convert rgb to cym                           */
/***************************************************************/

#define  MAX    255
#define  XSIZE  640
#define  YSIZE  480

unsigned char *ir,*ig,*ib;
unsigned char *oc,*om,*oy;

main()
  {
  long  int  x,y;

  /* allocate input and output memory buffers */
  ir = (unsigned char *) malloc (XSIZE*YSIZE);
  ig = (unsigned char *) malloc (XSIZE*YSIZE);
  ib = (unsigned char *) malloc (XSIZE*YSIZE);
  oc = (unsigned char *) malloc (XSIZE*YSIZE);
  om = (unsigned char *) malloc (XSIZE*YSIZE);
  oy = (unsigned char *) malloc (XSIZE*YSIZE);

  /* read the rgb input image */
  read_image("input",ir,ig,ib);

  /* convert each pixel to cym */
  for (y = 0; y < YSIZE; y = y++)
    {
    for (x = 0; x < XSIZE; x = x++)
      {
      oc[(y*XSIZE)+x] = MAX - ir[(y*XSIZE)+x];  /* cyan */
      om[(y*XSIZE)+x] = MAX - ig[(y*XSIZE)+x];  /* magenta */
      oy[(y*XSIZE)+x] = MAX - ib[(y*XSIZE)+x];  /* yellow */
      }
    }

  /* write the output image */
  /* note: if the output image is displayed on an rgb monitor
      it will appear like a negative, but if it is printed on
      a cym printer it will appear correct. */
  write_image("output",oc,oy,om);

  /* free memory buffers */
  free (ir);
  free (ig);
  free (ib);
  free (oc);
  free (om);
  free (oy);
  }
```

Program 2 RGB-to-CYM conversion.

added to give the correct shade. In addition to being more economical to produce, the printed image quality is increased because less ink is used overall, which in turn enhances drying and reduces the likelihood of smears.

Figure 2.8 shows an example of how the CYMK process works. A color has certain components of cyan, yellow, and magenta on an arbitrary scale. In this case, 7 units of cyan ink, 5 units of yellow ink, and 9 units of magenta ink are required, for a total of 21 units. That same color can then have its underlying gray, or *under color*, removed. To reproduce this same color now takes 5 units of black ink, with 2 units of cyan, no yellow, and 4 units of magenta. This makes a total of 11 units of ink, only 6 units of which are expensive colors.

Hue, saturation, intensity (HSI)

The RGB and CYM color spaces work very well for technical reproduction of color, but human vision tends to look at the world in a different fashion. We do not see things as quantities of primary colors mixed at preset proportions. We see the brilliant orange of a sunset or the dark, muted greens of a forest. We see things as colors, or *hues*, that either have a washed-out look or have deep, rich tones. This means having low or high *saturation,* respectively. A bright afternoon sun gives everything a high-intensity look, while dusk provides dark images of low intensity.

Artists tend to describe scenes not in terms of red, green, and blue, but as hue, saturation, and intensity (HSI). While still a three-dimensional

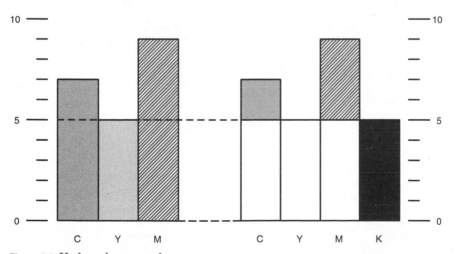

Figure 2.8 Under color removal.

color space, HSI is very different from RGB or CYM. And while there are many variations to describe it, Fig. 2.9 illustrates a common representation. The cone shape has one axis running down its center, representing intensity. Along this axis are all the gray values, with black at the pointed end of the cone and white at its widest opening. The greater the distance along this line from the pointed end, or origin, the brighter or higher the intensity.

If this cone is viewed from above, looking at its widest end, it becomes a circle. Different colors, or hues, are defined as having specific positions around this circle, as shown in Fig. 2.10. This is the standard, familiar color wheel used by artists. Note that we also can see the relationship between red/green/blue and cyan/yellow/magenta, and how they are the inverse of one another. Hues are determined by their angular location on this wheel, with red at 0 degrees and the others progressing as shown in Figure 2.10.

Saturation, or the richness of color, is defined as the distance perpendicular to the intensity axis. Colors near the central axis have low

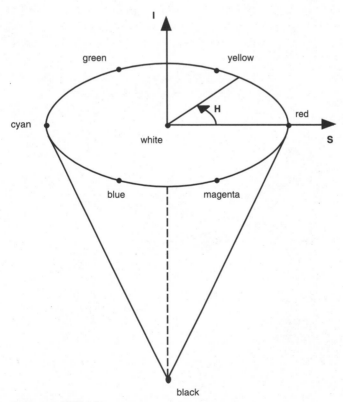

Figure 2.9 HSI color space.

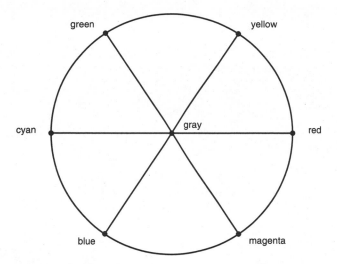

Figure 2.10 Hue color wheel.

saturation and look pastel. Colors near the edge of the cone have high saturation and are bold in appearance.

At times it is preferable to modify an image in HSI color space instead of RGB. For example, we might want to change the color of a bright yellow car moving down a road to blue, but we want to leave the rest of the scene, including highlights and shadows on the car, unaffected. This would be an impossible task in RGB, but it is relatively simple in HSI. Because the yellow pixels of the car have a specific range of hue, regardless of intensity or saturation, those pixels can be isolated easily and their hue component modified, thus giving a different-colored car.

Since almost all digital image processing systems operate on RGB images, the example described above would be performed in three steps. First, the original RGB image would be converted to HSI. Second, the hue (or saturation or intensity) would be modified. Finally, the image would be converted back to RGB. There are many techniques for transforming an image from RGB to HSI and back again, because the transformation is somewhat subjective. Program 3 provides an implementation of one of these methods, as described in *The Fundamentals of Interactive Computer Graphics*, by J. D. Foley and A. Van Dam.

This particular implementation, referred to as the *HSV* color model, generates a hue value of 0 degrees to 360 degrees, with red at the origin (Fig. 2.10). Saturation is in the range of 0 to 1, with 0 being no color (along the central axis) and 1 being on the outer edge of the cone. The value (a variation of intensity) also has a range of 0 to 1, where 0 is black and 1 is white. Note that these calculations require higher

```
/*************************************************************/
/*    program 3: convert RGB from/to HSV                  */
/*                                                        */
/*    note: no main program is supplied for this example, */
/*       only the routines to perform the conversions.    */
/*************************************************************/

#define UNDEFINED 999.0

void rgb2hsv();
void hsv2rgb();

/************************************************/
/*        rgb2hsv: RGB-to-HSV conversion      */
/************************************************/

void rgb2hsv(r,g,b,h,s,v)
int r,g,b;
float *h,*s,*v;
  {
  float min,max;
  float rc,gc,bc;
  float fr,fg,fb;

  /* determine maximum of R,G,B */
  if ((r >= g) && (r >= b)) max = (float)r;
  if ((g >= r) && (g >= b)) max = (float)g;
  if ((b >= r) && (b >= g)) max = (float)b;

  /* determine minimum of R,G,B */
  if ((r <= g) && (r <= b)) min = (float)r;
  if ((g <= r) && (g <= b)) min = (float)g;
  if ((b <= r) && (b <= g)) min = (float)b;

  /* calculate V (simply maximum of R,G,B) */
  *v = max;

  /* calculate S (if RGB is black, saturation is 0) */
  if (max != 0)
    *s = (max-min) / max;
  else
    *s = 0.0;

  /* calculate H (if no saturation, hue is undefined) */
  if (*s == 0)
    {
    *h = UNDEFINED;
    }
  else
    {
    rc = (max - ((float)r / 255.0)) / (max - min);
    gc = (max - ((float)g / 255.0)) / (max - min);
    bc = (max - ((float)b / 255.0)) / (max - min);
```

```
      if (r == (unsigned char)max)
        *h = bc - gc;                      /* hue between yellow—magenta */
      else
        if (g == (unsigned char)max)
          *h = 2.0 + rc - bc;              /* hue between cyan—yellow */
        else
          *h = 4.0 + gc - rc;              /* hue between magenta—cyan */
      *h = *h * 60.0;                      /* convert to degrees */
      if (*h < 0.0) *h = *h + 360.0;  /* make non-negative */
      }

  return;
  }

/***************************************************/
/*        hsv2rgb: HSV-to-RGB conversion           */
/***************************************************/

void hsv2rgb(h,s,v,r,g,b)
float h,s,v;
int *r,*g,*b;
  {
  long int i;
  float hh;
  float f,p,q,t;

  if (s == 0)
    {
    if (h == UNDEFINED)
      {
      *r = (unsigned char)v;   /* achromatic, RGB is grey  scale */
      *g = (unsigned char)v;
      *b = (unsigned char)v;
      }
    else
      {
      *r = 0;                  /* ERROR! this should never occur */
      *g = 0;
      *b = 0;
      }
    }

  else
    {
    hh = h;
    if (hh == 360) hh = 0;
    hh = hh / 60.0;
    i = (long)hh;
    f = hh - (float)i;
    p = v * (1.0 - s);
```

```
q = v * (1.0 - (s * f));
t = v * (1.0 - (s * (1.0 - f)));

switch(i)      {
  case 0:
    *r = (unsigned char) (v * 255.0);
    *g = (unsigned char) (t * 255.0);
    *b = (unsigned char) (p * 255.0);
    break;
  case 1:
    *r = (unsigned char) (q * 255.0);
    *g = (unsigned char) (v * 255.0);
    *b = (unsigned char) (p * 255.0);
    break;
  case 2:
    *r = (unsigned char) (p * 255.0);
    *g = (unsigned char) (v * 255.0);
    *b = (unsigned char) (t * 255.0);
    break;

  case 3:
    *r = (unsigned char) (p * 255.0);
    *g = (unsigned char) (q * 255.0);
    *b = (unsigned char) (v * 255.0);
    break;
  case 4:
    *r = (unsigned char) (t * 255.0);
    *g = (unsigned char) (p * 255.0);
    *b = (unsigned char) (v * 255.0);
    break;
  case 5:
    *r = (unsigned char) (v * 255.0);
    *g = (unsigned char) (p * 255.0);
    *b = (unsigned char) (q * 255.0);
    break;
  default:
    break;
  }
}

return;
}
```

Program 3 RGB-to-HSV conversion.

numerical precision than is offered by 8-bit integer arithmetic. It therefore is advisable to maintain the HSI image as floating-point numbers, or at least 16-bit or 32-bit integers, and reduce them to 8-bit values as they are being transformed back into RGB. Also note that Program 3 consists of two functions, one for RGB-to-HSV conversion and the other for HSV-to-RGB conversion. These functions would be invoked for converting each pixel in an image.

Luminance-chrominance

The last color spaces to be discussed are those based on *luminance* and *chrominance*, which correspond to brightness and color. These color spaces are denoted as YUV and YIQ. The YUV space is used for the PAL system of broadcast television in Europe and Japan, and YIQ for the NTSC broadcast standard in America. The two methods are nearly identical, using slightly different conversion equations to transform from RGB color space and back. In both situations, Y is the luminance, or brightness, component of a pixel, and the I and Q (or U and V) are the chrominance, or color, components. These are the variables that are changed by the brightness, color, and tint controls on a television.

The advantages of using YUV and YIQ for broadcast is that the amount of data needed to define a television picture is greatly reduced. But the price paid for this compression is that many colors that appear on a computer display cannot be recreated on television. High-definition television (HDTV) will remedy some of this problem, but the sharper, clearer picture of HDTV comes from higher spatial resolution, not from greater depth resolution.

Listed below are the equations for converting RGB colors into YUV and YIQ, and back to RGB. These equations are based on the red, green, and blue having values between 0 and 1, which means that typical 8-bit values of 0–255 must be scaled and processed as floating-point numbers:

RGB-to-YUV

$$Y = 0.299R + 0.587G + 0.114B$$

$$U = -0.147R - 0.289G + 0.437B$$

$$V = 0.615R - 0.515G - 0.100B$$

RGB-to-YIQ

$$Y = 0.299R + 0.587G + 0.114B$$

$$I = 0.596R - 0.274G - 0.322B$$

$$Q = 0.211R - 0.523G - 0.312B$$

YUV-to-RGB

$$R = 1.000Y + 0.000U + 1.403V$$

$$G = 1.000Y - 0.344U - 0.714V$$

$$B = 1.000Y + 1.773U + 0.000V$$

YIQ-to-RGB

$$R = -1.129\ Y + 3.306I - 3.000Q$$

$$G = 1.607Y - 0.934I + 0.386Q$$

$$B = 3.458Y - 3.817I + 5.881Q$$

Program 4 provides the functions for converting RGB pixels to and from YUV and YIQ. In this program, the fractional coefficients are represented as fixed-point numbers, with 16 bits to the right of the implied decimal point. This allows integer operations to be used instead of floating-point while still maintaining necessary precision. While in the YUV or YIQ color space, the values are maintained with 8 bits to the right of the decimal point so that overflows will not occur with they are converted back to RGB.

Histogram

A very important tool of digital image processing is the histogram. A *histogram* is a statistical representation of the data within an image that shows how many pixels there are at each of the possible values. Figure 2.11 shows an image and its histogram. The histogram is a bar chart where each entry on the horizontal axis is one of the possible values that a pixel can have. Since this is an 8-bit image, those values range from 0 to 255. Each vertical bar in the graph indicates the number of pixels at each value. This means that the sum of all vertical bars is equal to the total number of pixels in the image. Usually, the absolute value of each vertical bar, or number of pixels at a specific value, is not important. What is important is the number of pixels at a specific value relative to the number of pixels at other values. Therefore, the vertical scale of a histogram is usually normalized to some arbitrary value so that the resultant graph can be more easily viewed and interpreted.

Program 5 shows how to collect the histogram statistics and normalize them for display. An 8-bit image is used in this example, so there are 256 entries, or bins, into which possible values may fall. (If 12-bit data were being interrogated, there would be 4096 bins.) The values are normalized to a maximum value of 255. Thus, when the histogram is graphed by whatever means available, the result is a square (Fig. 2.11). The last portion of this program generates the graph as a digital image of size 256×256 pixels. Often, the histogram is never actually

```
/***************************************************************/
/*    program 4: RGB-to-YUV,YIQ conversion                  */
/*                                                          */
/*    note: no main program is supplied for this example,  */
/*     only the routines to perform the conversions.       */
/***************************************************************/

void rgb2yuv();
void rgb2yiq();
void yuv2rgb();
void yiq2rgb();

/*********************************************************/
/*        rgb2yuv: RGB-to-YUV conversion          */
/*********************************************************/

rgb2yuv(r,g,b,y,u,v)
unsigned char r,g,b;
long int *y,*u,*v;
  {
  *y = ((0x00004c8b * ((long)r & 0xff)) +
        (0x00009645 * ((long)g & 0xff)) +
        (0x00001d2f * ((long)b & 0xff))) > 8;

  *u = ((0xffffda5f * ((long)r & 0xff)) +
        (0xffffb605 * ((long)g & 0xff)) +
        (0x00006f6f * ((long)b & 0xff))) > 8;

  *v = ((0x00009d70 * ((long)r & 0xff)) +
        (0xffff7c29 * ((long)g & 0xff)) +
        (0xfffffe667 * ((long)b & 0xff))) > 8;

  return;
  }

/*********************************************************/
/*        rgb2yiq: RGB-to-YIQ conversion          */
/*********************************************************/

rgb2yiq(r,g,b,y,i,q)
unsigned char r,g,b;
long int *y,*i,*q;
  {
  *y = ((0x00004c8b * ((long)r & 0xff)) +
        (0x00009645 * ((long)g & 0xff)) +
        (0x00001d2f * ((long)b & 0xff))) > 8;

  *i = ((0x00009893 * ((long)r & 0xff)) +
        (0xffffb9dc * ((long)g & 0xff)) +
        (0xffffad92 * ((long)b & 0xff))) > 8;

  *q = ((0x00003604 * ((long)r & 0xff)) +
        (0xffff7a1d * ((long)g & 0xff)) +
        (0xffffb021 * ((long)b & 0xff))) > 8;
```

```
    return;
    }


/***************************************************/
/*       yuv2rgb: YUV-to-RGB conversion       */
/***************************************************/

yuv2rgb(y,u,v,r,g,b)
long int y,u,v;
unsigned char *r,*g,*b;
    {
    *r = (unsigned char)((((0x00010000 * y) > 24) & 0xff) +
                         (((0x00000000 * u) > 24) & 0xff) +
                         (((0x0001672b * v) > 24) & 0xff));

    *g = (unsigned char)((((0x00010000 * y) > 24) & 0xff) +
                         (((0xffffa7f0 * u) > 24) & 0xff) +
                         (((0xffff4938 * v) > 24) & 0xff));

    *b = (unsigned char)((((0x00010000 * y) > 24) & 0xff) +
                         (((0x0001c5e3 * u) > 24) & 0xff) +
                         (((0x00000000 * v) > 24) & 0xff));

    return;
    }

/***************************************************/
/*       yiq2rgb: YIQ-to-RGB conversion       */
/***************************************************/

yiq2rgb(y,i,q,r,g,b)
long int y,i,q;
unsigned char *r,*g,*b;
    {
    *r = (unsigned char)((((0xfffedefa * y) > 24) & 0xff) +
                         (((0x00034e56 * i) > 24) & 0xff) +
                         (((0x00030000 * q) > 24) & 0xff));

    *g = (unsigned char)((((0x00019b64 * y) > 24) & 0xff) +
                         (((0xfffff10e6 * i) > 24) & 0xff) +
                         (((0x000062d0 * q) > 24) & 0xff));

    *b = (unsigned char)((((0x0003753f * y) > 24) & 0xff) +
                         (((0xfffc2eda * i) > 24) & 0xff) +
                         (((0x0005e189 * q) > 24) & 0xff));

    return;
    }
```

Program 4 RGB-to-YIQ,YUV conversion.

Figure 2.11 Image with histogram. *(Image courtesy of Eastman Kodak Co.)*

graphed, but is processed by other software to make decisions as to how to manage an image.

What are the uses for the histogram of an image? Many will be discussed throughout this book. It is important to remember that a histogram represents a statistical analysis of an image; it indicates the distribution of the data. From this simple data array, the best contrast for an image can be determined. It also indicates, in an objective numerical fashion, the overall brightness or darkness of an image. A histogram can be used to determine how to apply a function, such as thresholding, to an image. It also can be used to judge the effectiveness of an algorithm, such as contrast enhancement, that has been applied to an image.

As an example, consider the image and its histogram illustrated in Fig. 2.12a. This image is flat and washed-out, as can be determined simply by looking at it. But we can also determine this from the histogram. Most of the pixels are clustered around the center of the graph, or the mid-tone region. There are few or no pixels that are very dark or very bright. Now consider the same image, shown in Figure 2.12b, after it has been processed using techniques that will be described in Chap. 4. The image has better contrast, which is reflected in its histogram as a more even distribution of pixels over the entire intensity range.

Arithmetic Mean, Standard Deviation, and Variance

Other useful statistical features of an image are its arithmetic mean, standard deviation, and variance. These are well-known mathematical constructs that, when applied to a digital image, can reveal important information. The values are calculated as shown below:

$$\text{mean} = \text{sum}(P_{x,y})/(x \times y)$$

$$\text{var} = (\text{sum}(P_{x,y} \times P_{x,y}) / (x \times y)) - (\text{mean} \times \text{mean})$$

$$\text{stdev} = \sqrt{(\text{var})}$$

```
/*************************************************************/
/*    program 5: histogram collection                        */
/*************************************************************/

#define   MAX     256
#define   XSIZE   640
#define   YSIZE   480

unsigned char *ir,*ig,*ib;
unsigned char *or,*og,*ob;

main()
  {
  long  int  i,x,y;
  long  int  maxr, maxg, maxb;
  long  int  hr[MAX], hg[MAX], hb[MAX];

  /* allocate input and histogram image memory buffers */
  ir = (unsigned char *) malloc (XSIZE*YSIZE);
  ig = (unsigned char *) malloc (XSIZE*YSIZE);
  ib = (unsigned char *) malloc (XSIZE*YSIZE);
  or = (unsigned char *) malloc (MAX*MAX);
  og = (unsigned char *) malloc (MAX*MAX);
  ob = (unsigned char *) malloc (MAX*MAX);

  /* read the input image */
  read_image("input",ir,ig,ib);

  /* be sure histogram collection bins start at zero */
  for (i = 0; i < MAX; i++)
    {
    hr[i] = 0;
    hg[i] = 0;
    hb[i] = 0;
    }

  /* collect histogram data for each color plane */
  for (y = 0; y < YSIZE; y++)
    {
    for (x = 0; x < XSIZE; x++)
      {
      hr[ir[(y*XSIZE)+x]]++;
      hg[ig[(y*XSIZE)+x]]++;
      hb[ib[(y*XSIZE)+x]]++;
      }
    }

  /* find maximum bin value of each color plane */
  maxr = 0;
  maxg = 0;
  maxb = 0;
  for (i = 0; i < MAX; i++)
    {
```

```
    if (hr[i] > maxr) maxr = hr[i];    if (hg[i] > maxg) maxg =
hg[i];
    if (hb[i] > maxb) maxb = hb[i];
    }


  /* normalize all bins to maximum */
  for (x = 0; x < MAX; x++)
    {
    hr[x] = hr[x] * (MAX - 1) / maxr;
    hg[x] = hg[x] * (MAX - 1) / maxg;
    hb[x] = hb[x] * (MAX - 1) / maxb;
    }

  /* generate rgb histogram image */
  for (x = 0; x < MAX; x++)
    {
    for (y = (MAX - 1); y >= 0; y—)
      {
      /* draw red line */
      if (y > hr[x])
        or[((MAX-y-1)*MAX)+x] = 0x00;
      else
        or[((MAX-y-1)*MAX)+x] = 0xff;

      /* draw green line */
      if (y > hg[x])
        og[((MAX-y-1)*MAX)+x] = 0x00;
      else
        og[((MAX-y-1)*MAX)+x] = 0xff;

      /* draw blue line */
      if (y > hb[x])
        ob[((MAX-y-1)*MAX)+x] = 0x00;
      else
        ob[((MAX-y-1)*MAX)+x] = 0xff;
      }
    }

  /* write the output image */
  write_image("histo",or,og,ob);

  /* free memory buffers */
  free (ir);
  free (ig);
  free (ib);
  free (or);
  free (og);
  free (ob);
  }
```

Program 5 Histogram collection.

(a) Low Contrast

(b) Contrast Enhanced

Figure 2.12 Low- and high-contrast image with histogram.

In these equations, sum($P_{x,y}$) respresents the summation of all pixel values in the image, and sum($P_{x,y} \times P_{x,y}$) is the sum of the squares of all pixel values.

The arithmetic mean indicates the image's *average* value. This is valuable, for example, in setting the exposure time of a scanning device. Suppose the light source of this scanner produced an illumination field such as the one shown in Fig. 2.13, which could be displayed

Figure 2.13 Image, histogram, and arithmetic mean.

on a computer monitor. The lighting is not perfectly even, with the center being slightly brighter than the edges and the outer corners being darker. If an operator were attempting to set the exposure time for this scanner by approaching a predetermined value under these conditions, which value is correct? Should an intensity at the center be regarded as correct? Or the top or side?

Figure 2.13 contains the histogram for this image, and it shows the distribution of data. The vertical line near the peak of the histogram is the arithmetic mean and provides the answer for the operator. This value can be considered the average value of all pixels in the image.

The *standard deviation* is a measure of the frequency distribution, or range of pixel values, of an image. If an image is supposed to be even throughout, as in this example, the standard deviation should be small. A small standard deviation indicates that the pixel intensities do not stray very far from the mean; a large value indicates a greater range. The *variance* is the square root of the standard deviation.

These values must be used with some caution when dealing with many applications, since more subjective analysis may be required to determine the "goodness" or "badness" of an image. For some applications, such as machine vision, these statistical values can be very accurate indicators of image quality and can be used to make automated decisions.

Input/Output Devices

Since digital images are a representation of the real world, it follows that the real world must somehow be brought into the computer. Similarly, after images have been processed, they must be extracted from the realm of bits and bytes for presentation in visual form. These tasks are accomplished by input and output devices, which are a critical link in the chain of digital image processing. Too often they are not viewed as important and, as a result, are the source of many technical errors. The old computer saying of "garbage in, garbage out" must be heeded in the field of digital image processing.

Why is this the case? It may seem like the simple procedure of scanning a photograph or generating a hardcopy output would not be fraught with danger, but it is. There are several reasons. First, there are no standard methods for converting analog signals—the real world—into digital values. The process of analog-to-digital conversion may be deterministic from an electronics point of view, but what to do with those digital signals to produce an acceptable image is another matter altogether.

Most sensors, the devices that actually perform the conversion, are *nonlinear* in nature. This means that if a certain number of photons translates to a specific digital value, doubling the number of photons may not necessarily result in conversion to a value twice as large. That human vision is nonlinear, as will be investigated more thoroughly in a later chapter, only compounds the problem.

Then there is the problem of viewing digital images on a computer screen. This is such an important function that a later chapter will be devoted to the subject. Let it suffice here to state that what is seen on the computer display, in respect to color or saturation, may be quite different than the original real-world image that was captured, or the tangible output that is eventually generated. One of the most difficult hurdles for engineers to overcome is to create a WYSIWYG (pronounced "Whizzy-wig") or "what you see is what you get" imaging system.

What follows is an overview of the various input and output devices available today. *Charge-coupled devices* (CCDs) are primarily used in digital cameras, *linear arrays* are used for flatbed scanners, *drum scanners* are used for high-resolution print scanning, and *laser scanners* are a newer technology used for high-resolution film scanning. The most common output devices are ink printers, but CRT and laser film recorders, along with wax transfer and dye sublimation printers, also are widespread.

Charge-Coupled Devices and Digital Cameras

A CCD is a silicon semiconductor that acts like a light detector. An interesting property of crystalline silicon is that the energy from photons causes the bonds between adjacent atoms to be broken, thus leaving electron-hole pairs. The resultant electrical charge is proportional to the amount of light, or number of photons, that strike the silicon. If the silicon chip is subdivided into a very fine grid, as shown in Fig. 3.1, and an image is focused on that grid, the result is a sensor in which each square holds a charge that is equivalent to the intensity of the light at that point. Each point corresponds to a pixel of the soon-to-be digital image.

This collection of subdivided silicon is referred to as a *parallel register*, since photons fall on each sensor simultaneously. Once the exposure to light is complete, the data must be retrieved from the parallel register. This is accomplished by shifting the collected charges, one row at a time, into another silicon buffer called the *serial register*. Once a row is captured in the serial register, it is then amplified and transported off the chip one cell, or pixel, at a time. Figure 3.2 illustrates how this propagation of data works. Note that the data may not emerge from the chip in the proper viewing organization and must be flipped either left to right, top to bottom, or both.

This is a very simple overview of how a CCD operates. The actual implementation is much more complicated, especially considering the intricate timing involved in the operations. These devices are very

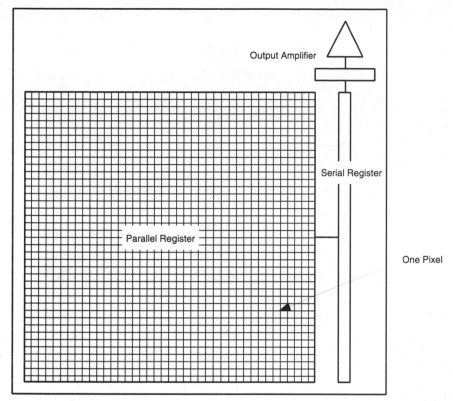

Figure 3.1 CCD chip.

susceptible to electromagnetic radiation other than visible light, and are especially sensitive to infrared, or heat, so they are usually cooled to very low temperatures, around -25 to -35 degrees Fahrenheit, during operation.

CCDs can be made with very fine grids. Common sizes are 512×512 pixels, 720×486, 1024×1024, 2048×2048, and even 4096×4096 pixels. CCDs are at the heart of digital cameras, which are becoming commonplace. Figure 3.3 shows how a digital camera is built around this technology. A digital camera looks like a normal 35mm camera but, instead of film, a CCD chip resides at the focal plane of the lens. And instead of being loaded with a canister of unexposed film, a removable disk holds the captured images. This disk may then be loaded into an appropriate computer for viewing.

Today, many professional newspaper photographers use digital cameras because of their compatibility with the digital image processing capabilities of the layout and production equipment. While other application areas, such as astronomy, are using digital cameras, there

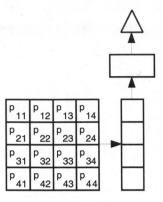

a) Exposed CCD holds
charge for each pixel

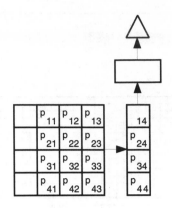

b) Shift a row of parallel
register into serial register

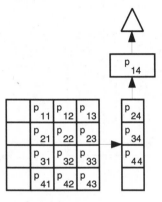

c) Shift one pixel of serial
register into output buffer

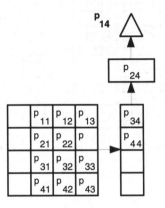

d) Move first pixel off chip while
next is shifted into output buffer

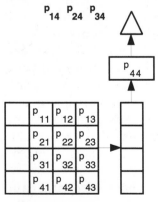

e) Remaining pixels in serial
register are shiffted off chip

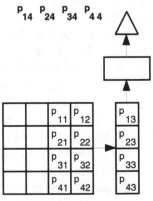

f) Next row of parallel register
is shifted into serial register

Figure 3.2 CCD data propagation.

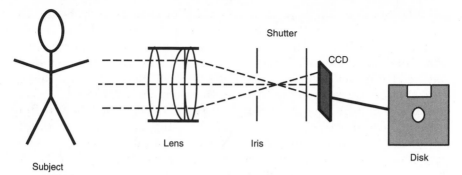

Figure 3.3 Digital camera.

is still widespread use of photographic film and will continue to be for the foreseeable future.

An important use of CCD technology is for scanning photographic film to create digital images that may then be processed by computers. Figure 3.4 shows the principal components of a film scanner. A light source is used to illuminate a film negative. (Film positives can be used, but negatives are better.) A lens then focuses the images of the film onto a CCD, which converts the light signals to digits, as in the previous description. Filters are placed in front of the light source so that individual exposures of the red, green, and blue film emulsions are captured to produce a color image. The light source illuminates a piece of film that is held in a gate to keep it stationary and flat. A lens focuses the image of the film onto a CCD in the same way a camera does. Finally, the captured digital image is processed and saved in computer or disk memory.

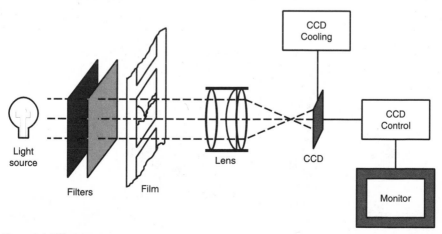

Figure 3.4 Film scanner.

While film scanning is a straightforward process, it must be tightly controlled to generate consistent and accurate results. Two major obstacles must be overcome before acceptable digital scans are generated: the unevenness of the illumination field and the nonlinear nature of film. Following are methods to solve these problems, along with sample source code to illustrate their implementation.

Unlike taking a picture under natural lighting conditions, a film scanner has an artificial light source that shines through, or *illuminates*, the film. Unfortunately, no source casts light perfectly evenly over a given area. In other words, the illumination field in not flat. This is a problem because an uneven illumination field will result in darker or brighter areas in the digital image; this is especially noticeable in areas of even or slowly changing color, such as a blue sky or a painted wall. Uneven illumination is eliminated by a processes called *flat field correction*.

Consider the image in Fig. 3.5a, which is the illumination field of a scanner with no film present. Note that there are darker and lighter areas. Figure 3.5b shows a scanned image using this illumination

(a) Illumination Field

(b) Uncorrected Scan

(c) Corrected Scan

Figure 3.5 Image scanned with uneven illumination field. *(Image courtesy of Eastman Kodak Co.)*

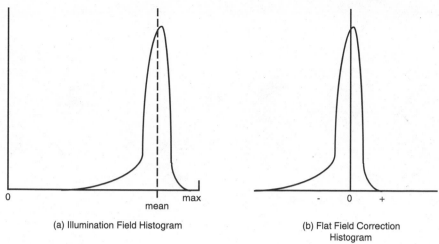

(a) Illumination Field Histogram

(b) Flat Field Correction Histogram

Figure 3.6 Flat field correction.

field, where the unevenness of the field has caused the corners of the image to become overly dark and the center too bright. Figure 3.5c is the same image, but scanned using flat field correction, yielding much better results.

The procedure to accomplish this is relatively easy. First, an image of the illumination field is captured. A histogram of this image is generated, as well as the arithmetic mean, as shown in Fig. 3.6a. If the mean value is subtracted from every pixel value in the illumination field image, the histogram in Fig. 3.6b. is the result. Notice that this image now has positive and negative values. This signed image is the flat field correction information that will be used to modify scans.

When the film is scanned, the following operation is applied to every pixel:

$$p = s - (f \times s/\text{max})$$

In this operation, p is the corrected pixel, s is the raw scanned value, and f is the flat field correction value at that location. Thus, a pixel in a bright area of the illumination field is slightly darkened, while one in a dim area is brightened. Note that f is scaled by the factor s/max, where max is the maximum value for a scanned pixel, which assures that darker pixels are not overcompensated by flat field correction. Program 6 shows how to generate the flat field correction image; Program 7 shows how to use it to correct a scan. Note that these programs assume the incoming signals from the camera are 12-bit values and that the resultant digital image has 8-bit pixel values.

The next problem of scanning, that of compensating for the nonlinearity of film, is more subjective and has no correct or incorrect solution. A link between the amount of exposure, or *density*, on the film

```
/**************************************************************/
/*    program 6: generate flat field correction image      */
/**************************************************************/

#include <math.h>
#define  XSIZE  640
#define  YSIZE  480

short int *in;
short int *out;

main()
  {
  long  int  x,y;
  double   sum,sum2,fsum,fsum2;
  double   mean,var,stdev;

  /* allocate input and output memory buffers */
  in  = (short int *) malloc (XSIZE*YSIZE);
  out = (short int *) malloc (XSIZE*YSIZE);

  /* read the 16-bit raw data file */
  read_image16("raw",in);

  /* calculate the arithmetic mean
  (and variance and standard deviation) */
  sum = sum2 = 0.0;
  for (y = 0; y < YSIZE; y = y++)
    {
    for (x = 0; x < XSIZE; x = x++)
      {
      sum  = sum +   in[(y*XSIZE)+x];
      sum2 = sum2 + (in[(y*XSIZE)+x] * in[(y*XSIZE)+x]);
      }
    }
  fsum  = sum  / (double)(XSIZE * YSIZE);
  fsum2 = sum2 / (double)(XSIZE * YSIZE);
  mean  = fsum;
  var   = fsum2 - (fsum * fsum);
  stdev = sqrt(var);

  /* subtract the arithmetic mean from each pixel */
  for (y = 0; y < YSIZE; y = y++)
    {
    for (x = 0; x < XSIZE; x = x++)
      {
      out[(y*XSIZE)+x] = in[(y*XSIZE)+x] - (short int)mean;
      }
    }
  /* write the output image */
  /* note: this is a signed image, 16 bits/pixel */
  write_image16("ffcorrect",out);

  /* free memory buffers */  free (in);
  free (out);
  }
```

Program 6 Generate flat field correction.

```
/**************************************************************/
/*    program 7: apply flat field correction              */
/**************************************************************/

#define  XSIZE  1280
#define  YSIZE  960

short int *ff;
long  int  scale,val;
unsigned char *ir,*ig,*ib;
unsigned char *or,*og,*ob;

main()
  {
  long  int  x,y;

  /* allocate input and output memory buffers */
  ff  = (short int *) malloc (2*XSIZE*YSIZE);
  ir = (unsigned char *) malloc (XSIZE*YSIZE);
  ig = (unsigned char *) malloc (XSIZE*YSIZE);
  ib = (unsigned char *) malloc (XSIZE*YSIZE);
  or = (unsigned char *) malloc (XSIZE*YSIZE);
  og = (unsigned char *) malloc (XSIZE*YSIZE);
  ob = (unsigned char *) malloc (XSIZE*YSIZE);

  /* read the 16-bit flat field correction image */
  read_image16("ffcorrect",ff);

  /* read the uncorrected field rgb input image */
  read_image("input",ir,ig,ib);

  /* correct the rgb image */
  for (y = 0; y < YSIZE; y++)
    {
    for (x = 0; x < XSIZE; x++)
      {
      /* correct red plane */
      scale = ((long)ir[(y*XSIZE)+x] * (long)ff[(y*XSIZE)+x]) >> 12;
      val = (long)ir[(y*XSIZE)+x] - scale;
        or[(y*XSIZE)+x] = (unsigned int)val;
        if (val <    0) or[(y*XSIZE)+x] = 0;
        if (val > 255) or[(y*XSIZE)+x] = 255;

      /* correct green plane */
      scale = ((long)ig[(y*XSIZE)+x] * (long)ff[(y*XSIZE)+x]) >> 12;
      val = (long)ig[(y*XSIZE)+x] - scale;
        og[(y*XSIZE)+x] = (unsigned int)val;
        if (val <    0) og[(y*XSIZE)+x] = 0;
        if (val > 255) og[(y*XSIZE)+x] = 255;

      /* correct blue plane */
      scale = ((long)ib[(y*XSIZE)+x] * (long)ff[(y*XSIZE)+x]) >> 12;
      val = (long)ib[(y*XSIZE)+x] - scale;
```

```
        ob[(y*XSIZE)+x] = (unsigned int)val;
        if (val <    0) ob[(y*XSIZE)+x] = 0;
        if (val > 255) ob[(y*XSIZE)+x] = 255;
    }
  }

/* write the corrected field rgb output image */
write_image("output",or,or,or);

/* free memory buffers */
free (ff);
free (ir);
free (ig);
free (ib);
free (or);
free (og);
free (ob);
}
```

Program 7 Apply flat field correction.

must be correlated to some given digital value. This is accomplished by scanning a precisely made set of frames where the film had been exposed to a known amount of light, yielding expected density values. Scanning this film produces input numbers that can be correlated to desired digital values in the computer image. Once these values are saved, they provide the basis for a table that can be used to translate any input value into the correct digital image pixel value, from which the nonlinearity of the film will be removed.

This procedure is illustrated in Fig. 3.7. The film shown is a series of 33 frames, each with a density decreasing from the previous frame. The numbers directly below the frames are the 12-bit values reported by the digital camera when each frame is scanned. The numbers below those are the 8-bit values that are chosen to correspond to those scanned input numbers. Note that in this example, the 8-bit values are equally spaced, which creates a linear digital image from the nonlinear film densities; this is not necessary, because any translation can be implemented. The digital values also are inverted in order to convert the negative film into a positive digital image. Finally, a graph of this translation table is shown. When an actual frame of film is scanned, each 12-bit value obtained from the digital camera is transformed through this table to create the 8-bit digital image.

Linear Arrays and Flatbed Scanners

A variation of the two-dimensional CCD chip used in digital cameras is the linear array. It uses the same silicon-based semiconductor technology that generates an electrical charge proportional to the amount

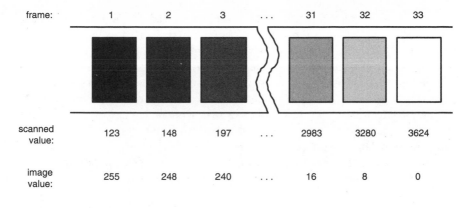

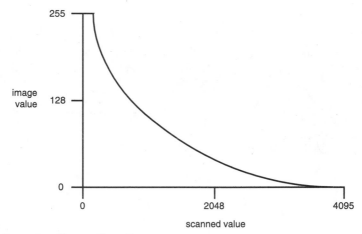

Figure 3.7 Removing film nonlinearity.

of light that falls on it. Linear arrays, as the name implies, are composed of a single row of sensors instead of the two-dimensional grid used in the chips in digital cameras. Because of this, they are easier and much cheaper to produce. Linear arrays are used in flatbed scanners that have a clear glass platen, just like a photostatic copier, onto which flat prints or transparencies are placed.

The fact that linear arrays are essentially one-dimensional, though, raises the question of how to scan in two dimensions. The problem is solved by moving the linear array along a fixed track while the data is continuously retrieved from the CCD. A prism-and-lens system is mounted with the chip, so that the projected image of the material being scanned is projected onto the CCD. The light source, which is a fluorescent or halogen tube, is moved along with the lens/CCD assembly. Thus, a two-dimensional image is constructed as a collection of lines. Figure 3.8 illustrates how a flatbed scanner is constructed.

For creating color digital images, either one or three scanning passes of the material on the platen are performed. In three-pass scanners, the lens/CCD assembly makes three individual passes, with a red, green, or blue filter placed in the light path (Fig. 3.9a). This generates three separate primary-color images, which are then combined to form the true-color image. This method must ensure that the mechanical track of the lens/CCD assembly remains perfectly registered during the three passes; otherwise a misalignment of color planes will result and destroy the image quality.

One-pass scanners perform a single mechanical scan of the material, thus eliminating the problem of registration between the color planes.

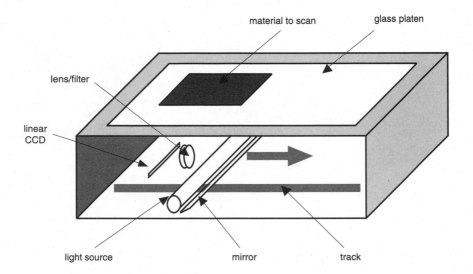

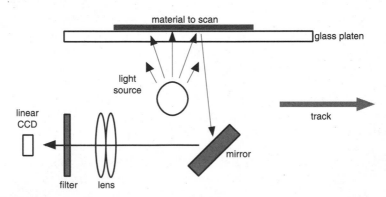

Figure 3.8 Flatbed scanner.

There are two techniques for one-pass scanners, as illustrated in Fig. 3.9b and 3.9c. The first method uses three light sources (namely red, green, and blue), which are flashed on and off very rapidly as the lens/CCD assembly passes under the platen. These flashes are coordinated with the data collection of the CCD to build the color image one line at a time. Alternatively, a full-spectrum light source, or white light, and prisms are used to split the red, green, and blue components of the reflected light into different paths, which are then collected by three different CCDs. This latter method is similar to the way a digital video camera works.

Surprisingly, there is little time difference in scanning material with a three-pass or a one-pass scanner. This is because the same amount of data is being collected, whether in one or three passes, and it is the collection and subsequent processing time that determines the speed of the scan. Both methods have their advantages, drawbacks, and related costs.

Many of the problems that arise with two-dimensional scanners do not occur with linear array flatbed scanners. Since lighting occurs only along a one-dimensional axis, and since the light source is a tube, achieving a flat field is much easier. Flatbed scanners generally are used in less-demanding applications than film scanners, so generating acceptable results is easier. Application software that controls the scanner may offer several fixed look-up tables, which makes calibration of the device much easier. Usually, the operator may select from a series of different scanning resolutions, both spatial and depth, which allows the scanning operation to be adjusted to meet the quality and speed requirements of the application.

Photomultiplier Tubes and Drum Scanners

The drum scanner is a type of image input device that uses photomultiplier tubes, instead of CCD, as the light sensors. Photomultipliers are used in such diverse applications as astronomy and subatomic physics, but work very well in drum scanners. Figure 3.10 shows a simplified diagram of a photomultiplier tube. A photomultiplier is a vacuum tube with an opaque cover, except for a small window that permits light to enter. Photons strike the cathode of the tube, which emits electrons. These negatively charged particles, in turn, are attracted to a positively charged dynode that produces a secondary emission of electrons than is greater than the input charge. The number of electrons increases as they cascade through a series (usually six to eight) of these dynodes, resulting in a signal that is amplified up to a million times from the initial number of photons that entered the device. This analog signal is then converted into a digital value that is proportional to the input light source.

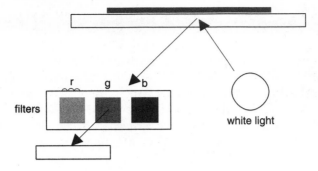

(a) 3-pass, white light, RGB filters

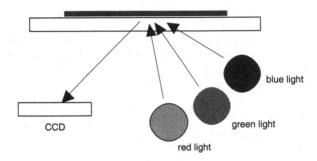

(b) 1-pass, RGB light sources

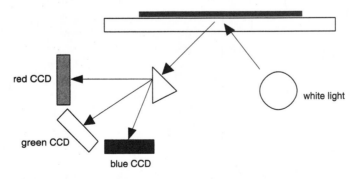

(c) 1-pass, RGB light sensors

Figure 3.9 Color flatbed scanner configurations.

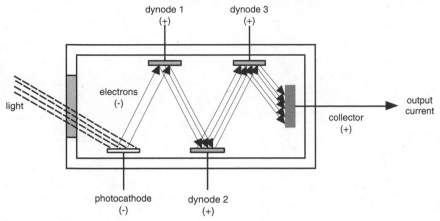

Figure 3.10 Photomultiplier tube.

Figure 3.11 shows how photomultipliers are used within a drum scanner. This type of device is designed to scan artwork that is attached to the inside of a plexiglass cylinder, or drum, that spins at speeds of about 600 to 1600 revolutions per minute. A very bright light source is placed at the axis of the rotating drum and is reflected 90 degrees and focused to illuminate a very small spot on the inside of the drum—where the artwork is attached. The light is attenuated at different frequencies corresponding to the colors of the artwork, and is reflected through a series of filters to separate it into red, green, and blue components. A separate photomultiplier detects the light intensity for each primary color, and from these signals a digital image is created. The rotation of the drum generates a line of the captured image, while the light source is moved down the axis of the drum to scan successive lines.

Drum scanners generally are used in the printing industry and are capable of converting hard copy into a very high-resolution digital image. Spatial resolutions of up to 8000 pixels per inch can be scanned. As with other input devices, drum scanners must be calibrated to ensure the best performance and highest-quality image capture.

Laser Scanners

A newer technology being used for scanning film and other transparency material uses a laser as a light source. Before discussing how a laser is used in this type of scanner, it is worthwhile to investigate what laser light is and how it differs from other light sources. In an incandescent lamp, an electrical current heats up a coiled filament inside an evacuated bulb (Fig. 3.12). As it becomes hotter, the filament glows, giving off both heat and light. A large quantity of heat, or

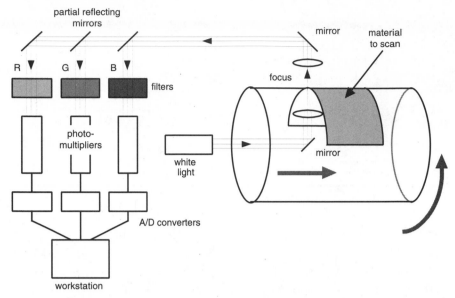

Figure 3.11 Drum scanner.

infrared radiation, is generated compared to a relatively small amount appearing in the form of visible light. The light that emerges does so in all directions and at many wavelengths, which is why a light bulb can illuminate an entire room in white light.

A laser (the word stands for *light amplification by stimulated emission of radiation*) operates very differently. A glass tube holds a gas whose atoms, when excited by an electrical current, move to a higher quantum energy state. Each atom wants to return to its lower energy state, and does so by emitting a photon. Some of these photons strike other atoms of the gas, which increases their energy levels and subsequent emission of more photons. One end of the tube is sealed with a mirror that reflects the light back through the excited gas, while the other end is sealed with a mirror that only partially reflects light. This end allows some of the light to exit the tube, and this is the laser light we see. As long as an electrical current is applied to the gas, the process continues.

But something unique happens to the photons as they bounce back and forth through the tube. All of the photons are of the exact same wavelength, or color, and are lined up in perfect synchronization with each other in a straight line. This property is called *coherence*, and is the reason a laser beam is pencil-thin over very long distances.

Lasers also are very efficient. While it is not advisable, a person can look directly at a 100-watt incandescent light bulb without causing any damage to his or her eyes. If a person were to look directly into a 0.5-mW (one-half of one-thousandth of a watt), it would be about the same as looking directly into the sun at noon. One should never look directly into any laser, since even the weakest of beams can cause permanent eye damage. Because of their efficiency, lasers do not generate much heat. All of these properties, namely coherency, intensity, efficiency, and monochromaticity, make lasers an ideal light source for creating scanners.

Figure 3.13 illustrates one possible configuration of a laser scanner. A laser is chosen that generates several discrete wavelengths of light,

(a) Incandescent light

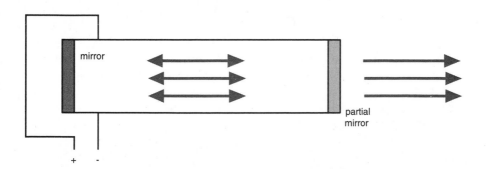

(b) Laser light

Figure 3.12 Incandescent vs. laser light.

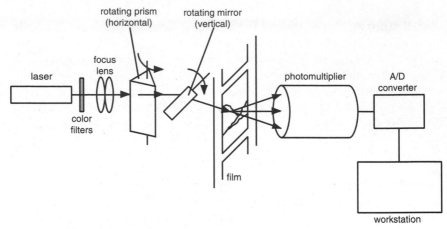

Figure 3.13 Laser film scanner.

namely red, green, and blue. A filter selects the desired wavelength, after which a lens precisely focuses the beam to a very small point. Unlike scanners with light sources that illuminate the entire area to be scanned, the laser beam must be accurately aimed at every point in the target. This is usually accomplished with a rotating prism and mirror that can move the beam horizontally and vertically.

Finally, the beam strikes the film and the intensity of the light is decreased, or *attenuated*, by an amount proportional to the density of the film. Therefore, a dark area on the film will allow less light to pass, while a light area will let more light through. The light that passes through the film is scattered in many directions and strikes a photomultiplier. The output from the photomultiplier is converted to digital values and becomes the pixels of an image. Even though laser scanners do not have uneven illumination fields like other film scanners, they do require precise calibration.

Ink Printers

Probably the most common form of image output devices are printers. They come in all shapes, sizes, and quality levels. Some output to paper, some to acetate, some to cloth. There are dot-matrix printers, inkjet printers, and laser printers. But they have one thing in common: They can either deposit or not deposit a dot of ink or toner at a specific spot. For text or simple graphics this works fine, but for images it creates a problem. Most printers cannot be commanded to output three-quarters intensity ink to simulate a pixel that has an 8-bit value of 192, let alone different amounts of ink for the remaining 255 intensity levels.

A seemingly obvious solution to the problem is to create a threshold image in which any pixel value less than, say, half the maximum value, becomes zero and no ink is output; anything over half the maximum results in a dot of ink. This solution does not work, however, because it creates the equivalent of a 1-bit-per-pixel image. That type of image, as was shown in the preceding chapter, is not pleasing to view.

Better solutions are provided by processes known as *halftoning* and *dithering*. While the two terms are sometimes used interchangeably, they involve different techniques. Both methods, though, make use of a particular phenomenon of human vision, called *spatial integration*, that causes us to see a group of very small objects as if they were a single large object, with a single intensity that is the average of all the smaller components.

Recall from the preceding chapter that digital images have both spatial and depth resolution. These two parameters are closely related and, if it is done properly, one can be traded off for the other. In other words, an image that has low depth resolution but high spatial resolution can look as good as one that has high depth resolution but lower spatial resolution. This is how a printer, with only 1-bit depth resolution, can acceptably reproduce an 8-bit image that normally is displayed on a CRT: The spatial resolution is increased to make up for the loss of depth. And halftoning and dithering are the means to perform that function.

Halftoning involves producing different patterns of ink dots that correspond to different intensity values of the digital image. Of course, most computer printers cannot generate dots of different sizes, so halftoning is governed by either printing or not printing dots within a localized group. Figure 3.14 illustrates how these groups could be arranged for different-sized dot groups. A 1×1 dot group can have two patterns, while 2×2 and 3×3 dot groups can have five and ten patterns, respectively. In general, the number of possible patterns that can be held by a group is given by the formula:

$$\text{Number of patterns} = (n \times n) + 1$$

In the above formula, n is the size of the dot matrix. Therefore, a dot group of 16 will yield 257 patterns, enough to hold all possible pixels values of an 8-bit image. This means that the depth resolution of an image has been reduced to 1 bit, but the spatial resolution has been increased by a factor of 256 (since each pixel now requires a 16×16 dot pattern). This means that a 1024×1024, 8-bit digital image becomes 16384×16384 dots. If the final output size of the print were to be 10×10 inches, the resolution would be more than 1600 dots per inch, or *dpi*. Since most printers have maximum resolution of only 300 or 600 dpi (newspapers print pictures at only 60 or 80 dpi), it is unnecessary

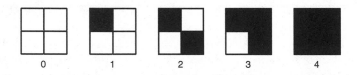

(a) 1x1 dot group

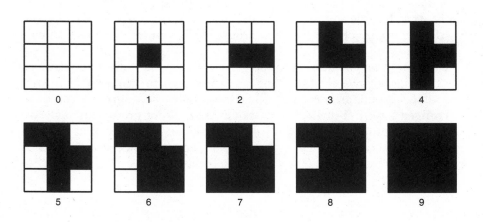

(b) 2x2 dot group

(c) 3x3 dot group

Figure 3.14 Halftoning dot groups.

to obtain anything greater than this. Thus, a 4×4 dot group would be sufficient for this example:

$$10 \text{ inches} \times 300 \text{ dpi} = 3000 \text{ dots}$$

$$3000 \text{ dots} / 1024 \text{ pixels} = 2.9 \text{ dots per pixel}$$

Therefore, a 4×4 dot group that yields 17 patterns will increase the spatial resolution sufficiently.

```
/************************************************************/
/*    program 8: halftone an image                         */
/************************************************************/

#define  HTONE  4
#define  XSIZE  640
#define  YSIZE  480

unsigned char *in;
unsigned char *out;

main()
  {
  long  int  x,y,h,hx,hy;
  char       mask;
  unsigned char p;

  /* initialize halftone group patterns */
  unsigned char htone[HTONE][HTONE*HTONE] =

{0x0,0x0,0x0,0x0,0x0,0x4,0x4,0x4,0x4,0x4,0x6,0x6,0x6,0x7,0x7,0xf,

0x0,0x4,0x4,0x6,0x6,0x6,0x7,0x7,0x7,0xf,0x7,0xf,0xf,0xf,0xf,0xf,

0x0,0x0,0x2,0x2,0x6,0x6,0x6,0xe,0xf,0x7,0xf,0xf,0xf,0xf,0xf,0xf,

0x0,0x0,0x0,0x0,0x0,0x0,0x0,0x0,0x0,0x2,0x2,0x2,0x6,0x6,0xe,0xf};

  /* allocate input and output memory buffers */
  in = (unsigned char *)malloc(XSIZE*YSIZE);
  out= (unsigned char *)malloc(XSIZE*YSIZE*HTONE*HTONE);

  /* read the grey scale input image */
  read_image_gs("input",in);

  /* halftone each pixel in the input image */
  for (y = 0; y < YSIZE; y++)
    {
    for (x = 0; x < XSIZE; x++)
      {

      /* get the input pixel to halftone
           note: for odd lines, offset the pattern by 1/2 the group
                                                         size */
      if ((y % 2) == 0)
        h = (long)in[(y*XSIZE)+x] >> 4;
      else
        h = ((long)in[(y*XSIZE)+x] + (long)in[(y*XSIZE)+x+1]) >> 5;

      /* generate the halftone pattern for this input pixel */
      for (hy = 0; hy < HTONE; hy++)
```

```
        {
      mask = htone[hy][h] << 4;
      for (hx = 0; hx < HTONE; hx++)
        {
        if ((mask & 0x80) != 0)
          p = 0xff;
        else
          p = 0x00;
        /* for odd lines, offset the pattern by 1/2 the group
                                                     size */
        if ((y % 2) == 0)
          out[(((y*HTONE)+hy)*XSIZE*HTONE)+(x*HTONE)+hx] = p;
        else

out[(((y*HTONE)+hy)*XSIZE*HTONE)+(x*HTONE)+hx+(HTONE/2)] = p;

        mask = mask << 1;
        }
      }
    }
  }

/* write the output image */
write_image_gs_ht("output",out,HTONE);

/* free memory buffers */
free(in);
free(out);
}
```

Program 8 Halftone operation.

Program 8 illustrates how to convert an 8-bit image, known as a *con-tinuous tone image,* into a halftoned image (stored as 8 bits per pixel for viewing) using a 4×4 dot group that yields 16 different patterns. Figure 3.15 shows a portion of an image that is enlarged to illustrate the effects of the process. Note that the array htone defines where the dots of the pattern for each pixel value will be placed. Small dots start at the center of the array and work out as the values increase. Also note that this pattern is only a sample; there has been much research into the process of halftoning that should be referenced before a programmer attempts to create an application.

In addition, some printers have the ability to output different ink levels for each dot. This fact can be incorporated into a halftone application that will reduce further the number of patterns necessary to generate acceptable results. Alternatively, multilevel printers can be used to increase the apparent resolution of the device.

Dithering is one of those ubiquitous terms that mean different things to different people in the field of image processing. There are numerous implementations of various algorithms, but all lead to the same basic solution. Dithering may be superior to halftoning when using a color printer because of the three independent color planes of an image. Unlike halftoning, dithering does not increase the spatial size of an image as depth resolution is reduced. Instead, it is a method for rounding the truncated pixel values up or down, depending on a pixel's position within a localized area. The best way to illustrate this is with an example.

Suppose an 8-bit color image is to be reduced to 1 bit for output on a color ink printer. If the pixel values were simply truncated, any 8-bit value less than 127 would be reduced to black (0), and any values greater than this would become white (1), creating the stark look previously observed. But think of this 8-bit number as a fixed-point number, having an integer portion of 1 bit and a fractional portion of 7 bits. The fractional portion that normally would be discarded can be used to

(a) Original image

(b) Halftoned image

Figure 3.15 Halftoned image. *(Image courtesy of Eastman Kodak Co.)*

make the decision to round the integer number up or down. Such a rounding decision usually occurs at a value of 0.5, but with dithering the rounding value changes depending on the pixel location.

The dither matrix defines the rounding values. Figure 3.16 shows a typical 2×2 matrix. The dither matrix is square and can be of any size, depending on the application. If x and y define the location of a pixel within an image, and n is size of the dither matrix D, then the correcting rounding value is:

$$D_{i,j} \text{ where } i = x \% n \text{ and } j = y \% n$$

In this formula the % symbol (the remainder operator in C) denotes a standard modulo operation. So if a pixel location corresponds to $D_{1,1}$, and its fractional value is less than or equal to 0.25, the resultant 1-bit integer value is rounded down. If it is greater than 0.25, the value is rounded up.

This process is called an *ordered dither* and has many variations and different matrix values. Program 9 is an implementation of the example described above. Figure 3.17 shows an 8-bit image that has been reduced to 1-bit values with dithering. Note that in areas of the image with a constant value, dithering may produce noticeable spatial patterns. Dithering is most helpful in transitional areas because it rounds off the "rough edges," giving a more pleasing look and generating more colors than would appear with simple truncation.

Thermal Wax Transfer Printers

Another type of image output device that employs different technology is the wax transfer printer. Here, the deposit of color is not ink, but a pigmented wax that adheres to paper. In order for this transfer to occur, the paper is brought into contact with a ribbon that contains a

	i = 0	i = 1
j = 0	0.00	0.50
j = 1	0.75	0.25

Figure 3.16 Dither rounding values.

(a) Original image

(b) Dithered image

Figure 3.17 Dithered image. *(Image courtesy of Eastman Kodak Co.)*

thin layer of wax, as shown in Fig. 3.18a. At the proper time, a precise heat source in the print head causes dots of wax to soften and transfer from the ribbon to the paper. The process is repeated for each of the subtractive color planes, namely cyan, yellow, magenta, and black, so that a true color image is reproduced.

Like ink printers, thermal wax transfer printers can transfer only the equivalent of a 1-bit image: a dot of wax is either deposited or not deposited. Therefore, digital images must be dithered before they are output.

Dye Sublimation Printers

A newer technology that is available for image output is called *dye sublimation,* which is also called *dye diffusion* or *dye transfer*.

```
/*****************************************************/
/*    program 9: dither an image                 */
/*****************************************************/

#define  DITH   2
#define  XSIZE  640
#define  YSIZE  480

unsigned char *ir,*ig,*ib;
unsigned char *or,*og,*ob;

main()
  {
  long  int  x,y,i,j,d,v;
  long  int  dith[DITH][DITH] = {0,3,2,1};

  /* allocate input and output memory buffers */
  ir = (unsigned char *) malloc (XSIZE*YSIZE);
  ig = (unsigned char *) malloc (XSIZE*YSIZE);
  ib = (unsigned char *) malloc (XSIZE*YSIZE);
  or = (unsigned char *) malloc (XSIZE*YSIZE);
  og = (unsigned char *) malloc (XSIZE*YSIZE);
  ob = (unsigned char *) malloc (XSIZE*YSIZE);

  /* read the input image */
  read_image("input",ir,ig,ib);

  /* for each pixel, round according to dither matrix */
  for (y = 0; y < YSIZE; y++)
    {
    j = y % DITH;
    for (x = 0; x < XSIZE; x++)
      {
      i = x % DITH;
      d = dith[i][j] << 4;
      v = ((long)ir[(y*XSIZE)+x] + d);
       if (v > 255) v = 255;
       or[(y*XSIZE)+x] = (unsigned char)((v >> 7) << 7);
      v = ((long)ig[(y*XSIZE)+x] + d);
       if (v > 255) v = 255;
       og[(y*XSIZE)+x] = (unsigned char)((v >> 7) << 7);
      v = ((long)ib[(y*XSIZE)+x] + d);
       if (v > 255) v = 255;
       ob[(y*XSIZE)+x] = (unsigned char)((v >> 7) << 7);
      }
    }
  /* write the output image */
  write_image("output",or,og,ob);

  /* free memory buffers */
  free(ir);
  free(ig);
  free(ib);
  free(or);
  free(og);
  free(ob);
  }
```

Program 9 Dither operation.

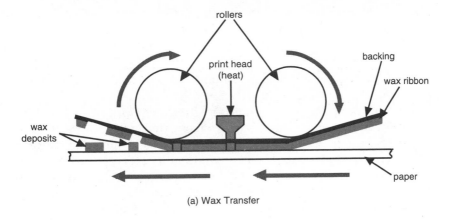

(a) Wax Transfer

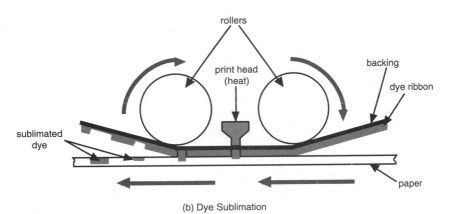

(b) Dye Sublimation

Figure 3.18 Wax transfer and dye sublimation printers.

Mechanically, these printers operate in a fashion similar to wax transfer printers. A roller brings the paper into contact with a special ribbon that is impregnated with the color dyes. A precisely controlled heat source at the print head causes the dye on the ribbon to transfer to the paper. The process is illustrated in Fig. 3.18b. Like wax transfer, there are four passes of the paper through the process in order to transfer the CYMK colors.

There are several important differences, though, between wax transfer and dye sublimation printers. While wax can be deposited only in discrete dots, either "on" or "off," dye can be transferred in incremental amounts. If more heat is applied, or if a constant amount of heat is applied for a longer period of time, more dye, or color, appears on the paper. This means that instead of being limited to dithered image outputs, dye sublimation printers can output *continuous tones*, a superior method for generating hard copy of digital images. Another advantage over wax is that the dye actually is diffused into the paper instead of merely being deposited on the surface. Thus, there is no waxy or "bumpy" feel to the final image, which looks more like a photograph.

Devices of this sort take advantage of different print head and ink technology. Since paper and ribbon are fed through the rollers at a constant speed, the print head must be precisely controlled and calibrated in order to allow for rapid heating and cooling. If this process, which is much more difficult than simply turning a heat source on and off, does not occur both at the correct time and with the proper amount of heat, the resultant images will not be acceptable. This also means that these devices are more expensive than wax transfer printers but, depending on the application, the quality can more than offset the cost.

CRT Film Recorders

The most common way to capture a digital image on photographic film is with a device known as a *CRT film recorder*. They come in many shapes and sizes, some small enough to fit on a desktop, and others that are large and stand on the floor. All work on the same principle, though, by having a camera mounted in front of a cathode-ray tube, or CRT, and taking a picture of its surface.

Figure 3.19 shows a simplified diagram of how this procedure works. A single color plane of a digital image is displayed on a CRT, and the CRT's phosphors emit photons in a wide range of visible frequencies, or white light. Thus, the image displayed on the CRT appears as a grayscale. A camera is placed pointing toward the CRT, and the lens of the camera focuses the image of the CRT on the film. A color filter, either red, green, or blue, is placed in front of the camera lens so that only the desired primary color is exposed on the film. In other words, when the red digital image data is displayed on the CRT, the red filter is placed over the camera lens; when the green data is displayed, the

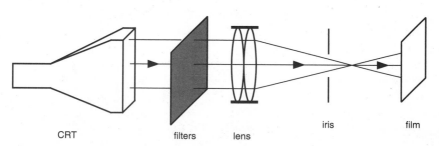

Figure 3.19 CRT film recorder.

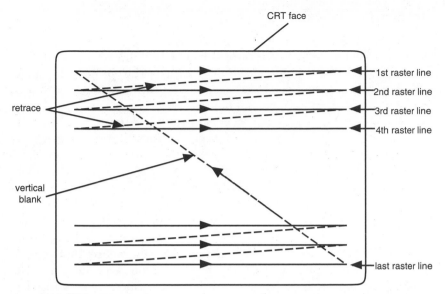

Figure 3.20 CRT raster display.

green filter is used; and the same happens for blue. Thus, a triple expo-sure is required to obtain a color image.

The CRT, which is the heart of these devices, is not like a normal tele-vision or computer monitor. While a television has only about 250 lines of resolution, a typical home computer about 500 to 600 lines, and a graphics workstation about 1000 lines of resolution, the CRTs in film recorders can have 4000 or even 8000 lines of resolution. Unlike televi-sion screens and computer monitors, which have a curved surface, these CRTs are designed with a perfectly flat face because any curvature would distort the image. The high resolution of these CRTs means they generally do not display an image in the same fashion as other monitors.

Figure 3.20 shows the standard method in which the electron beam is moved across the tube face, known as a *raster display*. The electron beam is energized as it traces along each horizontal line, and its inten-sity is modulated based on the data at each pixel. When the beam retraces to the start of the next line, it is turned off so that it is not seen. Similarly, when the display is completed in the lower-right cor-ner, the beam is turned off while it is returned to the upper-left corner to begin displaying the next image. For televisions and computer mon-itors, this process occurs 60 times every second so that the picture appears smooth and unbroken. Because of the massive amount of data that is displayed on high-resolution film recorders, it may take sever-al seconds for an entire image to be traced in the raster pattern. Therefore these devices are enclosed in light-tight cases so that extra-neous light does not interfere with the long film exposures.

Laser Film Recorders

As with laser scanners, laser film recorders will become more common in the future. They are quite different from CRT film recorders in that there is no conventional camera to capture the projected image. Instead, a laser beam directly exposes photographic film. Figure 3.21 illustrates the structure of such a device.

Unexposed film is positioned in a gate that is curved, not flat. The laser is capable of generating many wavelengths of light; red, green, or blue filters are placed in front of it to select the desired color for exposure. As with a laser scanner, a series of rotating prisms and mirrors causes the beam to traverse the face of the film while the beam is modulated as a function of pixel intensity.

Laser scanners are very fast and very expensive, but produce superior results when compared to other film recorders. The laser beam can be focused to an extremely small point, which means that images of very high resolution, 4000 or 8000 pixels, can be recorded. Since the beam is high-intensity, exposure times are short, increasing the throughput capacity of the device.

Input and Output Device Correlation

As this chapter has shown, there is a vast array of input and output devices from which designers of digital image systems may select. No one device is superior to another, given constraints of cost, speed, and quality considerations. What is important, though, is that all technologies be investigated before deciding on a specific device. Most applications are based on the old triad of input-process-output, and

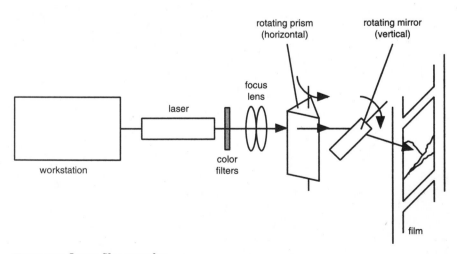

Figure 3.21 Laser film recorder.

therefore these devices should be chosen with care. It also is advisable to design with modularity in mind, since today's latest-and-greatest device will be tomorrow's antique.

Input and output devices, along with storage devices, are the most rapidly changing area of digital imaging. Constantly emerging new technologies provide higher quality or lower cost. As more and more people use digital pictures, they will expect only the best from scanners and recorders, so this fast-paced trend is likely to continue.

Point Operations

All image processing functions may be separated into three broad categories: *point, neighborhood,* and *morphological* operations. This chapter is concerned with the first type; the following two chapters will describe the others.

Point operations are defined as functions that are performed on each pixel of an image, independent of all other pixels in that image. Operations can be *unary*, meaning that a single image is modified, or they can be *binary*, which means that two images are combined in some manner. In certain situations, a point operation may be *tertiary*, implying that three images are used. On the surface, point operations might appear simple, but they are a very powerful class of image processing functions that can be cascaded one upon another to create interesting and useful results.

Look-Up Tables

Let us begin with the most powerful unary point operation, the *numeric transformation*. This operation is used in many situations and for many different purposes, and is frequently known by the data structure that implements it: a *look-up table,* or *LUT*. The operation is described by the following equation:

$$T_{x,y} = \text{lut}(P_{x,y})$$

where $P_{x,y}$ is the input pixel value, lut is the look-up table array, and $T_{x,y}$ is the transformed pixel value. Fig. 4-1 illustrates how this equation works. For every pixel in an image, $P_{x,y}$, the value, i, is used as an index into the LUT. The value in the table at that location, k, becomes the new, or transformed, pixel value. Program 10 shows how to perform this operation on an image. Note that the length of the LUT is exactly equal to the number of values that a pixel may have.

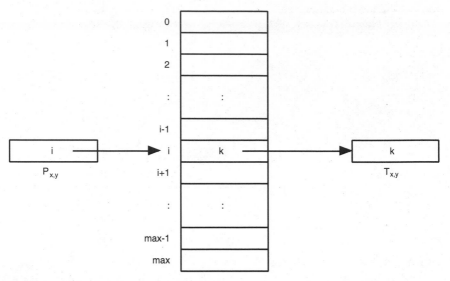

Figure 4.1 Look-up table operation.

For 8-bit digital images, LUTs are 256 entries long, whereas for 12-bit images they are 4096 entries long.

As Program 10 shows, performing this operation is trivial, especially when considering how important it is in digital image processing. The real science involved in numeric transformations is not in applying the look-up table, but in generating the data that's placed in the LUT. A LUT's data is also known as a *transfer function* and can be written in a mathematical fashion. For example, a look-up table that inverts an image to obtain a negative can be described by the function:

$$f(x) = \max - x$$

where max is maximum value that a pixel can have (255 for an 8-bit image) and $f(x)$ is the transformed value. Note that this is identical to the operation, described in a preceding chapter, that converts an image in RGB color space to CYM, but here the transformation is performed via a look-up table instead of being hard-coded in software. This is beneficial for the programmer because a single, simple subroutine can be implemented to perform the transformation, with different look-up tables and data buffers passed to the routine as parameters. This eliminates many specialized routines (such as RGB-to-CYM conversion) and provides for better code maintenance.

Any function that can be described in mathematical terms can be implemented as a look-up table. A few other examples are listed below:

```
/************************************************************/
/*    program 10: apply look-up table                      */
/************************************************************/

#define  XSIZE   640
#define  YSIZE   480

unsigned char *ir,*ig,*ib;
unsigned char *or,*og,*ob;

main()
  {
  long  int  x,y,i;
  unsigned char lut[256];

  /* allocate input and output memory buffers */
  ir = (unsigned char *)malloc(XSIZE*YSIZE);
  ig = (unsigned char *)malloc(XSIZE*YSIZE);
  ib = (unsigned char *)malloc(XSIZE*YSIZE);
  or = (unsigned char *)malloc(XSIZE*YSIZE);
  og = (unsigned char *)malloc(XSIZE*YSIZE);
  ob = (unsigned char *)malloc(XSIZE*YSIZE);

  /* read the input image */
  read_image("input",ir,ig,ib);

  /* initialize look-up table (invert, for this example) */
  for (i = 0; i <= 255; i++) lut[i] = 255 - i;

  /* apply look-up table to each pixel in image */
  for (y = 0; y < YSIZE; y++)
    {
    for (x = 0; x < XSIZE; x++)
      {
      or[(y*XSIZE)+x] = lut[ir[(y*XSIZE)+x]];
      og[(y*XSIZE)+x] = lut[ig[(y*XSIZE)+x]];
      ob[(y*XSIZE)+x] = lut[ib[(y*XSIZE)+x]];
      }
    }

  /* write the output image */
  write_image("output",or,og,ob);

  /* free memory buffers */
  free(ir);
  free(ig);
  free(ib);
  free(or);
  free(og);
  free(ob);
  }
```

Program 10 Look-up table operation.

$$f(x) = \quad x/2 \qquad \text{decrease intensity by half}$$

$$f(x) = \begin{cases} 0 & \text{for } x < 128, \text{ threshold an image} \\ 255 & \text{for } x \geq 128 \end{cases}$$

$$f(x) = \quad e^x \qquad \text{gamma modification}$$

It sometimes is easier to visualize these functions as graphs instead of as mathematical equations. Many image processing application programs provide graphical user interfaces with appropriate control handles that allow operators to modify the transfer function interactively. Figure 4.2 illustrates several typical functions, along with the results of applying each function to an image. The horizontal axis represents each value that an input pixel can have, and the vertical axis shows the output pixel value.

Figure 4.2a is known as the *unity LUT* because the output image is identical to the input image; it is linear with a slope of 1. Figure 4.2b inverts an image, having a slope of –1. These look-up tables are unique in that they do not cause any loss of information in the image, which is not true of other transfer functions.

The LUT described in Figure 4.2c will increase the contrast of an image. As can be seen, low-intensity values in the input image, say 0 to 31, are all mapped to 0. Similarly, high-intensity values, perhaps 224 to 255, all become 255. The remaining input values, 32 to 223, are linearly distributed over the output range of 0–255 and, as can be seen, this line has a slope greater than 1. The transfer function can be written in mathematical form as:

$$f(x) = \begin{cases} 0 & \text{for } x < 32 \\ (x - 32) \times (256/(224 - 32)) & \text{for } 32 \leq x \leq 223 \\ 255 & \text{for } x > 223 \end{cases}$$

If we think about how this affects what we perceive visually, we realize that the dark areas of the input image become darker, while the bright areas become brighter, causing the difference between these areas to become more pronounced. The LUT in Fig. 4.2d has the opposite effect, by decreasing image contrast. Its transfer function, which has a slope less than 1, is as follows:

$$f(x) = (x \times (\text{max} - \text{min})/256) + \text{min})$$

The variables min and max have been used to represent the desired minimum and maximum output values. It is important to note how easily one can be lulled into a false sense of security with digital

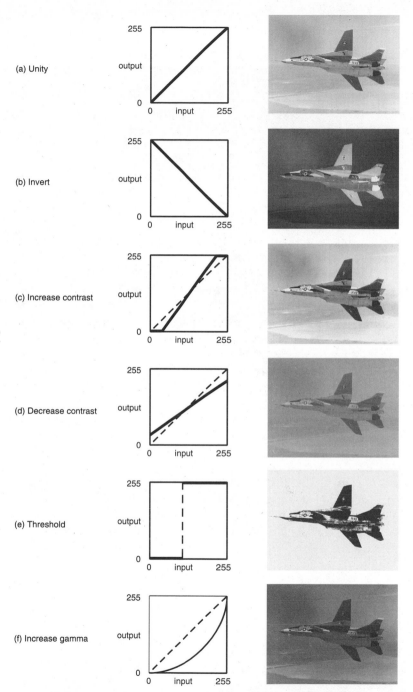

Figure 4.2 Typical transfer functions. *(Image courtesy of NASA.)*

images, only to find out later that a drastic mistake has occurred. At first glance, it appears that increasing and decreasing contrast are complementary functions, so an operator could, for example, increase contrast, then decrease it, and expect the resultant image to be the same as the one he or she started with.

This is not true, unfortunately. Numeric transformations such as these—in fact, nearly every image processing technique—always causes information to be lost irrevocably. In the preceding example of increasing contrast, all of the input values between 0 and 31 become 0 in the output image; attempting to decrease the contrast of that image will not restore the lost data. Programmers therefore must make sure that operators of their systems do not inadvertently destroy the images they are trying to enhance.

Figure 4.2e illustrates a *threshold operation*, which means that below some input value, all output pixels are set to the minimum (black), and above some value they all become the maximum value (white). Figure 4.2f illustrates that transfer functions are not necessarily linear, but may take on any shape or curve that can be generated. This example, referred to as *increasing gamma*, is similar to contrast enhancement. Pixel values of 0 and 255 in the input image map to the same output values, but the darker portions have their contrast lowered and the brighter portions have contrast increased. The image, overall, is darkened. Gamma modification, a useful tool when dealing with image display monitors, will be discussed further in Chap. 9.

Another important use of look-up tables in digital image processing is to perform color correction and modification. Just as a photographic processing laboratory can modify a particular color within a picture by altering the exposures of different primary colors, an image processing program can control the color of a digital picture. Figure 4.3 shows how this is done. Because a color image is composed of three primary colors (red, green, and blue, each of which can be thought of as a grayscale image), the data of each color plane can be operated upon independently.

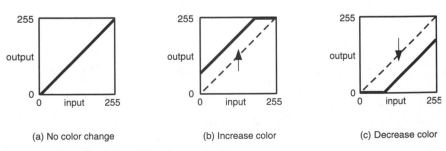

(a) No color change   (b) Increase color   (c) Decrease color

Figure 4.3 Digital color modification.

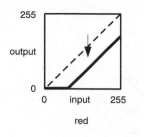
red

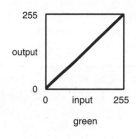
green

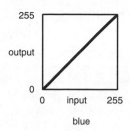
blue

(a) Make less red

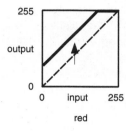
red

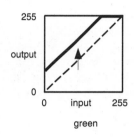
green

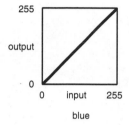
blue

(b) Make more yellow

Figure 4.4 Color modification examples.

If a color plane has the unity look-up table applied to it, that color remains unchanged. Application of a look-up table such as that shown in Figure 4.3b will increase the pixel values for a color plane linearly, while that shown in Fig. 4.3c will decrease pixel values for a color plane. As with other digital image operations, this is a simple process that has far-reaching results: A simple change in pixel values can greatly alter the look of an image.

Figure 4.4 illustrates two examples of color modification. The first shows how to make an image less red, while the second set of LUTs will make an image more yellow (or less blue). When implementing an application program of this sort, the designer should not force users to operate with pixel intensity values, unless that is their customary method of working. Instead, terminology should be incorporated that is more applicable to the field. For example, an operator accustomed to working with photographic film would feel more comfortable with film density units, while an operator in the printing industry might prefer percentages of cyan, yellow, and magenta. In addition to color intensity modification, the same principles are used to control features of brightness and darkness by modifying all three color planes in unison and, as was shown earlier, contrast is controlled by changing the slope of the line.

Look-up tables are used not only when processing images with software, but also are frequently implemented in hardware, as in the case of CRT display monitors. Many computer systems allow the user to modify the transfer function of a monitor in order to change its color or contrast. This is useful because the actual image data is not modified, only how is displayed to the user. Calibration of display monitors then can occur, so that one CRT will match another, or so that a monitor will match a different output device such as a color printer.

It should be remembered that look-up tables affect an entire image. They are not adaptive, which means they operate on all portions of an image in the same way. As was described earlier, application of a look-up table is not reversible, so the programmer must take precautions to avoid losing critical original data. One way to think of the process is to compare it to making prints from a photographic negative. Through the printing process, different tones and colors can be produced, but the original negative remains unchanged. The same holds true with digital images. The original data, like an original negative, is never altered, but new images, with various characteristics and modifications, are created from that original.

Arithmetic Operations

Since digital images are composed of numeric values, arithmetic operations can be performed on them. These are classified as *binary* operations because two images are used to create a resultant image. This can be expressed in the following equation:

$$C_{x,y} = A_{x,y} \text{ <operation> } B_{x,y}$$

where C is the resultant output image, A and B are the input images, and <operation> is the arithmetic operation performed between them, namely addition, subtraction, multiplication, or division. The values of each pixel in the images, locations of which are denoted by x,y, are independent of all other pixels in the image. Program 11, an example of performing the addition operation between two images, easily can be modified to perform subtraction, multiplication, and division.

There are many applications for these functions. For example, consider the image of the planet Saturn in Figure 4.5a. Notice the many superfluous bright and dark pixels, referred to as *noise*, that detract from the fine detail of the scene. If several images of the same scene are captured, the noise (which is random) will appear in different locations and with different intensities in each image. This fact can be

```
/**************************************************************/
/*    program 11: perform arithmetic point operation    */
/**************************************************************/

#define  XSIZE  640
#define  YSIZE  480

unsigned char *i1r,*i1g,*i1b;
unsigned char *i2r,*i2g,*i2b;
unsigned char *or,*og,*ob;

main()
  {
  long  int  x,y,i;
  unsigned char lut[256];

  /* allocate input and output memory buffers */
  i1r = (unsigned char *)malloc(XSIZE*YSIZE);
  i1g = (unsigned char *)malloc(XSIZE*YSIZE);
  i1b = (unsigned char *)malloc(XSIZE*YSIZE);
  i2r = (unsigned char *)malloc(XSIZE*YSIZE);
  i2g = (unsigned char *)malloc(XSIZE*YSIZE);
  i2b = (unsigned char *)malloc(XSIZE*YSIZE);
  or  = (unsigned char *)malloc(XSIZE*YSIZE);
  og  = (unsigned char *)malloc(XSIZE*YSIZE);
  ob  = (unsigned char *)malloc(XSIZE*YSIZE);

  /* read the input images */
  read_image("input1",i1r,i1g,i1b);
  read_image("input2",i2r,i2g,i2b);

  /* perform the arithmetic operation
     note: this example adds to images together to reduce noise */
  for (y = 0; y < YSIZE; y++)
    {
    for (x = 0; x < XSIZE; x++)
      {
      or[(y*XSIZE)+x] = (i1r[(y*XSIZE)+x] + i2r[(y*XSIZE)+x]) / 2;
      og[(y*XSIZE)+x] = (i1g[(y*XSIZE)+x] + i2g[(y*XSIZE)+x]) / 2;
      ob[(y*XSIZE)+x] = (i1b[(y*XSIZE)+x] + i2b[(y*XSIZE)+x]) / 2;
      }
    }

  /* write the output image */
  write_image("output",or,og,ob);

  /* free memory buffers */
  free(i1r);
  free(i1g);
  free(i1b);
  free(i2r);
  free(i2g);
  free(i2b);
  free(or);
  free(og);
  free(ob);
  }
```

Program 11 Arithmetic operation.

used to eliminate the noise by adding the images together then dividing by the number of images:

$$R_{x,y} = (A_{1x,y} + A_{2x,y} + \ldots + A_{nx,y}) / n$$

where A_1, A_2, etc., are the single input images, n is the number of input images, and R is the resultant image. This process is called *image averaging*, and the results are shown in Fig. 4.b. All random noise has been eliminated, the final image is much clearer, and it yields finer detail. High-quality results can be achieved by averaging three or four images, but even two will remove a large amount of noise.

As an example of image subtraction, consider Fig. 4.6. In machine vision or robotics applications it is common to have objects (such as screws, bolts, or other well-defined objects) on a conveyor belt passing a digital camera. A number of operations may be performed on that object, and the first step usually is to isolate it from background. Figure 4.6a shows an image captured by the camera, several screws

(a) Single Image with Noise

(b) Multiple Images Averaged

Figure 4.5 Image addition. *(Image courtesy of NASA-NSSDC.)*

(a) Image with Objects

(b) Reference Image

(c) Image Difference
(Enhanced)

Figure 4.6 Image subtraction.

distributed on the hard surface of a table. While it is easy for the human eye to distinguish the objects of interest, i.e., the screws, a computer can not do so. Figure 4.6b shows an image of the table with no screws present; this is called the *reference image*. By taking the absolute difference between the two images and increasing the contrast, Fig. 4.6c is generated. The screws are now isolated on a nearly black field and now can be further operated upon, as will be discussed in a later chapter.

Two other operators, not strictly arithmetic but very useful, are the minimum and maximum functions. The minimum operator compares the pixel values of the input images and assigns the lesser of the two to the output image. Similarly, the maximum operator assigns the greater of the two values to the output image.

A programmer performing these operations must be aware of several pitfalls. First, the processing in Program 11 assumes that the input images are of the same spatial and depth resolution. This might not always be the case. If the input images are different sizes, the programmer must decide whether they will be aligned at their centers, one of their corners, or some arbitrary offset. The programmer also might need to resize one or both images before the operations occur. In some situations, the input or output images may be of different depth resolutions; a numeric transformation must be performed before the arithmetic operators can be applied.

The programmer must be aware that the pixel values are usually integer numbers of a limited range. For 8-bit images, this range is 0 to 255. If a pixel of one input image has a value of 150 and the other input image is has a value of 130, and if the values are added together, the resultant value of 280 is outside the range of an 8-bit integer. If the programmer allows this operation to occur, most computers will handle this overflow condition by wrapping the number and maintaining only the least significant bits.

In this example, the resultant pixel would be assigned a value of 24 (280 less 256) and a very dark pixel would appear where a bright one was expected. Similarly, the programmer must be conscious of possible underflow conditions when subtracting two images. The programmer must be aware of the precision of the data and clip the results to the minimum or maximum allowable pixel value. In the above example, the resultant pixel value of 280 would be clipped to 255. Similar numeric considerations exist for multiplication and division.

Logical Operations

Another set of binary point operations are those involving the logic functions: AND, OR, NAND, NOR, XOR, and XNOR. The equation to implement them is the same as that for the arithmetic operators:

$$C_{x,y} = A_{x,y} \text{ <operator> } B_{x,y}$$

In this situation, though, the operations are performed on a bit level between the pixel values of the input images in order to generate the resultant image. Figure 4.7 provides the truth tables for each operator.

Image Composite

Seldom will the invocation of a single function described in this chapter be sufficient to satisfy the requirements of an application. As an example, consider the images in Fig. 4.8. It might be required to combine, or *composite*, the image of two people holding hands with garden

AND		
A	B	C
0	0	0
0	1	0
1	0	0
1	1	1

OR		
A	B	C
0	0	0
0	1	1
1	0	1
1	1	1

NAND		
A	B	C
0	0	1
0	1	1
1	0	1
1	1	0

NOR		
A	B	C
0	0	1
0	1	0
1	0	0
1	1	0

XOR		
A	B	C
0	0	0
0	1	1
1	0	1
1	1	0

XNOR		
A	B	C
0	0	1
0	1	0
1	0	0
1	1	1

Figure 4.7 Logical operator truth tables.

scenery in the distance. In this situation a third image, called a *matte*, is used. The operation is known as an *alpha filter*.

$$C_{x,y} = (A_{x,y} \times M_{x,y}) + (B_{x,y} \times (\max - M_{x,y}))$$

Every pixel in the image of the hands, A, which is also referred to as the foreground image, is multiplied by its corresponding value of the matte image, M. The same pixel in scenery image, B, or background image, is multiplied by the inverse of M. The results of these two multiplications are then added together to form the composite image, C. Where the matte is full intensity (255 for an 8-bit image), all of the foreground image pixel value is used and none of the background is seen. Similarly, wherever the matte is black, no foreground image is seen.

The image becomes interesting at the transition between the white and black areas of the matte. If the matte image is not thresholded, i.e., if it does not instantaneously transition from black to white, the resulting composite image will have a mixture, or *merging*, of the foreground and background images at those pixels. This mixing is important

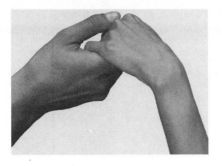

(a) Foreground Image

(b) Background Image

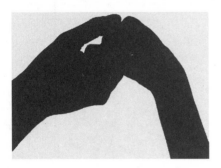

(c) Matte Image

(d) Composite Image

Figure 4.8 Alpha filter composite.

because it makes the foreground appear more naturally integrated with the background, as opposed to looking "pasted on." Program 12 provides an implementation of this process.

Another important technique for merging a foreground and background image is called *blue screen compositing*. As can be seen from Program 12, the actual processing involved in creating a composite image is relatively simple. The difficulty arises in generating the matte. A traditional method for accomplishing this is to capture the foreground subject in front of a brightly illuminated blue screen. Then, either by electronic means for video cameras or photographic means for film cameras, a matte is generated that allows the subject to be composited over the desired background.

This is the process used during a television news broadcast that permits a meteorologist to walk in front of maps and satellite photographs

```
/***********************************************************/
/*    program 12: alpha filter composite                   */
/***********************************************************/

#define  MAX    255
#define  XSIZE  640
#define  YSIZE  480

unsigned char *fgr,*fgg,*fgb;
unsigned char *bgr,*bgg,*bgb;
unsigned char *or,*og,*ob;
unsigned char *m;

main()
  {
  long  int  x,y;
  long  int  r,g,b,a;

  /* allocate input, output and matte memory buffers */
  fgr = (unsigned char *) malloc (XSIZE*YSIZE);
  fgg = (unsigned char *) malloc (XSIZE*YSIZE);
  fgb = (unsigned char *) malloc (XSIZE*YSIZE);
  bgr = (unsigned char *) malloc (XSIZE*YSIZE);
  bgg = (unsigned char *) malloc (XSIZE*YSIZE);
  bgb = (unsigned char *) malloc (XSIZE*YSIZE);
  or  = (unsigned char *) malloc (XSIZE*YSIZE);
  og  = (unsigned char *) malloc (XSIZE*YSIZE);
  ob  = (unsigned char *) malloc (XSIZE*YSIZE);
  m   = (unsigned char *) malloc (XSIZE*YSIZE);

  /* read the foreground, background, and matte images */
  read_image("hands",fgr,fgg,fgb);
  read_image("mountain",bgr,bgg,bgb);
  read_image_matte("hands_matte",m);

  /* perform alpha filter for each pixel */
  for (y = 0; y < YSIZE; y = y++)
    {
    for (x = 0; x < XSIZE; x = x++)
      {
      /* calculate alpha value (which is simply inverse of matte) */
      a = MAX - (long)m[(y*XSIZE)+x];

      /* calculate composite rgb values */
      r = ((long)fgr[(y*XSIZE)+x] * a) +
          ((long)bgr[(y*XSIZE)+x] * (MAX - a));
      g = ((long)fgg[(y*XSIZE)+x] * a) +
          ((long)bgg[(y*XSIZE)+x] * (MAX - a));
      b = ((long)fgb[(y*XSIZE)+x] * a) +
          ((long)bgb[(y*XSIZE)+x] * (MAX - a));

      /* normalize composite to 8-bit values and save */
      or[(y*XSIZE)+x] = (unsigned char)(r / (MAX + 1));
```

```
    og[(y*XSIZE)+x] = (unsigned char)(g / (MAX + 1));
    ob[(y*XSIZE)+x] = (unsigned char)(b / (MAX + 1));
    }
  }
/* write the composite output image */
write_image("output",or,og,ob);

/* free memory buffers */
free(fgr);
free(fgg);
free(fgb);
free(bgr);
free(bgg);
free(bgb);
free(or);
free(og);
free(ob);
free(m);
}
```

Program 12 Alpha filter composite.

with apparent ease. In reality, the person is standing in front of a blue (or sometimes a green) screen, while the person's image is composited with the desired background. In television, this technique is called *chroma key*.

Program 13 shows an implementation of this process as applied to digital images. While there are many nuances that can be added to enhance the look of the final composite, this program illustrates the basic steps that must be performed:

1. Invert the red channel data.

2. Multiply the blue and inverted red data.

3. Invert and contrast enhance to create the matte.

4. Replace the blue data with the minimum of green or blue.

5. Perform alpha filtering to generate the composite image.

While the process may at first seem complicated or magical, it is actually just a series of point operations that have been discussed in this chapter.

The images in Fig. 4.9 illustrate this process. Because the blue screen of the foreground image is very blue, by definition it has very little red intensity at those pixel locations. When the red channel is inverted in step 1, the blue screen areas become very bright. When the inverted red data are multiplied by the blue data in step 2, the bright areas (blue screen) become brighter and the dark areas (subject) become darker and form the basis for the matte. Step 3 enhances the matte by making the dark areas black and the bright areas white, and inverts the entire image to give the matte the correct "sense." This is

```
/****************************************************************/
/*    program 13: blue screen composite                       */
/****************************************************************/

#define  XSIZE   640
#define  YSIZE   480
#define  LUTMIN 80
#define  LUTMAX 150

unsigned char *fgr,*fgg,*fgb;
unsigned char *bgr,*bgg,*bgb;
unsigned char *or,*og,*ob;
unsigned char *m;

main()
  {
  long  int  x,y;
  long  int  i;
  float val,incr;
  unsigned char lut[256];

  /* allocate input and output memory buffers */
  fgr = (unsigned char *) malloc (XSIZE*YSIZE);
  fgg = (unsigned char *) malloc (XSIZE*YSIZE);
  fgb = (unsigned char *) malloc (XSIZE*YSIZE);
  bgr = (unsigned char *) malloc (XSIZE*YSIZE);
  bgg = (unsigned char *) malloc (XSIZE*YSIZE);
  bgb = (unsigned char *) malloc (XSIZE*YSIZE);
  or  = (unsigned char *) malloc (XSIZE*YSIZE);
  og  = (unsigned char *) malloc (XSIZE*YSIZE);
  ob  = (unsigned char *) malloc (XSIZE*YSIZE);
  m   = (unsigned char *) malloc (XSIZE*YSIZE);

  /* read the foreground and background images */
  read_image("foreground",fgr,fgg,fgb);
  read_image("background",bgr,bgg,bgb);

  /* build the lut that will generate mask in step 3 */
  for (i = 0; i < LUTMIN; i++) lut[i] = 255;
  incr = 255.0 / (float)(LUTMAX - LUTMIN);
  val = 255;
  for (i = LUTMIN; i < LUTMAX; i++)
    {
    lut[i] = (unsigned char)(val + 0.5);
    val = val - incr;
    }
  for (i = LUTMAX; i < 256; i++) lut[i] = 0;

  /* perform composite for all pixels in image */
  for (y = 0; y < YSIZE; y = y++)
    {
    for (x = 0; x < XSIZE; x = x++)
      {

      /* step 1: r = -r */
      m[(y*XSIZE)+x] = -fgr[(y*XSIZE)+x];
```

```
        /* step 2: r = r * b / 256 */
        m[(y*XSIZE)+x] = (unsigned char)
          ((long)m[(y*XSIZE)+x] * (long)fgb[(y*XSIZE)+x] >> 8);

        /* step 3: invert/contrast enhance r */
        m[(y*XSIZE)+x] = lut[m[(y*XSIZE)+x]];

        /* step 4: generate synthetic blue (min g,b) */
        if (fgg[(y*XSIZE)+x] < fgb[(y*XSIZE)+x])
          fgb[(y*XSIZE)+x] = fgg[(y*XSIZE)+x];

        /* step 5: alpha filter */
        bgr[(y*XSIZE)+x] = (unsigned char)
          ((((long)fgr[(y*XSIZE)+x] * (long)m[(y*XSIZE)+x]) +
            ((long)bgr[(y*XSIZE)+x] * (255-(long)m[(y*XSIZE)+x]))) >> 8);
        bgg[(y*XSIZE)+x] = (unsigned char)
          ((((long)fgg[(y*XSIZE)+x] * (long)m[(y*XSIZE)+x]) +
            ((long)bgg[(y*XSIZE)+x] * (255-(long)m[(y*XSIZE)+x]))) >> 8);
        bgb[(y*XSIZE)+x] = (unsigned char)
          ((((long)fgb[(y*XSIZE)+x] * (long)m[(y*XSIZE)+x]) +
            ((long)bgb[(y*XSIZE)+x] * (255-(long)m[(y*XSIZE)+x]))) >> 8);
      }
    }

  /* write the output image */
  write_image("output",bgr,bgg,bgb);

  /* free memory buffers */
  free (fgr);
  free (fgg);
  free (fgb);
  free (bgr);
  free (bgg);
  free (bgb);
  free (or);
  free (og);
  free (ob);
  free (m);
  }
```

Program 13 Blue screen composite.

the most subjective part of the process. In an actual application, the programmer should supply the operator with interactive controls to vary the contrast, since different lighting and exposure of the blue screen will yield different results.

Once step 3 is complete, the actual composite may proceed, but first the original foreground image must be modified. Step 4 yields an image with a synthetic blue channel, meaning that there will be no predominately blue cast to any pixel. While this may give the foreground image

Foreground Image

Background Image

Step 1: Inverted Red

Step 2: Red * Blue

Step 3: Alpha Filter Matte

Step 4: Synthetic Blue

Step 5: Composite Image

Figure 4.9 Blue screen composite.

a slightly washed-out (or *desaturated*) look, it must be performed; otherwise the composite will have a blue fringe around the edges of the foreground subject. Finally, step 5 is the application of an alpha filter, as described in the preceding example, which produces the composite.

There can be many variations on the techniques presented here that will yield optimum composite image quality. It also is possible to use a green screen instead of a blue one, in which case the same operations are performed, except substituting the green channel for the blue.

5

Neighborhood Operations

Neighborhood operations are those that in some form or fashion combine a small area of pixels, or *neighborhood,* to generate an output pixel. This is different from point operations, which rely only on a single pixel (or single pixels from multiple images) to perform a function. The uses and consequences of neighborhood operators are wide-ranging; this chapter will discuss how they work and demonstrate their use for practical applications.

The most important neighborhood operator is *convolution*. To convolve something means to roll together. In digital imagery, this means that a local area of pixels are "rolled together" in various ways to achieve some desired result. Almost as important as convolution is the process of *sampling*; many neighborhood operators result in sub-pixel addressing, which means that data values that exist *between* the discrete pixels of a digital image must be derived. Different methods of sampling allow this to occur.

The applications of neighborhood operators are diverse. This chapter will discuss many of the most popular of these, ranging from digital filters to techniques for sharpening, transforming, and warping.

Convolution

One of the most powerful techniques in all of image processing is convolution. It takes many forms and can be used to perform many functions. The general convolution equation, shown in Fig. 5.1, is computationally intensive. Figure 5.2 illustrates the same equation in a pictorial fashion.

At the heart of this operation is the *convolution mask* or *kernel*, shown as M in these figures, which has individual mask elements labeled mi,j. It is an array of numbers that has, just like a digital image, a

$$C_{x,y} = \frac{\sum\limits_{i=1}^{m}\sum\limits_{j=1}^{n} p_{i,j} * m_{i,j}}{\sum\limits_{i=1}^{m}\sum\limits_{j=1}^{n} m_{i,j}}$$

Figure 5.1. Convolution equation.

horizontal and vertical dimension, with size usually denoted as $m \times n$. Each element in the mask is multiplied by the corresponding pixel value in the neighborhood of the input image, P, that has elements $p_{x,y}$. The results of all the multiplications are added together, and this summation is divided by the summation of the mask values. This denominator is known as the *weight* of the mask. The result of the division is a pixel, $c_{x,y}$, in the convolved image, C.

Convolution requires a lot of computational power. To calculate a pixel for a given mask of size $m \times n$, $m \times n$ multiplications, $m \times n - 1$ additions, and one division are required. So to perform a 3×3 convolution on a 1024×1024 color image (which is a minimal convolution on an average-size image), 27 million multiplications, 24 million additions, and 3 million divisions are performed. For more substantial convolutions, such as 5×5 or 8×8, on larger images the numbers become astronomical.

Convolution also illustrates the close relationship of image processing to signal processing. Consider the images in Fig. 5.3. The first shows an undulating pattern of pixels increasing and decreasing in intensity, from left to right, in a sinusoidal pattern. The accompanying graph shows the corresponding pixel values along a line of the image. Figure 5.3a shows an image that is said to have a "low frequency," since the change in intensity from one pixel to the next is small. This also is apparent from the graph, since the sinusoidal wave is very elongated.

Figure 5.3b shows an image that has a higher frequency. Here, the change in intensity between adjacent pixels along the horizontal axis is greater than the first image. The graph of this image also indicates the higher frequency.

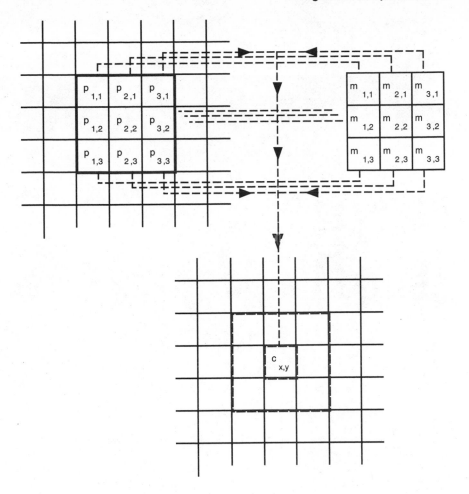

$$c_{x,y} = [(p_{1,1} * m_{1,1}) + (p_{2,1} * m_{2,1}) + (p_{3,1} * m_{3,1}) +$$

$$(p_{1,2} * m_{1,2}) + (p_{2,2} * m_{2,2}) + (p_{3,2} * m_{3,2}) +$$

$$(p_{1,3} * m_{1,3}) + (p_{2,3} * m_{2,3}) + (p_{3,3} * m_{3,3})] /$$

$$(m_{1,1} + m_{2,1} + m_{3,1} + m_{1,2} + m_{2,2} + m_{3,2} + m_{1,3} + m_{2,3} + m_{3,3})$$

Figure 5.2 Convolution illustrated.

In signal processing, the frequency of a signal is a measure of how often its amplitude cycles from 0 through both opposing peaks and back to 0, expressed per unit of time. In digital imagery, frequency is

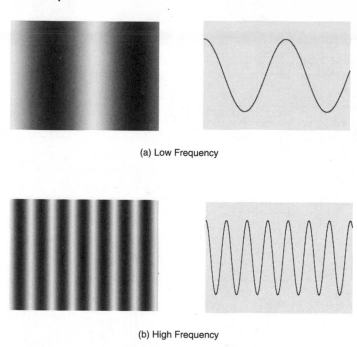

(a) Low Frequency

(b) High Frequency

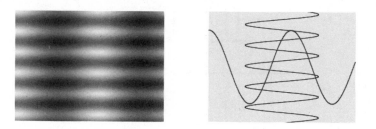

(c) Low Horizontal Frequency,
High Vertical Frequency

Figure 5.3 Spatial frequency.

determined by the raising or lowering of pixel intensities in spatial
directions. The image in Fig. 5.3c illustrates an image that has a low
frequency component in the horizontal dimension but a high frequency one in the vertical dimension. Note that spatial frequencies occur
within an image at any given angle, not just along the horizontal or
vertical axes. As will be shown in this chapter, the existence of these
spatial frequencies permits many interesting and useful operations to
be performed.

Program 14 is an implementation of the generalized convolution equation stated above. Several things should be noted when constructing

```
/*********************************************************/
/*    program 14: generalized convolution                */
/*********************************************************/

#define   XSIZE   640
#define   YSIZE   480
#define   XMASK   3
#define   YMASK   3

#define   RED     0
#define   GREEN   1
#define   BLUE    2

main()
  {
  unsigned char *ir,*ig,*ib;
  unsigned char *or,*og,*ob;
  unsigned char *i,*i1,*i2,*i3;
  unsigned char *o,*o1;
  long   int   x,y,c;
  long   int   xm,ym;
  long   int   *m1;
  long   int   val;
  long   int   w;
  long   int   m[XMASK][YMASK] = {-1,-1,-1,
                                  -1, 9,-1,
                                  -1,-1,-1};

  /* allocate input and output memory buffers */
  ir = (unsigned char *) malloc (XSIZE*YSIZE);
  ig = (unsigned char *) malloc (XSIZE*YSIZE);
  ib = (unsigned char *) malloc (XSIZE*YSIZE);
  or = (unsigned char *) malloc (XSIZE*YSIZE);
  og = (unsigned char *) malloc (XSIZE*YSIZE);
  ob = (unsigned char *) malloc (XSIZE*YSIZE);

  /* read the input image */
  read_image("input",ir,ig,ib);

  /* calculate weight of the mask */
  w = 0;
  for (ym = 0; ym < YMASK; ym++)
    {
    for (xm = 0; xm < YMASK; xm++)
      {
      w = w + m[xm][ym];
      }
    }

  /* process the red, green, and blue planes one at a time */
  for (c = RED; c <= BLUE; c++)
    {
    /* initialize pointers for current color plane */
    if (c == RED  ) i = ir;
    if (c == GREEN) i = ig;
```

```
    if (c == BLUE ) i = ib;
    if (c == RED  ) o = or;
    if (c == GREEN) o = og;
    if (c == BLUE ) o = ob;

    /* process all lines in the image
         (ignoring lines that would produce edge effects) */
    for (y = (YMASK/2); y < (YSIZE-(YMASK/2)); y++)
      {
      i1 = i + (y*XSIZE) + (XMASK/2);
      o1 = o + (y*XSIZE) + (XMASK/2);

      /* process all pixels in the line
           (ignoring pixels that would produce edge effects) */
      for (x = (XMASK/2); x < (XSIZE-(XMASK/2)); x++)
        {
        i2 = i1 - ((YMASK/2)*XSIZE) - (XMASK/2);
        m1 = &m[0][0];
        val = 0;

        /* generate convolution equation numerator */
        for (ym = 0; ym < YMASK; ym++)
          {
          i3 = i2 + (ym*XSIZE);
          for (xm = 0; xm < XMASK; xm++)
            {
            val = val + (((long int)*i3++ & 0xff) * *m1++);
            }
          }

        /* divide numerator by kernel weight and scale if needed */
        if (w  !=   0) val = val / w;
        if (val > 255) val = 255;
        if (val <   0) val = 0;

        /* save convoluted output pixel */
        *o1++ = (unsigned int)val;
        i1++;
        }
      }
    }

/* write the output image */
write_image("output",or,og,ob);

/* free memory buffers */
free(ir);
free(ig);
free(ib);
free(or);
free(og);
free(ob);
}
```

Program 14 Generalized convolution.

programs involving neighborhood operations. When implementing the point operations discussed in the preceding chapter, it is possible to perform a given function and, if desired, save the resulting pixels in the same memory buffer, thereby destroying the original input pixels. For point operations this is allowable, because once an input pixel has been processed its original value is no longer needed. This is not possible with neighborhood operators because, even after an output pixel has been calculated, the corresponding input pixel at that location will be included in other neighborhoods. Therefore no input pixels can be overwritten until all relevant output pixels have been calculated.

While point operation programs are generally a series of two nested for loops (one for the horizontal dimension and one for the vertical), neighborhood operation programs are usually four nested for loops: two for the horizontal and vertical processing of the image, and two for the horizontal and vertical processing of the neighborhood.

For clarity, previous sample programs have accessed images as two-dimensional arrays but, beginning with Program 14, addressing will be performed with pointers. This is usually more efficient in compiled languages. As with previous programs, the reader is encouraged to modify the sample programs presented here to obtain maximum efficiency for a particular application. Execution speed in routines performing convolution and other neighborhood operations can be increased substantially by taking advantage of special addressing schemes or eliminating unnecessary calculations, instead of implementing the generalized method shown here.

Low-Pass and High-Pass Filters

What are some of the applications that use convolution? There are many. Some of the most common are digital filters. As noted earlier, images can be thought of as signals that have detectable frequencies. In an image of a bright white picket fence against a dark foliage background, for example, the transitions between the edges of the pickets and the foliage produce high frequencies: The pixel values change from high to low values very quickly. Conversely, if color changes slowly across a large area, such as a sky at sunset, that image has a low frequency. Digital signal processing techniques can be applied to images to accentuate or diminish their characteristic frequencies. They are performed via convolution using different kernels.

Figure 5.4 shows a 3×3 kernel for performing a low-pass filter operation. This is a simple kernel that allows easy investigation of the effect it will have on an image. Since each element in the kernel has a value of 1, all pixels in the input neighborhood will contribute an equal amount of their intensity to the convoluted output pixel. In other words, the output pixel is just the simple average of the input pixels.

In regions of low spatial frequency (where a neighborhood's pixel values are about the same), the output pixel is nearly identical to the input pixels. Hence the name *low-pass*, implying that low-frequency areas are unchanged. High-frequency regions, though, will experience the same averaging of pixels, which tends to eliminate the rapid changes from dark to light. Figure 5.4b illustrates the frequency response of this filter, indicating that low frequencies are permitted to pass through unchanged but high frequencies are rejected.

Figure 5.4d shows the result of performing a convolution on an image with this low-pass kernel. By diminishing high frequencies, which define the sharp edges, the image becomes blurred. Applying a low-pass filter also has the effect of eliminating noise from an image, such as film grain in a scanned image—since noise is nothing more

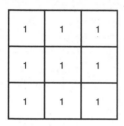

(a) Kernel (weight=9)

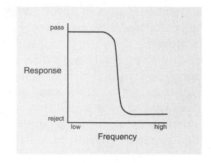

(b) Frequency Response

(c) Original Image

(d) Filtered Image

Figure 5.4 Low-pass filter. *(Image courtesy of Eastman Kodak Co.)*

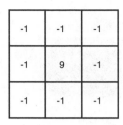

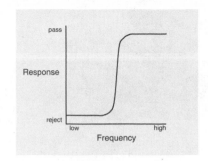

(a) Kernel (weight=1)   (b) Frequency Response

(c) Original Image   (d) Filtered Image

Figure 5.5 High-pass filter. *(Image courtesy of Eastman Kodak Co.)*

than very localized high frequencies. Unfortunately, using this method to eliminate grain also causes loss of sharp edge definition, which usually is unacceptable; another method of grain removal that provides better results will be discussed later in this chapter.

Since low-pass filtering can be accomplished using convolution, it follows that high-pass filters also exist. Figure 5.5 shows a common high-pass kernel. The 9 in the central mask location means that the corresponding input pixel will add a far greater amount of its value to the output pixel than the surrounding pixels, which have values of –1. The frequency response of this kernel is shown, along with the effect it has on an image. The high frequencies, or edges, of the image are highlighted, while the low frequencies are diminished. The visual impact of this is to make the image appear sharpened. Unfortunately, this type of filtering is usually quite severe and might not give desirable results.

(a) 100% Original,
0% Sharpened

(b) 75% Original,
25% Sharpened

(c) 50% Original,
50% Sharpened

(d) 25% Original,
75% Sharpened

(e) 0% Original,
100% Sharpened

Figure 5.6 Graduated high-pass filter. *(Image courtesy of Eastman Kodak Co.)*

One way to resolve this problem is by graduating the amount of sharpening incorporated into the original image. Once the high-pass convolution is performed on an image, the sharpened image can be merged with the original using the alpha filtering technique described in the preceding chapter. The result is a final image that is sharpened by an amount proportional to the percentage of the merging. The results of this technique are shown in Fig. 5.6. Software developers should allow the operator to select interactively the percentage of merging that occurs, since different subjects may require different degrees of sharpening. Another technique for sharpening will be presented later in this chapter.

Edge Detection Filters

Often there is a need to detect or enhance just the edges that appear within an image. There are many ways to do this using convolution. One common method is to use a *Laplacian edge enhancement* filter, the kernel shown in Fig. 5.7. Note that, unlike the convolution kernels previously discussed, the weight of the Laplacian operator is equal to zero; if pondered for a moment, this makes sense for edge detection. Suppose that this kernel, or mask, is "passed over" an image that has the same value at every pixel. The resulting image will be black, because the sum of each pixel times its mask value will yield zero. It also should be obvious that the final step of the convolution equation, dividing by the weight, must be ignored because dividing by zero is undefined. Also note how similar this kernel is to the high-pass filter discussed earlier; only the center value is different, being 8 instead of 9. This indicates that edge detection looks for high frequencies in images. It also should indicate just how powerful the convolution operation is, because completely different results are obtained by changing one number by the smallest possible increment.

Neighborhoods of constant intensity will become zero while those having a high frequency will yield pixels of positive or negative values. Because images usually have pixels with positive values, the programmer must make a decision about how to handle negatives. As usual, the decision depends on the application, but one of three methods usually is selected.

First, the resultant image can be assumed to consist of signed values. This may be most appropriate for machine vision applications in which another program interprets the results of the edge detection operation, and a human operator does not view the image. If this method is chosen, the programmer must be aware that the range of pixel values for, say, an 8-bit image, is no longer 0 to 255. It is now −128 (or hexadecimal 0x80) through +127 (0x7F).

The second method involves simply setting any negative values to zero and working only with positive values. This might provide the best viewing results because it will highlight edges as white pixels on a black background.

The third method involves offsetting the calculated value so that any negative pixels are moved into the positive range. For an 8-bit image, this is done by adding 128, or half the possible intensity range, to every calculated pixel. This results is a gray image in which intensities are not changing, and bright and dark pixels appear where edges

-1	-1	-1
-1	8	-1
-1	-1	-1

(a) Kernel (weight=0)

(b) Original Image

(c) Value Range: -128 to +127

(d) Ignore Negative Values

(e) Add 128 to Results

Figure 5.7 Laplacian edge enhancement filter.

occur. The images in Fig. 5.7 show these methods applied after Laplacian edge detection.

Program 15 is an implementation of the Laplacian edge detection algorithm and utilizes the three methods of handling resultant pixels described above (based on the setting of an internal variable).

Note that overflow and underflow conditions may be quite common because, theoretically, an output pixel can take on any value within the range −2040 (which is −8 × 255) to +2040 (8 × 255). Here again, the programmer must decide how to handle these conditions. The values either can be clipped to a range of −128 to 127, or can be scaled to fit into the allowable range. This sample program uses the latter method.

It also may be beneficial to use a mixture of these two because, as the reader should realize by now, there are very few hard-and-fast rules in the field of image processing, and the important thing is to produce results that are most appropriate for the application. This program also takes advantage of the fact that all convolution mask values are either 8 or −1, which means that all multiplications can be eliminated from the processing and replaced with a 3-bit left shift or a subtraction, respectively.

Using a priori knowledge of a specific situation is common in image processing applications since it can greatly reduce the number and type of calculations and, therefore, increase execution speed. This same operation could be performed with Program 14 (albeit with changes to handle negative numbers). The shortcuts taken here in Program 15 will make it run much faster. There is a down side, though, in that Program 15 is not a generalized convolution program; it is specifically designed to solve a program more efficiently. Changes to the kernel require program changes, not merely new input data.

Many other edge detection filters can be implemented, and all have benefits and drawbacks. Figure 5.8 shows variations on the standard Laplacian operator and the results one can expect to achieve with them. Note that filters can be constructed to detect edges in specific directions. Due to their limited size, these kernels can only detect edges along the horizontal, vertical, and diagonals. With larger masks it is possible to detect edges at any given angle, which can be useful in applications such as satellite photo-reconnaissance, where it is desirable to isolate roadways (which are generally straight for a given distance), or high-energy physics, where barely discernible traces of subatomic particles are captured when collisions occur.

As stated earlier, edge detection is closely related to high-pass filtering. It is possible to combine these two operations in a single convolution kernel that will produce the effect of embossing. Figure 5.9 shows these kernels and the effects they have when applied to an image. In this situation, edges are detected, but since the weight of the kernel is 1 (not 0), the bulk of the image content is retained. Because one side of the kernel contains positive numbers and the other contains negative numbers, however, any intensity gradients that correlate to this

```
/*********************************************************/
/*    program 15: laplacian edge enhancement            */
/*********************************************************/

#define  XSIZE   640
#define  YSIZE   480

#define  LSIGN   1      /* treat result as signed pixels */
#define  LPOS    2      /* ignore negative values */
#define  LGREY   3      /* offset negative values */

main()
  {
  unsigned char *in;
  unsigned char *out;
  unsigned char *i1,*i2,*i3;
  unsigned char *o;
  long  int  x,y;
  long  int  val,method;

  /* indicate how to interpret results */
  method = LSIGN;

  /* allocate input and output memory buffers */
  in  = (unsigned char *) malloc (XSIZE*YSIZE);
  out = (unsigned char *) malloc (XSIZE*YSIZE);

  /* read the input image (one plane) */
  read_image("input",in);

  /* process all lines in the image */
  for (y = 1; y < (YSIZE-1); y++)
    {
    i1 = in + ((y-1)*XSIZE);
    i2 = i1 + XSIZE;
    i3 = i2 + XSIZE;
    o  = out + (y*XSIZE) + 1;

    /* process all pixels in the line */
    for (x = 1; x < (XSIZE-1); x++)
      {
      val = (((long int)*(i2+1) & 0xff)<< 3) -
             ((long int)*(i1+0) & 0xff) -
             ((long int)*(i1+1) & 0xff) -
             ((long int)*(i1+2) & 0xff) -
             ((long int)*(i2+0) & 0xff) -
             ((long int)*(i2+2) & 0xff) -
             ((long int)*(i3+0) & 0xff) -
             ((long int)*(i3+1) & 0xff) -
             ((long int)*(i3+2) & 0xff);

      /* interpret results of output pixel */
      switch (method)
          {        case LSIGN:
```

```
      val = val / 24;
      break;
   case LPOS:
      if (val > 255) val = 255;
      if (val <   0) val = 0;
      break;
   case LGREY:
      if (val >  127) val =  127;
      if (val < -128) val = -128;
      val = val + 128;
      break;
   default:
      break;
   }

 /* save processed output pixel */
 *o++ = (unsigned int)val;
 i1++;
 i2++;
 i3++;
 }
}

/* write the output image (one plane) */
write_image("output",out);

/* free memory buffers */
free(in);
free(out);
}
```

Program 15 Laplacian edge enhancement.

direction will be enhanced, any that are opposite to it are diminished, and any that occur perpendicular to the direction of interest are ignored.

Two other types of directional edge detection methods are Sobel and Prewitt filters, illustrated in Fig. 5.10 and 5.11, respectively. Like the Laplacian operator, they detect edges, or gradients, in images, and differ only in the numbers that are used in the convolution masks. Unlike the omnidirectional Laplacian filter, these filters can only detect gradients in a single direction. To create an omnidirectional effect, the directional images are merged or added together.

Object Correlation

Filters based on convolutions need not be limited to detecting frequencies within an image. It is possible to use convolution actually to detect objects within an image. Consider the geometric objects that are strewn around within Fig. 5.12a. If we are asked to find all of the

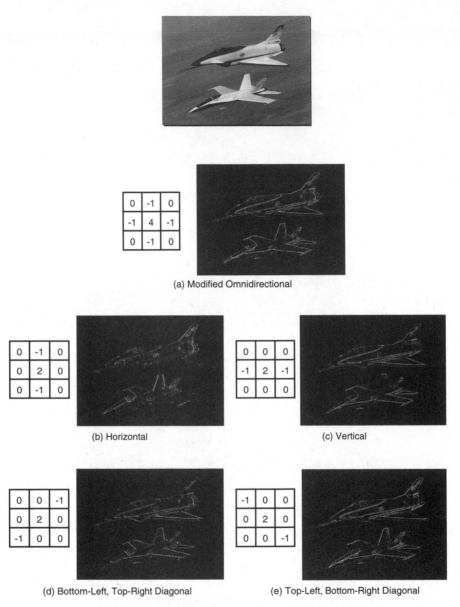

(a) Modified Omnidirectional

(b) Horizontal

(c) Vertical

(d) Bottom-Left, Top-Right Diagonal

(e) Top-Left, Bottom-Right Diagonal

Figure 5.8 Other Laplacian filters. *(Image courtesy of NASA.)*

diamonds, it is a simple matter for us to identify each one visually and point to it. If we ask a computer to do this, we must make the request in a different fashion.

The convolution kernels we have used so far have had some underpinning based on mathematics. But convolution masks can be created that correlate to specific object shapes, such as that shown

(a) Top-Bottom

(b) Bottom-Top

(c) Left-Right

(d) Right-Left

Figure 5.9 Embossing filter. *(Image courtesy of NASA.)*

Original Image

1	2	1
0	0	0
-1	-2	-1

(a) Up

-1	-2	-1
0	0	0
1	2	1

(b) Down

1	0	-1
2	0	-2
1	0	-1

(c) Left

-1	0	1
-2	0	2
-1	0	1

(d) Right

Composite Sobel Image

Figure 5.10 Sobel edge enhancement filter. *(Image courtesy of NASA.)*

Original Image

-1	-1	-1
1	-2	1
1	1	1

(a) North

1	-1	-1
1	-2	-1
1	1	1

(b) Northeast

1	1	-1
1	-2	-1
1	1	-1

(c) East

1	1	1
1	-2	-1
1	-1	-1

(d) Southeast

1	1	1
1	-2	1
-1	-1	-1

(e) South

1	1	1
-1	-2	1
-1	-1	1

(f) Southwest

-1	1	1
-1	-2	1
-1	1	1

(g) West

-1	-1	1
-1	-2	1
1	1	1

(h) Northwest

Composite Prewitt Image

Figure 5.11 Prewitt edge enhancement filter. *(Image courtesy of NASA.)*

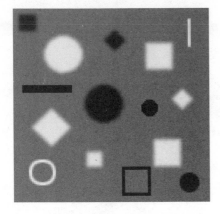

(a) Objects of Interest

(b) Correlation Mask

Figure 5.12 Object correlation.

in Fig. 5.12b. In fact, this mask was generated from an actual portion of the image in Fig. 5.12a, and has been magnified so that its individual components can be discerned. By performing the convolution operation with this mask, the resulting image is black everywhere except where the objects of interest occur, and these are identified as bright points. Note that objects that are similar in shape to the items of interest will produce some correlation, but with less intensity.

In real life, finding geometrical objects such as these is not very challenging. But this same technique can be applied in various application areas to generate useful results. For example, a machine vision system might need to find all objects in its field of view that have a specific shape. Medical images from a microscope might show higher numbers of cells that have a unique deformity when diseased. Satellite images could be used to monitor activity at hostile airfields by counting the number of aircraft on the tarmac.

It is important to note that object correlation using convolution can become very computationally expensive, since the process usually involves large convolution kernels. It would not be unreasonable to have correlation masks that are 20×20 or 50×50 pixels in size and, as illustrated earlier in this chapter, convolution operations of this size require many calculations.

Nonlinear Filters

Thus far, all of the filters discussed have been *linear*: Each is a summation of weighted pixel intensities, which then is divided by a constant value, or weight. Filters that modify their operation as the data elements change also can be constructed. This class of filter is known as *nonlinear* filters, also referred to as *rank* or *statistical* filters.

Consider the 3×3-pixel neighborhood illustrated in Fig. 5.13. Each pixel can be ordered, or ranked, based on its intensity compared to the others in the group. Nonlinear filters use this statistical information to select the final output pixel. Figure 5.14 shows an image after applying three different filters. The median filter will choose the middle value to become the output pixel, while the minimum and maximum filters choose the smallest and greatest values, respectively. Program 16 shows an implementation of these filters.

The results can be rather unexpected, as illustrated in this image. The minimum filter causes the woman's face to become dark and gaunt, with matted, flattened hair. In reality, the bright highlights of the hair and teeth have become thinner, while the dark areas, such as the corners of the mouth and eyebrows, become more pronounced.

	i=1	2	3
j=1	23	65	64
2	120	187	90
3	47	209	72

Rank: **23**, 47, 64, 65, **72**, 90, 120, 187,**209**

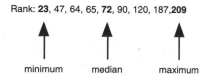

minimum   median   maximum

Figure 5.13 Pixel intensity rankings.

(a) Original Image   (b) Median Filter

(c) Minimum Filter   (d) Maximum Filter

Figure 5.14 Statistical filters. *(Image courtesy of Eastman Kodak Co.)*

Similarly, the maximum filter causes the face to appear brighter and fuller, and the hair thicker and shinier.

The median filter can be used to remove high-frequency noise from an image, but can introduce unwanted artifacts, especially in color images where the three planes of information are somewhat independent and the filter works on them accordingly. The minimum filter, also known as an *erosion* filter, will cause bright objects in an image to become thinner, while the maximum (or *dilation*) filter will cause bright areas to grow larger. Erosion and dilation are important morphological functions that will be discussed further in the next chapter.

Some of the harsh effects of applying these filters can be limited by not selecting the pixel value with a specific rank, but by taking the average of a few adjacent values to generate the output pixel. Averaging three pixels usually is sufficient, because doing more than that will have a blurring effect on the image. In fact, if all pixels in the

```
/*************************************************************/
/*    program 16: statistical filter                        */
/*************************************************************/

#define  XSIZE  640
#define  YSIZE  480
#define  XMASK  5
#define  YMASK  5

#define  RED    0
#define  GREEN  1
#define  BLUE   2

#define  MIN    1
#define  MED    2
#define  MAX    3

main()
  {
  unsigned char *ir,*ig,*ib;
  unsigned char *or,*og,*ob;
  unsigned char *i,*i1,*i2,*i3;
  unsigned char *o,*o1;
  unsigned char *pg,*p;
  unsigned char min,med,max;
  long  int  x,y,c;
  long  int  xm,ym;
  long  int  filter;

  /* indicate type of filter to perform */
  filter = MAX;

  /* allocate input and output memory buffers */
  ir = (unsigned char *) malloc (XSIZE*YSIZE);
  ig = (unsigned char *) malloc (XSIZE*YSIZE);
  ib = (unsigned char *) malloc (XSIZE*YSIZE);
  or = (unsigned char *) malloc (XSIZE*YSIZE);
  og = (unsigned char *) malloc (XSIZE*YSIZE);
  ob = (unsigned char *) malloc (XSIZE*YSIZE);
  pg = (unsigned char *) malloc (XMASK*YMASK);

  /* read the input image */
  read_image("input",ir,ig,ib);

  /* process the red, green, and blue planes one at a time */
  for (c = RED; c <= BLUE; c++)
    {
    /* initialize pointers for current color plane */
    if (c == RED  ) i = ir;
    if (c == GREEN) i = ig;
    if (c == BLUE ) i = ib;
    if (c == RED  ) o = or;
    if (c == GREEN) o = og;
    if (c == BLUE ) o = ob;

    /* process all lines in the image */
    for (y = (YMASK/2); y < (YSIZE-(YMASK/2)); y++)
```

```
        {
        i1 = i + (y*XSIZE) + (XMASK/2);
        o1 = o + (y*XSIZE) + (XMASK/2);

        /* process all pixels in the line */
        for (x = (XMASK/2); x < (XSIZE-(XMASK/2)); x++)
          {
          i2 = i1 - ((YMASK/2)*XSIZE) - (XMASK/2);
          p  = pg;

          /* get the input pixels for this group */
          for (ym = 0; ym < YMASK; ym++)
            {
            i3 = i2 + (ym*XSIZE);
            for (xm = 0; xm < XMASK; xm++)
              {
              *p++ = *i3++;
              }
            }

          /* sort the pixels by intensity value */
          sort(pg,(XMASK*YMASK),&min,&med,&max);

          /* save correct value to perform requested filter */
          switch (filter)
            {
            case MIN:
              *o1++ = min;
              break;
            case MED:
              *o1++ = min;
              break;
            case MAX:
              *o1++ = min;
              break;
            default:
              break;
            }
          i1++;
          }
        }
      }

  /* write the output image (one plane) */
  write_image("stat_max.bw",or,og,ob);

  /* free memory buffers */
  free(ir);
  free(ig);
  free(ib);
  free(or);   free(og);
  free(ob);
  free(pg);
  }

/**** sort function ****/
sort(pixel_group,elements,min,med,max)
```

```
unsigned char *pixel_group;
long int elements;
unsigned char *min,*med,*max;
  {
  unsigned char *p;
  unsigned char t;
  long int e,n;

  /* perform bubble sort until all elements are in order */
  n = 1;
  while (n > 0)
    {
    p = pixel_group;
    n = 0;
    for (e = 1; e < elements; e++)
      {
      if (*p > *(p+1))
        {
        t = *p;
        *p = *(p+1);
        *(p+1) = t;
        n++;
        }
      p++;
      }
    }

  /* save minimum, median, and maximum values */
  *min = pixel_group[0];
  *med = pixel_group[(elements+1)/2-1];
  *max = pixel_group[elements-1];

  return;
  }
```

Program 16 Statistical filter.

group were averaged, the results would be identical to the low-pass filter discussed earlier in this chapter.

Sharpening

A high-pass filter was used earlier to sharpen an image. This method
has disadvantages in that a convolution like this can produce severe
alterations in an image and result in undesirable visual artifacts.
These effects can be minimized by merging the convoluted image with
the original, as was done earlier, but the artifacts remain. A more
sophisticated technique for sharpening an image is through a multi-
step process called *unsharp masking*.

This technique not only produces a sharpened image, but is control-
lable with processing parameters. The process can be summarized in
the following equation:

$$S_{x,y} = (c/(2c - 1)) \times A_{x,y} - ((1 - c)/(2c - 1)) \times A'_{x,y}$$

In this equation, A is the original image, A' is the original image that has been processed with a low-pass filter, and c is a weighting constant used to produce the resultant sharpened image, S. Program 17 is an implementation of this equation, and Fig. 5.15 shows an image with this process applied to it. Unsharp masking is an interesting filter because it combines the use of a low-pass filter, which is a neighborhood operator, with multiplication and division, which are point operators. Upon examination, the equation for unsharp masking is similar to that for the alpha filter presented in the previous chapter. But instead of merging two different scenes with a mask to create a composite image, this process combines two versions of the same image via a constant.

As with many image processing techniques, unsharp masking does not actually sharpen the image, but increases the apparent sharpness by modifying the contrast between bright and dark areas. Figure 5.16a

(a) Original Image

(b) Sharpened Image

(c) Original Zoomed

(d) Sharpened Zoom

Figure 5.15 Unsharp masking. *(Image courtesy of Eastman Kodak Co.)*

```
/***********************************************************/
/*    program 17: unsharp masking filter                   */
/***********************************************************/

#define   XSIZE   640
#define   YSIZE   480

#define   RED     0
#define   GREEN   1
#define   BLUE    2

#define   LPASS   3    /* 3, 5, 7, 9, ... */
#define   WEIGHT 0.7   /* between 0.6 and 0.9 */

main()
  {
  unsigned char *ir,*ig,*ib;
  unsigned char *lr,*lg,*lb;
  unsigned char *or,*og,*ob;
  unsigned char *i,*i1,*i2,*i3;
  unsigned char *l,*l1;
  unsigned char *o;
  long  int   x,y,c;
  long  int   xm,ym;
  long  int   val;
  float       cp,cl,fval;

  /* allocate input and output memory buffers */
  ir = (unsigned char *) malloc (XSIZE*YSIZE);
  ig = (unsigned char *) malloc (XSIZE*YSIZE);
  ib = (unsigned char *) malloc (XSIZE*YSIZE);
  lr = (unsigned char *) malloc (XSIZE*YSIZE);
  lg = (unsigned char *) malloc (XSIZE*YSIZE);
  lb = (unsigned char *) malloc (XSIZE*YSIZE);
  or = (unsigned char *) malloc (XSIZE*YSIZE);
  og = (unsigned char *) malloc (XSIZE*YSIZE);
  ob = (unsigned char *) malloc (XSIZE*YSIZE);

  /* read the input image */
  read_image("input",ir,ig,ib);

  /* create low-pass filtered image */
  for (c = RED; c <= BLUE; c++)
    {
    if (c == RED  ) i = ir;
    if (c == GREEN) i = ig;
    if (c == BLUE ) i = ib;
    if (c == RED  ) l = lr;
    if (c == GREEN) l = lg;
    if (c == BLUE ) l = lb;
    for (y = (LPASS/2); y < (YSIZE-(LPASS/2)); y++)
      {
      i1 = i + (y*XSIZE) + (LPASS/2);
      l1 = l + (y*XSIZE) + (LPASS/2);
      for (x = (LPASS/2); x < (XSIZE-(LPASS/2)); x++)
        {
        i2 = i1 - ((LPASS/2)*XSIZE) - (LPASS/2);
        val = 0;
        for (ym = 0; ym < LPASS; ym++)
```

```
        {
        i3 = i2 + (ym*XSIZE);
        for (xm = 0; xm < LPASS; xm++)
          {
          val = val + ((long int)*i3++ & 0xff);
          }
        }
      *l1++ = (unsigned char)(val / (LPASS*LPASS));
      i1++;
      }
    }
  }

/* calculate constants for image merge */
cp = WEIGHT / ((2.0 * WEIGHT) - 1.0);
cl = (1.0 - WEIGHT) / ((2.0 * WEIGHT) - 1.0);

/* process the red, green, and blue planes one at a time */
for (c = RED; c <= BLUE; c++)
  {
  /* initialize pointers for current color plane */
  if (c == RED  ) i = ir;
  if (c == GREEN) i = ig;
  if (c == BLUE ) i = ib;
  if (c == RED  ) l = lr;
  if (c == GREEN) l = lg;
  if (c == BLUE ) l = lb;
  if (c == RED  ) o = or;
  if (c == GREEN) o = og;
  if (c == BLUE ) o = ob;

  /* merge the original and low-pass images */
  for (y = 0; y < YSIZE; y++)
    {
    for (x = 0; x < XSIZE; x++)
      {
      fval = (cp * (float)*i++) - (cl * (float)*l++);
      if (fval < 0.0)   fval = 0.0;
      if (fval > 255.0) fval = 255.0;
      *o++ = (unsigned char)fval;
      }
    }
  }

/* write the output image */
write_image("output",or,og,ob);

/* free memory buffers */
free(ir);
free(ig);   free(ib);
free(lr);
free(lg);
free(lb);
free(or);
free(og);
free(ob);
}
```

Program 17 Unsharp masking filter.

shows the graph of pixel intensities along a line of an image as the transition is made between a dark area and a bright area. Figure 5.16b shows the same transition of the low-pass filtered image. In this second graph, the length of the transition from dark to bright is longer, which is what would be expected knowing that this function reduces higher frequencies. But the graph in Fig. 5.16c shows the transition in the final "sharpened" image. The slope of the transition is about the same as in the original image, but there is a slight undershoot and overshoot of intensities at the edges. This subtle change causes the boundaries between dark and bright areas to be accentuated—which, in turn, causes our vision system to perceive a sharper image.

The low-pass filter applied to the image is the same one shown earlier in this chapter. The degree of sharpening increases as the size of the convolution becomes greater. In other words, a 9×9 low-pass filter will generate more sharpening than a 3×3 filter. The weighting constant, c, should have a value of between 0.6 and 0.85; a lower value for this constant will produce more sharpening. The programmer should allow the operator to control these parameters independently so that optimum results can be achieved. This operation is a good example of how digital image processing is a very subjective science. What one person might consider acceptable results, someone else might find unacceptable. It is important that the application software does not restrict this freedom of choice.

Degraining

Degraining is another specialized operation that often must be applied to digital images that originate from scanned photographic film. All film has grain, which causes small bright and dark spots to appear in digital images. Many schemes have been devised to eliminate this grain, some of which have already been discussed. The technique discussed here generates good results with minimal deterioration of image quality.

The technique is known as *pseudomedian* filtering and, as the name suggests, it is a form of median filtering that was discussed earlier in this chapter. It is described by W. Pratt in *Digital Image Processing*. Recall that a median filter interrogates and ranks all pixels in a neighborhood, then selects the median value to become the new output pixel intensity. Unfortunately, this is also a form of low-pass filtering, so sharp detail could be lost during the process.

Pratt's degraining algorithm considers a pixel group, which in the example shown in Fig. 5.17 is 5×5 pixels, to be made up of a vertical and a horizontal vector. The sequence of pixels along the horizontal line are labeled a through e, and those along the vertical are f through i. The center pixel, c, is included in both sequences. These two one-

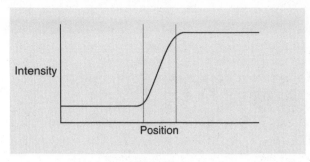

(a) Original Image

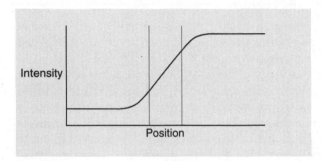

(b) Low-Pass Filtered

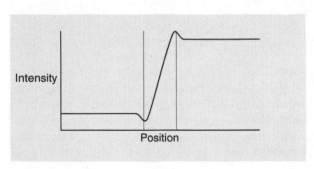

(c) "Sharpened"

Figure 5.16 Apparent sharpness using contrast.

dimensional sequences can be combined to form a single sequence, written as:

$$(a,b,c,d,e,f,g,c,h,i)$$

This sequence can be divided into subsequences of three adjacent pixels, namely, (a,b,c), (b,c,d), (c,d,e), and so forth, until the final subsequence, (c,h,i). The minimum value of each of these subsequences can be found, which creates a new sequence. Finally, the maximum value of this new sequence of minima can be found. This is known as the *maximin* operator and is defined as:

$$\text{maximin} = \max[(\min(a,b,c), \min(b,c,d), \min(c,d,e), \ldots, \min(c,h,i))]$$

When applied to an image, this operator will remove isolated bright areas of noise. Conversely, the *minimax* operator, which is the minimum value of the maximum of the subsequences, has the form:

$$\text{minimax} = \min[(\max(a,b,c), \max(b,c,d), \max(c,d,e), \ldots, \max(c,h,i))]$$

The minimax operator will remove dark noise from an image. To remove both bright and dark noise, one operator must be applied to an image, followed by the other. The order of the application does not matter. Program 18 is an implementation of this filter; Fig. 5.18 shows an enlarged portion of an image to which cascaded minimax and maximin operators have been applied.

While this technique can reduce grain without being overly destructive, it does have limits and might not solve all grain problems in scanned images. It does tend to maintain overall sharpness, something that previously discussed techniques do not. This example uses a 5 × 5 pixel group, but smaller and larger groups can be used. The larger the pixel groups, generally the more grain that is removed — but the cost of more grain reduction is also more action as a low-pass filter. In addition, because the operation is performed on a plus-signed

Figure 5.17 Pseudomedian filter pixel neighborhood.

(a) Original Image   (b) Minimax-Maximin

(c) Original Zoomed   (d) Minimax-Maximin Zoom

Figure 5.18 Cascaded minimax and maximin filters. *(Image courtesy of Eastman Kodak Co.)*

array of pixels rather than on a square area, some unwanted vertical or horizontal attributes of the image (Fig. 5.18) are enhanced or diminished.

Sampling

All neighborhood operators mentioned so far in this chapter have been based on convolution or ranking. There is another set of operators, called *geometric transformations*, that are based on sampling. The most common of these functions are image *rotation, scaling,* and *translation*. Others include *perspective* and *nonlinear warping*. Before these can be presented, however, it is necessary to grasp the underlying concept of sampling on which they are all based.

Up until now, pixels have been presented as squares that are adjacent to one another. Another way to visualize them is as points of light that are separated from one another by a discrete distance. These two

```
/************************************************************/
/*   program 18: degrain filter                          */
/************************************************************/

#define  XSIZE   640
#define  YSIZE   480
#define  NSIZE   5

#define  RED     0
#define  GREEN   1
#define  BLUE    2

void degrain();
void degrain_seq();
unsigned char minimax();
unsigned char maximin();
unsigned char mini();
unsigned char maxi();

main()
  {
  unsigned char *ir,*ig,*ib;
  unsigned char *or,*og,*ob;

  /* allocate input and output memory buffers */
  ir = (unsigned char *) malloc (XSIZE*YSIZE);
  ig = (unsigned char *) malloc (XSIZE*YSIZE);
  ib = (unsigned char *) malloc (XSIZE*YSIZE);
  or = (unsigned char *) malloc (XSIZE*YSIZE);
  og = (unsigned char *) malloc (XSIZE*YSIZE);
  ob = (unsigned char *) malloc (XSIZE*YSIZE);

  /* read the input image */
  read_image("input",ir,ig,ib);

  /* perform degrain function on each color plane */
  degrain(ir,or);
  degrain(ig,og);
  degrain(ib,ob);

  /* write the output image */
  write_image("output",or,og,ob);

  /* free memory buffers */
  free(ir);
  free(ig);
  free(ib);
  free(or);
  free(og);
  free(ob);
  }

/************************************************************/
/*    degrain: apply degrain filter to an image plane    */
/************************************************************/

void degrain(p,d)
```

```
unsigned char *p,*d;
{
unsigned char *i,*o;
unsigned char s[100];
long int  x,y;
long int  l,m;
long int  pass;

/* set pixel group and sequence sizes */
m = NSIZE;
l = (2 * m) + 1;

/* pass 1: minimax, pass 2: maximin */
for (pass = 1; pass <= 2; pass++)
  {
  /* perform the degrain (minimax or maximin) on every pixel */
  for (y = 0; y < YSIZE; y++)
    {
    i = p + (y * XSIZE);
    o = d + (y * XSIZE);
    for (x = 0; x < XSIZE; x++)
      {
      if ((y<m) || (y>(YSIZE-m-1)) || (x<m) || (x>(XSIZE-m-1)))
        {
        *o = *i;
        }
      else
        {
        degrain_seq(i,s,m);
        if (pass == 1) *o = minimax(s,m,l);
        if (pass == 2) *o = maximin(s,m,l);
        }
      i++;
      o++;
      }
    }

  /* results of pass 1 are copied to input buffer for pass 2 */
  if (pass == 1)
    {
    i = p;
    o = d;
    for (y = 0; y < YSIZE; y++)
      for (x = 0; x < XSIZE; x++)
        *i++ = *o++;
    }
  }

return;
}

/**************************************************************/
/*    degrain_seq: extract a sequence of pixels             */
/**************************************************************/

void degrain_seq(p,s,m)
  unsigned char *p;      /* image buffer pointer */
```

```
unsigned char *s;        /* extracted pixel sequence pointer */
long  int  m;            /* pixel group size */
{
unsigned char *o;
long  int  x,y;

o = s;

/* copy horizontal pixels to sequence */
for (x = -m; x <= m; x++) *o++ = *(p+x);

/* copy vertical pixels to sequence */
for (y = -m; y <= m; y++) *o++ = *(p+(y*XSIZE));

return;
}
/*************************************************************/
/*    minimax: perform minimax function on a sequence     */
/*************************************************************/
unsigned char minimax(s1,m,l)
  unsigned char *s1;      /* pixel sequence pointer */
  long  int  m;           /* pixel group size */
  long  int  l;           /* pixel sequence length */
  {
  unsigned char *i,*o,*s;
  unsigned char s2[100];
  unsigned char v;
  long  int  x,y,z;
  long  int  mm;

  /* find maximum of each horizontal sub-sequence */
  o = s2;
  i = s1;
  for (x = 1; x <= (m+1); x++)
    {
    s = i;
    v = *s++;
    for (mm = 0; mm < m; mm++)
      if (*s++ > v) v = *(s-1);
    *o++ = v;
    i++;
    }

  /* find maximum of each vertical sub-sequence */
  i = s1 + (l+1);  for (y = 1; y <= (m+1); y++)
    {
    s = i;
    v = *s++;
    for (mm = 0; mm < m; mm++)
      if (*s++ > v) v = *(s-1);
    *o++ = v;
    i++;
    }

  /* find minimum of the maximums */
  s = s2;
  v = *s++;
  for (z = 1; z < l+1; z++)
```

```
    if (*s++ < v)
      v = *(s-1);

  /* return minimax value */
  return(v);
  }

/********************************************************/
/*    maximin: perform maximin function on a sequence   */
/********************************************************/

unsigned char maximin(s1,m,l)
  unsigned char *s1;      /* pixel sequence pointer */
  long  int  m;           /* pixel group size */
  long  int  l;           /* pixel sequence length */
  {
  unsigned char *i,*o,*s;
  unsigned char s2[100];
  unsigned char v;
  long  int  x,y,z;
  long  int  mm;

  /* find minimum of each horizontal sub-sequence */
  o = s2;
  i = s1;
  for (x = 1; x <= (m+1); x++)
    {
    s = i;
    v = *s++;
    for (mm = 0; mm < m; mm++)
      if (*s++ < v) v = *(s-1);
    *o++ = v;
    i++;
    }

  /* find minimum of each vertical sub-sequence */
  i = s1 + (l+1);
  for (y = 1; y <= (m+1); y++)
    {
    s = i;    v = *s++;
    for (mm = 0; mm < m; mm++)
      if (*s++ < v) v = *(s-1);
    *o++ = v;
    i++;
    }

  /* find maximum of the minimums */
  s = s2;
  v = *s++;
  for (z = 1; z < l+1; z++)
    if (*s++ > v)
      v = *(s-1);

  /* return maximin value */
  return(v);
  }
```

Program 18 Degrain filter.

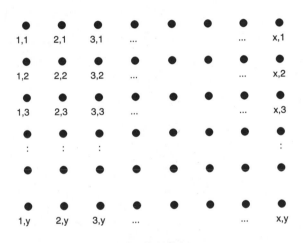

1,1	2,1	3,1	...			...	x,1
1,2	2,2	3,2	...			...	x,2
1,3	2,3	3,3	...			...	x,3
:	:	:					:
1,y	2,y	3,y	...			...	x,y

(a) Pixels as Squares

(b) Pixels as Points

Figure 5.19 Pixels as intersections.

methods of visualization are shown in Fig. 5.19. Consider what happens when an image is reduced in size by some arbitrary amount, as shown in Fig. 5.20a. Obviously, one could think of each pixel as getting smaller, or, in the new way of visualization, as the distance between pinpoints becoming less. Unfortunately, image display devices do not work this way: The resolution of a device is fixed and a pixel is a pixel. An even more abstract concept is the digital image itself: a 1024 × 1024 image has a defined spatial resolution, and just wanting to think of it as half the size, or 512 × 512, does not make it so.

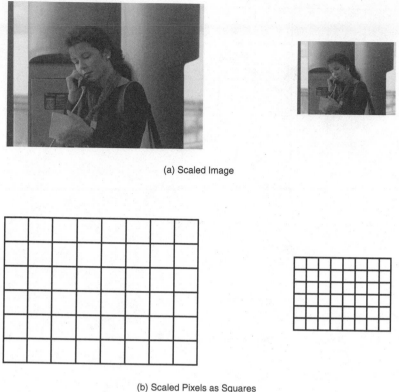

(a) Scaled Image

(b) Scaled Pixels as Squares

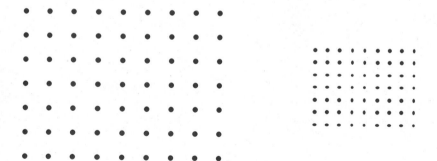

(c) Scaled Pixels as Points

Figure 5.20 Image reduction. *(Image courtesy of Eastman Kodak Co.)*

Consider the grid of pixels shown in Fig. 5.21. If we wished to reduce the size of the larger grid by one half, we simply could ignore every other pixel in the horizontal and vertical dimensions, as shown, producing a new and smaller grid. This new grid, or image, has only one-quarter the number of pixels as the original. This is called a *geometric transformation,* or in this example, a *scale operation.* Since we selectively discarded or kept pixels of the old image to form the new, smaller image, we sampled the data of the original image in some predetermined method (in this case by ignoring every other pixel).

The transformation of pixel locations from the original, or *source,* image into resultant, or *destination*, image is called *mapping.* A frame of reference for mapping must be defined. Figure 5.22 illustrates two ways to look at mapping. In the first, each pixel in the source image is transformed to its new location in the destination, called a *forward transform.* Alternatively, each pixel in the destination image is transformed to find where it was in the source image, which is an *inverse transform.* Either method can be used, but in forward transforms the programmer must be careful that all pixels in the destination image get filled in, or "holes" will appear. Inverse transforms never result in holes, because every destination pixel is addressed and filled in. This, then, is the method that will be illustrated.

Most of the time, geometric transformations result in mappings that land between pixels. This phenomenon leads to the last concept that must be discussed, which is sampling an image in a sub-pixel fashion. There are basically two ways of doing this: *nearest neighbor* sampling

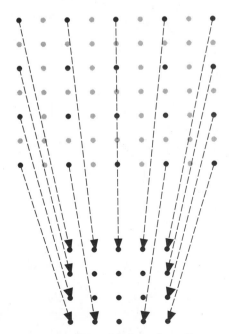

Figure 5.21 Geometric transformation.

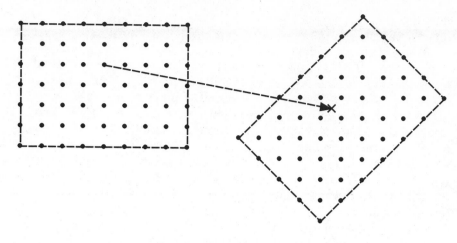

(a) Forward Transform

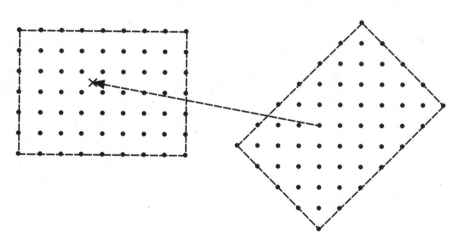

(b) Inverse Transform

Figure 5.22 Forward and inverse transforms.

and *interpolated* sampling. Suppose that an inverse transform determines the location of a required pixel in a source image to be that shown in Fig. 5.23. Somewhere between these four actual pixels $P_{x,y}$, $P_{x+1,y}$, $P_{x,y+1}$, and $P_{x+1,y+1}$, that have intensity values of a, b, c, and d, respectively, is the calculated location given by the inverse transform.

No pixel exists at this location, so the output pixel must be created from the four that do exist. The easiest way to do this is with nearest neighbor sampling. This method simply selects the actual pixel that is closest to the desired location. If the fractional portion of the desired location is less than 0.5, select the preceding pixel; if it is greater, select the next pixel. This decision is performed for both the horizontal and vertical dimension, resulting in the pixel closest to the desired location being selected. In Fig. 5.23, the pixel at location $P_{x+1,y}$ would be selected, and the output pixel would have the value b.

Nearest neighbor sampling is fast, but it can result in jagged edges and loss of apparent resolution. A much better method is interpolated sampling, which means to use proportional amounts of the surrounding four-pixel neighborhood in order to arrive at the output value. There are many ways to perform interpolation between these values, based on various mathematical techniques such a quadratic or cubic curve or *spline*. A common method that produces acceptable results is called *bilinear interpolation*. It is described below.

Figure 5.24 shows the same pixels used in the previous example, except that now the various pixel intensities are indicated by different heights. If d_x is the sub-pixel distance from pixel Px,y to the desired location in the horizontal dimension, then that distance is proportional to the difference in pixel intensities a and b. This interpolated intensity is called ab. Similarly, that distance is proportional to the difference of intensities c and d, so cd can be calculated. The vertical sub-pixel distance d_y is then proportional to the difference in pixel

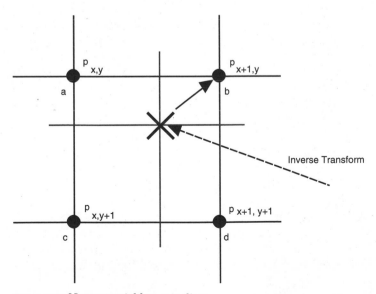

Figure 5.23 Nearest neighbor sampling.

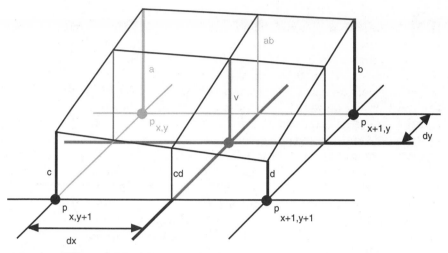

Figure 5.24 Bilinear interpolation sampling.

interpolated intensities *ab* and *cd*, so that the final bilinear interpolation intensity value, *v*, can be calculated and becomes the value of the output pixel.

Rotate, Scale, Translate

The most common form of geometric transformations are rotate, scale, and translate, which also are known as *affine transforms* because lines that are straight and parallel in the source image remain so in the destination image. These transformations can be applied individually or in unison. If the application is designed to perform them at the same time, the programmer and operator must be careful about the order in which they are done. The order of the individual transformations often will be referred to by the first letters in the action, namely RST for *rotate*, *scale*, and *translate*. If the order is scale, then rotate followed by translate, the abbreviation would be SRT. As an exercise, you can prove to yourself how the order of the transformations will affect the resultant image drastically.

Rotation has two operational properties that must be defined by the programmer. First, the direction of the rotation must be decided. Usually, a positive angle means a counterclockwise rotation and a negative value means clockwise. The point of rotation also must be decided. Rotation occurs either around the center, or around the origin (upper-left corner) of the image. For rotation around the origin, the inverse transform for each point is given by the following equations:

$$x_s = [x_d \times \cos(a)] - [y_d \times \sin(a)]$$

$$y_s = [x_d \times \sin(a)] + [y_d \times \cos(a)]$$

In these equations, *sin* and *cos* are the sine and cosine functions of the angle of rotation, a. The address for each pixel in the output, or destination, image is x_d, y_d and the source address is x_s, y_s. Remember, these calculations produce floating-point source addresses, which are then used for sub-pixel sampling of the source image. If rotation about the center of the image is desired, use the following equations:

$$x_s = [x_d \times \cos(a)] - [y_d \times \sin(a)] + [x_c \times (1-\cos(a))] + [y_c \times \sin(a)]$$

$$y_s = [x_d \times \sin(a)] + [y_d \times \cos(a)] - [x_c \times \sin(a)] + [y_c \times (1-\cos(a))]$$

Here, x_c, y_c is the center address of the source image. Program 19 is an implementation of these rotation equations and illustrates rotation around the center and origin. It includes both nearest neighbor and bilinear interpolation sampling. Figure 5.25 shows a rotated image, along with enlarged areas that show the difference between the sampling techniques.

(a) Original Image

(b) Rotated Image

(c) Original Zoomed

(d) Nearest Neighbor

(e) Bilinear Interpolation

Figure 5.25 Rotated image. *(Image courtesy of Eastman Kodak Co.)*

```
/****************************************************************/
/*    program 19: rotation                                    */
/****************************************************************/

#define   XSIZE   640
#define   YSIZE   480

#define   RED     0
#define   GREEN   1
#define   BLUE    2

#define   PI      3.141592654
#define   ANGLE   20      /* rotation angle in degrees */
#define   CENTER  0
#define   INTERP  1

main()
  {
  unsigned char *ir,*ig,*ib;
  unsigned char *or,*og,*ob;
  unsigned char *i,*o;
  long   int   ix,iy,c;
  long   int   ix0,iy0;
  long   int   ix1,iy1;
  long   int   ox,oy;
  long   int   cx,cy;
  double       angle;
  double       cosa,sina;
  double       X,Y;
  double       DX,DY;
  double       A,B,C,D,AB,CD;
  double       v;

  /* allocate input and output memory buffers */
  ir = (unsigned char *) malloc (XSIZE*YSIZE);
  ig = (unsigned char *) malloc (XSIZE*YSIZE);
  ib = (unsigned char *) malloc (XSIZE*YSIZE);
  or = (unsigned char *) malloc (XSIZE*YSIZE);
  og = (unsigned char *) malloc (XSIZE*YSIZE);
  ob = (unsigned char *) malloc (XSIZE*YSIZE);

  /* read the input image */
  read_image("input",ir,ig,ib);

  /* calculate image center */
  cx = XSIZE / 2;
  cy = YSIZE / 2;

  /* calculate sine and cosine of rotation angle */
  angle = (2 * PI / 360) * ANGLE;
  cosa = cos(angle);
  sina = sin(angle);

  /* process all lines of image */
```

```
for (oy = 0; oy < YSIZE; oy++)
  {
  for (ox = 0; ox < XSIZE; ox++)
    {
    if (CENTER == 0)
      {
      /* rotate around origin */
      X = ( ox*cosa) - (oy*sina);
      Y = ( ox*sina) + (oy*cosa);
      }
    else
      {
      /* rotate around center */
      X = ( ox*cosa) - (oy*sina) + ( cx*(1-cosa) + cy*sina);
      Y = ( ox*sina) + (oy*cosa) + (-cx*sina    + cy*(1-cosa));
      }

    /* process the red, green, and blue planes one at a time */
    for (c = RED; c <= BLUE; c++)
      {
      /* initialize pointers for current color plane */
      if (c == RED  ) i = ir;
      if (c == GREEN) i = ig;
      if (c == BLUE ) i = ib;
      if (c == RED  ) o = or;
      if (c == GREEN) o = og;
      if (c == BLUE ) o = ob;

      if (INTERP == 0)
        {
        /* nearest neighbor */
        ix = (long)(X + 0.5);
        iy = (long)(Y + 0.5);
        if ((ix >= 0) && (ix < XSIZE) && (iy >= 0) && (iy < YSIZE))
          o[(oy*XSIZE)+ox] = i[(iy*XSIZE)+ix];
        else
          o[(oy*XSIZE)+ox] = 0x0;
        }
      else
        {
        /* bilinear interpolation */
        if (X >= 0.0)
          ix0 = (long)X;
        else
          ix0 = (long)(X-1.0);

        if (Y >= 0.0)
          iy0 = (long)Y;
        else
          iy0 = (long)(Y-1.0);

        ix1 = ix0 + 1;
        iy1 = iy0 + 1;
```

```
            DX = X - (double)ix0;           DY = Y - (double)iy0;
            A = 0.0;
            B = 0.0;
            C = 0.0;
            D = 0.0;

            if ((ix0 >= 0)&&(ix0 < XSIZE)&&(iy0 >= 0)&&(iy0 < YSIZE))
              A = (float)i[(iy0*XSIZE)+ix0];
            if ((ix1 >= 0)&&(ix1 < XSIZE)&&(iy0 >= 0)&&(iy0 < YSIZE))
              B = (float)i[(iy0*XSIZE)+ix1];
            if ((ix0 >= 0)&&(ix0 < XSIZE)&&(iy1 >= 0)&&(iy1 < YSIZE))
              C = (float)i[(iy1*XSIZE)+ix0];
            if ((ix1 >= 0)&&(ix1 < XSIZE)&&(iy1 >= 0)&&(iy1 < YSIZE))
              D = (float)i[(iy1*XSIZE)+ix1];

            AB = (A * (1.0-DX)) + (B * DX);
            CD = (C * (1.0-DX)) + (D * DX);
            v  = (AB * (1.0-DY)) + (CD * DY);

            o[(oy*XSIZE)+ox] = (unsigned char)v;
            }
          }
        }
      }

  /* write the output image */
  write_image("output",or,og,ob);

  /* free memory buffers */
  free(ir);
  free(ig);
  free(ib);
  free(or);
  free(og);
  free(ob);
  }
```

Program 19 Rotation.

Scaling is a function that either enlarges an image, referred to as *scaling up*, or shrinks it, called *scaling down*. The inverse transform equations for scaling about the origin are as follows:

$$x_s = x_d \, / \text{ scale } x$$

$$y_s = y_d \, / \text{ scale } y$$

Again, x_s, y_s and x_d, y_d are source and destination addresses and scale x and scale y are the scale factors. Scale factors that are greater than 1.0 will enlarge the source image, while factors of less than 1 will shrink an image. Though scaling in the horizontal and vertical dimensions are independent of one another, the scale factors usually are set to the same value to maintain proper pixel *aspect ratio*. Sometimes different scale factors for the two dimensions are needed to correct for input devices that do not create square pixels. The inverse transform equations for scaling about the center of the source image are:

$$x_s = x_d \, / \, \text{scale } x - [(x_c \, / \, \text{scale } x) - x_c]$$

$$y_s = y_d \, / \, \text{scale } y - [(y_c \, / \, \text{scale } y) - y_c]$$

Program 20 is an implementation of these equations, with nearest neighbor and bilinear interpolation sampling. Figure 5.26 shows a scaled image.

There is a limit to how much an image can be enlarged before it becomes unusable. Remember that any group of scaled-up pixels are created from only four source pixels, and there is only so much information that exists. Surprisingly, shrinking an image can create unforeseen problems for a programmer, problems that do not appear when scaling up. The equations defined above operate perfectly well if the scale factor is not less than 0.5 or, in other words, if the resolution is reduced by no more than half. For reductions greater than this, certain source pixels will not be included at all in the transformation, resulting in overly bright or overly dark spots appearing in the destination image. This is especially true in images that have high frequencies in them; some edges may be completely skipped in the transformation process.

To alleviate this anomaly, it may be prudent to precompute a series of images in which each member is exactly one-half the resolution of the previous one, as shown in Fig. 5.27. Then, during scaling operations, the application program can select the appropriate member that will require nothing smaller than a 0.5 scale factor to achieve the final scaled-down image.

(a) Original Image   (b) Scaled Image

Figure 5.26 Scaled image. *(Image courtesy of Eastman Kodak Co.)*

```
/**********************************************************/
/*    program 20: scale                                   */
/**********************************************************/

#define  XSIZE  640
#define  YSIZE  480

#define  RED    0
#define  GREEN  1
#define  BLUE   2

#define  XSCALE 0.1
#define  YSCALE 0.1
#define  CENTER 0
#define  INTERP 1

main()
  {
  unsigned char *ir,*ig,*ib;
  unsigned char *or,*og,*ob;
  unsigned char *i,*o;
  long  int  ix,iy,c;
  long  int  ix0,iy0;
  long  int  ix1,iy1;
  long  int  ox,oy;
  long  int  cx,cy;
  double     X,Y;
  double     DX,DY;
  double     A,B,C,D,AB,CD;
  double     v;

  /* allocate input and output memory buffers */
  ir = (unsigned char *) malloc (XSIZE*YSIZE);
  ig = (unsigned char *) malloc (XSIZE*YSIZE);
  ib = (unsigned char *) malloc (XSIZE*YSIZE);
  or = (unsigned char *) malloc (XSIZE*YSIZE);
  og = (unsigned char *) malloc (XSIZE*YSIZE);
  ob = (unsigned char *) malloc (XSIZE*YSIZE);

  /* read the input image */
  read_image("input",ir,ig,ib);

  /* calculate image center */
  cx = XSIZE / 2;
  cy = YSIZE / 2;

  /* process all lines of image */
  for (oy = 0; oy < YSIZE; oy++)
    {
    for (ox = 0; ox < XSIZE; ox++)
      {
      if (CENTER == 0)
        {         /* scale around origin */
        X = ox / XSCALE;
        Y = oy / YSCALE;
```

```
    }
else
  {
  /* scale around center */
  X = (ox / XSCALE) - ((cx / XSCALE) - cx);
  Y = (oy / YSCALE) - ((cy / YSCALE) - cy);
  }

/* process the red, green, and blue planes one at a time */
for (c = RED; c <= BLUE; c++)
  {
  /* initialize pointers for current color plane */
  if (c == RED  ) i = ir;
  if (c == GREEN) i = ig;
  if (c == BLUE ) i = ib;
  if (c == RED  ) o = or;
  if (c == GREEN) o = og;
  if (c == BLUE ) o = ob;

  if (INTERP == 0)
    {
    /* nearest neighbor */
    ix = (long)(X + 0.5);
    iy = (long)(Y + 0.5);
    if ((ix >= 0) && (ix < XSIZE) && (iy >= 0) && (iy < YSIZE))
      o[(oy*XSIZE)+ox] = i[(iy*XSIZE)+ix];
    else
      o[(oy*XSIZE)+ox] = 0x0;
    }
  else
    {
    /* bilinear interpolation */
    if (X >= 0.0)
      ix0 = (long)X;
    else
      ix0 = (long)(X-1.0);

    if (Y >= 0.0)
      iy0 = (long)Y;
    else
      iy0 = (long)(Y-1.0);

    ix1 = ix0 + 1;
    iy1 = iy0 + 1;
    DX = X - (double)ix0;
    DY = Y - (double)iy0;
    A = 0.0;
    B = 0.0;
    C = 0.0;
    D = 0.0;

    if ((ix0 >= 0)&&(ix0 < XSIZE)&&(iy0 >= 0)&&(iy0 < YSIZE))
      A = (float)i[(iy0*XSIZE)+ix0];
    if ((ix1 >= 0)&&(ix1 < XSIZE)&&(iy0 >= 0)&&(iy0 < YSIZE))
      B = (float)i[(iy0*XSIZE)+ix1];
    if ((ix0 >= 0)&&(ix0 < XSIZE)&&(iy1 >= 0)&&(iy1 < YSIZE))
      C = (float)i[(iy1*XSIZE)+ix0];
```

```
        if ((ix1 >= 0)&&(ix1 < XSIZE)&&(iy1 >= 0)&&(iy1 < YSIZE))
          D = (float)i[(iy1*XSIZE)+ix1];

        AB = (A * (1.0-DX)) + (B * DX);
        CD = (C * (1.0-DX)) + (D * DX);
        v  = (AB * (1.0-DY)) + (CD * DY);

        o[(oy*XSIZE)+ox] = (unsigned char)v;
        }
      }
    }
  }

/* write the output image */
write_image("output",or,og,ob);

/* free memory buffers */
free(ir);
free(ig);
free(ib);
free(or);
free(og);
free(ob);
}
```

Program 20 Scale.

Translation of an image is the easiest of the geometric transformations. The inverse transform equations are as follows:

$$x_s = x_d - \text{trans } x$$

$$y_s = y_d - \text{trans } y$$

The source and destination address are x_s, y_s and x_d, y_d, respectively, and the horizontal and vertical translation values are trans x and trans y. Program 21 implements this function, and its effects are

1.00x   0.50x   0.25x

Figure 5.27 Prescaled images. *(Image courtesy of Eastman Kodak Co.)*

(a) Original Image   (b) Translated Image

Figure 5.28 Translated image. *(Image courtesy of Eastman Kodak Co.)*

shown in Fig. 5.28. This operation might seem trivial, but keep in mind that translation offsets of a fraction of a pixel are possible, allowing sub-pixel image movement that is crucial for many applications. In addition, the programmer must be aware of the addressing involved in translations for the reason shown in Fig. 5.28. The function can result in attempts to access nonexistent source addresses, which can cause program execution errors or abnormal termination if not handled properly.

Polynomial Warp

An interesting and powerful geometric transformation is *warping*. All transformation are generalizations of polynomial functions which can be expressed by the equations:

$$x' = a_0 + a_1 y + a_2 x + a_3 xy$$

$$y' = b_0 + b_1 y + b_2 x + b_3 xy$$

Note that these are identical to the rotation, scale, and translate equations stated above, except that the sine and cosine functions and scale factors and other constants have been replaced by coefficients, labels a_1 and b_1 and the cross term, xy, is nonexistent. This is known as a *first-order polynomial*, since no term contains a power of x or y greater than 1. A generalized first-order polynomial warp equation can be generated if, as shown in Fig. 5.29, four points in the source image are mapped to desired locations in the output image. These points, labeled d_1, d_2, d_3, and d_4, are called *control points*. If the corners of the source image are used as the control points, the coefficients in the polynomial equation become:

$$a_0 = x_1 \qquad a_1 = x_2 - x_1 \qquad a_3 = x_4 - x_1 \qquad a_3 = x_1 - x_2 + x_3 - x_4$$

$$b_0 = y_1 \qquad b_1 = y_2 - y_1 \qquad b_3 = y_4 - y_1 \qquad b_3 = y_1 - y_2 + y_3 - y_4$$

```
/**************************************************************/
/*    program 21: translate                                 */
/**************************************************************/

#define  XSIZE  640
#define  YSIZE  480

#define  RED    0
#define  GREEN  1
#define  BLUE   2

#define  XOFF   65.4
#define  YOFF   24.8
#define  INTERP 1

main()
  {
  unsigned char *ir,*ig,*ib;
  unsigned char *or,*og,*ob;
  unsigned char *i,*o;
  long  int  ix,iy,c;
  long  int  ix0,iy0;
  long  int  ix1,iy1;
  long  int  ox,oy;
  long  int  cx,cy;
  double     X,Y;
  double     DX,DY;
  double     A,B,C,D,AB,CD;
  double     v;

  /* allocate input and output memory buffers */
  ir = (unsigned char *) malloc (XSIZE*YSIZE);
  ig = (unsigned char *) malloc (XSIZE*YSIZE);
  ib = (unsigned char *) malloc (XSIZE*YSIZE);
  or = (unsigned char *) malloc (XSIZE*YSIZE);
  og = (unsigned char *) malloc (XSIZE*YSIZE);
  ob = (unsigned char *) malloc (XSIZE*YSIZE);

  /* read the input image */
  read_image("input",ir,ig,ib);

  /* process all lines of image */
  for (oy = 0; oy < YSIZE; oy++)
    {
    for (ox = 0; ox < XSIZE; ox++)
      {
      /* process the red, green, and blue planes one at a time */
      for (c = RED; c <= BLUE; c++)
        {
        /* initialize pointers for current color plane */
        if (c == RED  ) i = ir;
        if (c == GREEN) i = ig;
        if (c == BLUE ) i = ib;
        if (c == RED  ) o = or;
        if (c == GREEN) o = og;
        if (c == BLUE ) o = ob;

        if (INTERP == 0)
          {
          /* nearest neighbor */
          ix = ox - (long int)(XOFF + 0.5);
```

```
            iy = oy - (long int)(YOFF + 0.5);
            if ((ix >= 0) && (ix < XSIZE) && (iy >= 0) && (iy < YSIZE))
              o[(oy*XSIZE)+ox] = i[(iy*XSIZE)+ix];
            else
              o[(oy*XSIZE)+ox] = 0x0;
            }

        else
          {
          /* bilinear interpolation */
          X = (double)ox - XOFF;
          if (X >= 0.0)
            ix0 = (long)X;
          else
            ix0 = (long)(X-1.0);

          Y = (double)oy - YOFF;
          if (Y >= 0.0)
            iy0 = (long)Y;
          else
            iy0 = (long)(Y-1.0);

          ix1 = ix0 + 1;
          iy1 = iy0 + 1;
          DX = X - (double)ix0;
          DY = Y - (double)iy0;
          A = 0.0;
          B = 0.0;
          C = 0.0;
          D = 0.0;

          if ((ix0 >= 0)&&(ix0 < XSIZE)&&(iy0 >= 0)&&(iy0 < YSIZE))
            A = (float)i[(iy0*XSIZE)+ix0];
          if ((ix1 >= 0)&&(ix1 < XSIZE)&&(iy0 >= 0)&&(iy0 < YSIZE))
            B = (float)i[(iy0*XSIZE)+ix1];
          if ((ix0 >= 0)&&(ix0 < XSIZE)&&(iy1 >= 0)&&(iy1 < YSIZE))
            C = (float)i[(iy1*XSIZE)+ix0];
          if ((ix1 >= 0)&&(ix1 < XSIZE)&&(iy1 >= 0)&&(iy1 < YSIZE))
            D = (float)i[(iy1*XSIZE)+ix1];

          AB = (A * (1.0-DX)) + (B * DX);
          CD = (C * (1.0-DX)) + (D * DX);
          v  = (AB * (1.0-DY)) + (CD * DY);

          o[(oy*XSIZE)+ox] = (unsigned char)v;
          }
        }
      }
    }
  /* write the output image */
  write_image("output",or,og,ob);

  /* free memory buffers */
  free(ir);
  free(ig);
  free(ib);
  free(or);
  free(og);
  free(ob);
  }
```

Program 21 Translation.

By defining where the control points are mapped, the image thus can be rotated, scaled, or translated in any fashion. But, as Fig. 5.29 shows, the warping does not need to be an affine warp. Perspective can be added to the image by defining different control points for mapping.

Program 22 shows an implementation of these equations. Unlike the previous transformations, this program illustrates a forward transform and, because of this, the calculation of destination address must occur at a finer granularity than one pixel (0.5 pixels was chosen for this example). As mentioned earlier, this is necessary when implementing forward transforms because every source pixel might not map to a destination, and unless this sub-pixel addressing is forced, "holes" would appear in the destination image. With the application of linear algebra, it is possible to generate the inverse transforms for these polynomials. Also note that, for clarity, this program only performs nearest neighbor sampling, but the programmer should remember that bilinear interpolation also can be applied in warping to create a higher-quality image.

Polynomials can have orders higher than one. The equations for a second order polynomial are as follows:

$$x' = a_0 + a_1 x + a_2 y + a_3 xy + a_4 x^2 + a_5 y^2$$

$$y' = b_0 + b_1 x + b_2 y + b_3 xy + b_4 x^2 + b_5 y^2$$

In addition to the terms in the first-order polynomial, there are now terms that include x^2 and y^2. More control points are needed to define these polynomials, but by doing so the image can be made to bend and twist as if it were made out of a pliable material. This technique, sometimes known as *rubbersheeting*, can be used for many applications, such as correcting for spherical aberration of optical lens systems, or warping satellite images into Mercator or other map

(a) Original Image   (b) Warped Image

Figure 5.29 First-order polynomial warped image. *(Image courtesy of Eastman Kodak Co.)*

```
/************************************************************/
/*    program 22: first-order polynomial warp              */
/************************************************************/

#define  XSIZE  640
#define  YSIZE  480

main()
  {
  unsigned char *ir,*ig,*ib;
  unsigned char *or,*og,*ob;
  long  int  ix,iy;
  long  int  ox,oy;
  long  int  x1,x2,x3,x4;
  long  int  y1,y2,y3,y4;
  double     xa0,xa1,xa2,xa3;
  double     ya0,ya1,ya2,ya3;
  double     IX,IY;
  double     OX,OY;
  double     DX,DY;

  /* set corner warp control points */
  x1 = 140; y1 = 10;
  x2 = 535; y2 = 105;
  x3 = 610; y3 = 360;
  x4 = -30; y4 = 400;

  /* calculate X coefficients */
  xa0 = (double)x1;
  xa1 = (double)(x4 - x1) / (double)YSIZE;
  xa2 = (double)(x2 - x1) / (double)XSIZE;
  xa3 = (double)(x1-x2+x3-x4) / (double)XSIZE / (double)YSIZE;

  /* calculate Y coefficients */
  ya0 = (double)y1;
  ya1 = (double)(y4 - y1) / YSIZE;
  ya2 = (double)(y2 - y1) / XSIZE;
  ya3 = (double)(y1-y2+y3-y4) / XSIZE / YSIZE;

  /* allocate input and output memory buffers */
  ir = (unsigned char *) malloc (XSIZE*YSIZE);
  ig = (unsigned char *) malloc (XSIZE*YSIZE);
  ib = (unsigned char *) malloc (XSIZE*YSIZE);
  or = (unsigned char *) malloc (XSIZE*YSIZE);
  og = (unsigned char *) malloc (XSIZE*YSIZE);
  ob = (unsigned char *) malloc (XSIZE*YSIZE);

  /* read the input image */
  read_image("input",ir,ig,ib);

  /* process all lines of image */
  /* note: since this is a forward transform,
        compute location every 1/2 pixel */
  for (IY = 0; IY < YSIZE; IY = IY + 0.5)
    {
```

```
for (IX = 0; IX < XSIZE; IX = IX + 0.5)
  {
  /* compute output pixel location */
  OX = xa0 + (xa1 * IY) + (xa2 * IX) + (xa3 * IX * IY);
  OY = ya0 + (ya1 * IY) + (ya2 * IX) + (ya3 * IX * IY);

  /* reduce input and output pixel locations to integer */
  ix = (long)IX;
  iy = (long)IY;
  ox = (long)(OX + 0.5);
  oy = (long)(OY + 0.5);

  /* select nearest neighbor */
  /* note: bilinear interpolation could also be performed */
  if ((ox >= 0) && (ox < XSIZE) && (oy >= 0) && (oy < YSIZE))
    {
    or[(oy*XSIZE)+ox] = ir[(iy*XSIZE)+ix];
    og[(oy*XSIZE)+ox] = ig[(iy*XSIZE)+ix];
    ob[(oy*XSIZE)+ox] = ib[(iy*XSIZE)+ix];
    }
  }
}

/* write the output image */
write_image("output",or,og,ob);

/* free memory buffers */
free(ir);
free(ig);
free(ib);
free(or);
free(og);
free(ob);
}
```

Program 22 First-order polynomial warp.

projections. Second-order polynomials usually are sufficient for most image processing applications; third-, fourth-, or higher-order warps are sometimes necessary.

Another example of using higher-ordered polynomial warping is to implement the function known as *morphing*, which is not to be confused with the morphological operators to be discussed in the next chapter. Morphing has become commonplace in music videos, television commercials, and many other products of the entertainment industry where digital imagery is used. It is the method which makes one object appear to change into another in a short period of time. The process is accomplished in multiple steps.

The first step is to warp one image so that the its control points map to similar points of the second object and, conversely, define control points of the second object that map to the first. From these control points, an animated sequence (or a series of digital images) of both objects is created that incrementally warps each "normal" image into the desired "warped" image. The animation sequence for the desired final image is in reverse order, because we want to end with a "normal" image of the second object.

Finally, the images of the sequences are blended together (via the alpha filtering presented as a point operator), using a slightly different percentage of one object to the other, so that the first object appears to become the second. In other words, the first merged image in the sequence uses 100 percent of the first object and 0 percent of the second object. By the middle of the sequence, the image is generated with 50 percent of either object. (Also note that in the middle of the morph the final image is a combination of both warped images.) The last image in the sequence uses 0 percent of the first object and 100 percent of the second to complete the transformation. Naturally, the effect does not have visual impact unless the sequence is seen in motion, but Fig. 5.30 shows a few frames of one object morphing into another.

These types of morphs are unique in their implementation and many times require specialized manipulation to give the desired effect. For example, instead of a simple merge or cross-dissolve between images of the two sequences, certain features may dissolve before others. If two human faces are being morphed, perhaps the merging of the eyes and nose will precede the dissolving of the mouth and ears. This requires generating specialized merging masks for each frame of the sequence.

Figure 5.30 Morphed image sequence.

Similarly, the transitional warped images might not be simple linear interpolations between the starting and ending locations of the control points. There might be curves or even hesitations in the speed of the warps that combine to give the desired effect. What the programmer must remember is that, no matter how complex the implementation, morphing is always a combination of polynomial warping and alpha filtering.

Morphological Operations

Morphological operations are the last principal group of digital image processing techniques to be discussed. While point and neighborhood operations are generally designed to alter the look or appearance of an image for visual considerations, morphological operations are used to understand the structure, or form, of an image. This usually means identifying objects or boundaries within an image. Morphological operations therefore play a key role in such applications as machine vision and automatic object detection.

There are three primary morphological functions: *erosion, dilation,* and *hit-or-miss*. Others are special cases of these primary operations or are cascaded applications of them. Morphological operations usually are performed on binary images where pixels are either 0 or 1 (or true/false, on/off, black/white, or whatever other nomenclature is used to identify these two unique logical states). For simplicity, this chapter will refer to pixels as 0 or 1, and in diagrams will show a value of zero as black and a value of 1 as white. While most morphological operations center on binary images, some also can be applied to grayscale images; these will be discussed later in this chapter.

Before describing these functions, it is important to introduce the concepts of *segmentation* and *connectivity*, and slightly redefine what a *pixel neighborhood* is. Consider the binary image in Fig. 6.1(a), which shows an array of large pixels. The predominant field of white pixels is divided (or *segmented*) into two parts by the black line. In this image there are three segments: the top group of white pixels, the bottom group of white pixels, and the group of black pixels that form the dividing line.

The image in Fig. 6.1(b) also has three segments: the outer border of white pixels, the black pixels that form the square, and the group of white pixels within the square. From these images we can see that all pixels of a segment are directly adjacent to at least one other pixel of the same classification. In other words, they are all connected. But what about the image shown in Fig. 6.1(c)? Are there still only three segments? Or are there six, namely the white outer pixels, the inner white pixels, and four segments of detached black pixels?

The answer is both, depending on how *connectivity* is defined. Most morphological functions operate on 3×3 pixel neighborhoods. The pixels in a neighborhood are identified in one of two ways (and sometimes interchangeably), as shown in Fig. 6.2. The pixel of interest lies at the center of the neighborhood and is labeled X. The surrounding pixels are referred to as either $X0$ through $X7$, or by their compass coordinates E, NE, N, NW, W, SW, S, and SE. A pixel is called *four-connected* if at least one of its neighbors in positions $X0$, $X2$, $X4$, or $X6$ (E, N, W, or S) is the same value. The pixel is *eight-connected* if all neighbors are the same value.

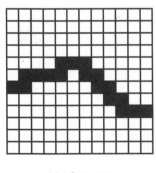

(a) 3 Segments

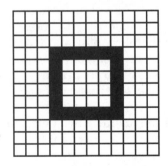

(b) 3 Segments

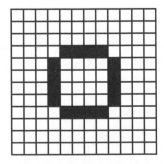

(c) How Many Segments?

Figure 6.1 Image segmentation.

X_3	X_2	X_1
X_4	X	X_0
X_5	X_6	X_7

NW	N	NE
W	X	E
SW	S	SE

Figure 6.2 Pixel neighborhood.

By using the four-connected method as a discriminator, there are four disconnected black lines in Fig. 6.1(c). If the more common eight-connected method is used, there is one black region. Under eight-connectivity, a string of pixels is said to be *minimally connected* if the loss of a single pixel causes the remaining pixels to lose connectivity.

Binary Erosion and Dilation

Erosion and dilation are related to convolution but, due to their specific nature, are oriented more towards logical decision-making than towards numeric calculation. Like convolution, binary morphological operators such as erosion and dilation combine a local neighborhood of pixels with a mask to achieve a result. Figure 6.3 shows this relationship. The output pixel, O, is set to either a hit (1) or a miss (0) based on the following relationship:

$$
\begin{aligned}
\text{if} \quad X &= M & \text{and} \\
X0 &= M0 & \text{and} \\
X1 &= M1 & \text{and} \\
X2 &= M2 & \text{and} \\
X3 &= M3 & \text{and} \\
X4 &= M4 & \text{and} \\
X5 &= M5 & \text{and} \\
X6 &= M6 & \text{and} \\
X7 &= M7 & \text{and}
\end{aligned}
$$

then $O = X$
else $O = $ not X

Binary erosion uses the following for its mask:

$$1 \ 1 \ 1$$

$$1 \ 1 \ 1$$

$$1 \ 1 \ 1$$

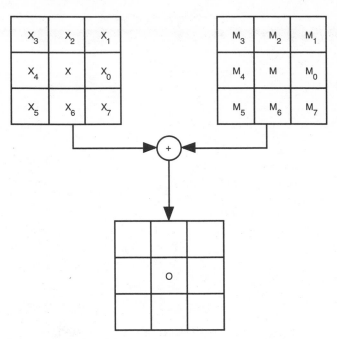

Figure 6.3 Neighborhood operation.

This means that every pixel in the neighborhood must be 1 in order for the output pixel to be 1; otherwise, the pixel will become 0. Figure 6.4 shows how this operator will work on several sample pixel neighborhoods. The first example shows that no matter what value the neighboring pixels have, if the central pixel is 0 the output pixel is 0. The second example shows that just a single 0 pixel anywhere within the neighborhood will cause the output pixel to become 0. The third condition is a special case called an *isolated pixel* and illustrates one of the powerful uses of erosion. It can be used to eliminate unwanted white noise pixels from an otherwise black area. The last example shows the only condition in which a white pixel will remain white in the output image: All of its neighbors must be white.

The effect this has on a binary image is to diminish, or *erode,* the edges of a white area of pixels. Figure 6.5(a), which is a low-resolution representation of simple objects created from large pixels, shows the original binary image. Figure 6.5(b) shows the image after the erosion operator has been applied once. (For readability, the extents of the original objects are shown in gray.) The objects have been uniformly reduced, or eroded, from all sides by one pixel. Figure 6.5(c) shows the same image after three applications of the erosion operator. If the operator were applied any more, the objects would disappear altogether.

Dilation is the opposite of erosion. Its mask is as follows:

0 0 0

0 0 0

0 0 0

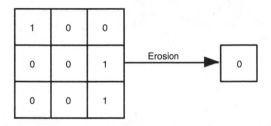

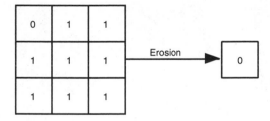

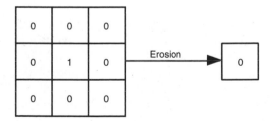

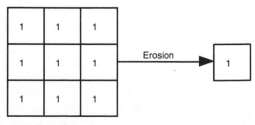

Figure 6.4 Erosion sample cases.

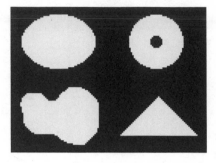

(a) Original Image

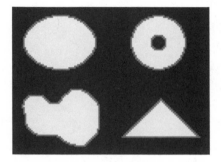

(b) Erode, 1 Application

(c) Erode, Multiple Applications

Figure 6.5 Binary erosion.

As would be expected, this mask will make white areas grow, or *dilate*. Figure 6.6 illustrates several instances of applying the dilation operator to pixel neighborhoods. The same rules that applied to erosion conditions apply to dilation, but the logic is inverted. Figure 6.7 shows application of the dilation operator. The original extents of the objects are again shown in gray. Being the opposite of erosion, dilation will allow a black pixel to remain black only if all of its neighbors are black. This operator is useful for removing isolated black pixels, or noise, from an image.

Program 23 shows an implementation of the erode and dilate operators. Specific code does not need to be generated for the two operators. Like convolution, the desired function can be implemented by providing different data in the mask.

Outlining and Opening/Closing

As mentioned earlier, other functions can be performed using erosion and dilation as their basic operation. One of these is *outlining*. In pre-

ceding examples, multiple iterations of the dilation or erosion operators
were cascaded to generate a more severe effect. It also is possible to perform a single erode and subtract the resultant image from the original.
The result will be an image that shows a one-pixel outline of all objects.

  Figure 6.8(a) is a binary image of a portion of an electronic circuit
board. The result of the outline operator is shown in Fig. 6.8(b). If two

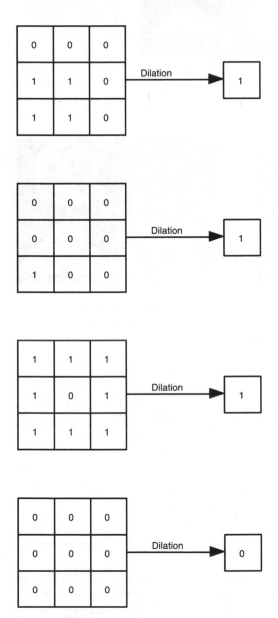

Figure 6.6 Dilation sample cases.

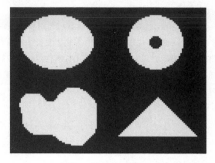

(a) Original Image

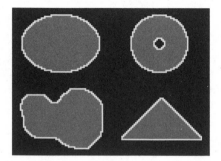

(b) Dilate, 1 Application

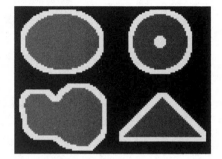

(c) Dilate, Multiple Applications

Figure 6.7 Binary dilation.

erode operators are performed before the subtraction, a two-pixel out-line would be created. If desired, a dilation operation can be performed before the erosion as a way to clear up any unwanted "holes" in the white areas and may produce a cleaner outline image. This is an optional operation because, while making the image cleaner, it might also affect the border of the original image.

Outlining produces an effect similar to edge detection, which was discussed in the preceding chapter. If you are working with binary images, though, it is less computationally expensive to use morphological techniques instead of using convolution. In addition, outlining will produce a better image because it is not as susceptible to noise produced from film grain or other scanning imperfections.

Another function can be performed with erosion and dilation. Figure 6.8(c) shows an example of *closing,* which can be helpful in the manufacturing process for printed circuit boards. If etches or solder joints are too close together, a short circuit can result. Determining how far

```
/***********************************************************/
/*    program 23: erosion and dilation                     */
/***********************************************************/

#define   XSIZE   640
#define   YSIZE   480

main()
  {
  unsigned char *ip;
  unsigned char *op;
  unsigned char *i1,*i2,*i3;
  unsigned char *o1,*o2,*o3;
  long   int   x,y;

  /* erode mask: */
  unsigned char m[3][3] = {0,0,0,0,0,0,0,0,0};

  /* dilate mask:
  unsigned char m[3][3] = {255,255,255,255,255,255,255,255,255};
  */

  /* allocate input and output memory buffers */
  ip = (unsigned char *) malloc (XSIZE*YSIZE);
  op = (unsigned char *) malloc (XSIZE*YSIZE);

  /* read the input image (one plane image) */
  read_image("input",ip);

  /* initialize pointers into buffers */
  i2 = ip;
  i3 = ip + XSIZE;
  o2 = op;
  o3 = op + XSIZE;

  /* process all lines of image */
  for (y = 1; y < (YSIZE-1); y++)
    {
    /* set pointers for this line */
    i1 = i2;
    i2 = i3;
    i3 = i3 + XSIZE;
    o1 = o2;
    o2 = o3;
    o3 = o3 + XSIZE;

    /* process all pixels in line */
    for (x = 1; x < (XSIZE-1); x++)
      {
      /* check neighborhood */
      if ((*(i1+x-1)==m[0][0]) &&
          (*(i1+x+0)==m[0][1])  &&
          (*(i1+x+1)==m[0][2])  &&
          (*(i2+x-1)==m[1][0])  &&
          (*(i2+x+0)==m[1][1])  &&
```

```
                (*(i2+x+1)==m[1][2])  &&
                (*(i3+x-1)==m[2][0])  &&
                (*(i3+x+0)==m[2][1])  &&
                (*(i3+x+1)==m[2][2]))
              {
              *(o2+x) = m[1][1];
              }
           else
              {
              *(o2+x) = 255 - m[1][1];
              }
           }
        }

    /* write the output image */
    write_image("output",op);

    /* free memory buffers */
    free(ip);
    free(op);
    }
```

Program 23 Erosion and dilation.

apart connections must be from one another can be related to pixel size of the scanned image. In this example, assume that *physical dimension* translates to 5 pixels. Thus, if two successive dilation operations are performed, etches farther apart than 4 pixels will not touch. Any objects that are closer than this minimum allowable space will "grow together."

Now, if the same number of erosion operations is performed on the dilated image, any areas that initially were too close together will leave a telltale pattern, since they will not separate properly. Simply subtracting the resultant image from the original will identify the problem areas. In Fig. 6.8(c) a problem area located by the closing operator is highlighted.

The same image can be processed for *opening*. In this example, the etches of the circuit board must be at least the equivalent of 3 pixels in width. To perform this function, the image is eroded; to catch etches that are 2 or fewer pixels wide, only one erode operation is required. The image is then dilated. If any objects are too thin, they are erased by the erosion and will not be regenerated by the dilation. The resultant image, with a potential break highlighted, is shown in Fig. 6.8(d).

Binary Hit-or-Miss Operators

Only two masks have been discussed so far, one filled with 1's to perform erosion and another filled with 0's to perform dilation. This brings up the question of whether there are other masks that could be useful for other types of conditional processing. The answer is yes. For example, the following masks can be used to check to see if a pixel is four-connected to its neighbors:

```
0 0 0       0 1 0       0 0 0       0 0 0

0 1 1       0 1 0       1 1 0       0 1 0

0 0 0       0 0 0       0 0 0       0 1 0
```

A similar set of masks can be used to check for eight-connectivity. Bridges, which are defined to be single-pixel connections between groups of similar pixels, can be identified by the following masks:

```
1 0 1       1 1 1

1 1 1       0 1 0

1 0 1       1 1 1
```

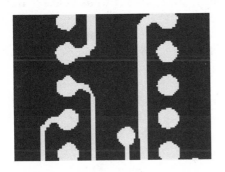

(a) Original Image

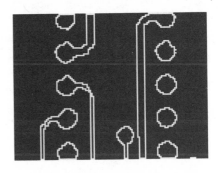

(b) Outlining

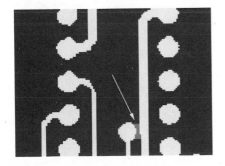

(c) Closing

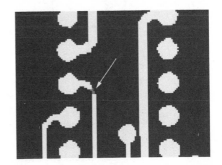

(d) Opening

Figure 6.8 Outlining, closing, and opening.

There also are masks that check for corners or interior pixels or other conditions. Sometimes it might be desirable to determine if an output pixel is set to black or white if most neighbors are of the same value. Performing multiple passes on the same image to check for every possible condition of interest can become extremely time-consuming.

To solve this problem, a function can be borrowed from the image processing point operators: look-up tables. Because each pixel in a binary image is either one or zero, it can become a bit that is grouped with other pixels in the neighborhood to form a numerical value, as shown in Fig. 6.9. The neighborhood of 9 binary pixels becomes a 9-bit number that can be used as an index into a look-up table to determine if the output pixel should be a hit or a miss. This table is known as a *9-to-1 LUT* since the 9-bit input value results in a 1-bit output value. Moreover, the table has 512 entries, the number of possible conditions of the 3×3 binary pixel neighborhood. Program 24 is an implementation of this function. For this example, the LUT is set up to perform the same erosion process that was implemented in Program 23.

Obviously, the difficulty of using this technique is generating the proper look-up table, because all possible conditions of pixel neighborhoods must be considered for whether a hit or a miss is generated. Once this task is completed, however, the resultant processing is much faster. Some computer systems perform the conversion of pixel groups into 9-bit values by using special hardware, in which case the programmer simply supplies the look-up table.

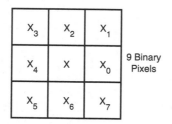

9 Binary Pixels

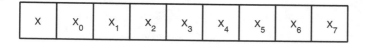

9-Bit Integer

Figure 6.9 Look-up table address generation.

```
/******************************************************/
/*    program 24: hit-and-miss LUT erosion and dilation    */
/******************************************************/


#define  XSIZE   640
#define  YSIZE   480

main()
  {
  unsigned char *ip;
  unsigned char *op;
  unsigned char *i1,*i2,*i3;
  unsigned char *o1,*o2,*o3;
  unsigned char lut[512];
  long  int  x,y;
  long  int  l;

  /* generate erode lut: */
  for (x = 0; x < 512; x++) lut[x] = 0x00;
  lut[0x1ff] = 0xff;

  /* generate dilate lut:
  for (x = 0; x < 512; x++) lut[x] = 0xff;
  lut[0x000] = 0x00;
  */

  /* allocate input and output memory buffers */
  ip = (unsigned char *) malloc (XSIZE*YSIZE);
  op = (unsigned char *) malloc (XSIZE*YSIZE);

  /* read the input image (one plane image) */
  read_image("input",ip);

  /* initialize pointers into buffers */
  i2 = ip;
  i3 = ip + XSIZE;
  o2 = op;
  o3 = op + XSIZE;

  /* process all lines of image */
  for (y = 1; y < (YSIZE-1); y++)
    {
    /* set pointers for this line */
    i1 = i2;
    i2 = i3;
    i3 = i3 + XSIZE;
    o1 = o2;
    o2 = o3;
    o3 = o3 + XSIZE;

    /* process all pixels in line */
    for (x = 1; x < (XSIZE-1); x++)
      {
      /* generate index into lut from binary pixels */
      l = ((*(i2+x+0) & 0x01) << 8) +
```

```
          ((*(i2+x+1) & 0x01) << 7) +
          ((*(i1+x+1) & 0x01) << 6) +
          ((*(i1+x+0) & 0x01) << 5) +
          ((*(i1+x-1) & 0x01) << 4) +
          ((*(i2+x-1) & 0x01) << 3) +
          ((*(i3+x-1) & 0x01) << 2) +
          ((*(i3+x+0) & 0x01) << 1) +
           (*(i3+x+1) & 0x01);

      /* perform look-up table operation */
      *(o2+x) = lut[l];
      }
   }

  /* write the output image */
  write_image("output",op);

  /* free memory buffers */
  free(ip);
  free(op);
  }
```

Program 24 Hit-and-miss LUT erosion and dilation.

Pipelined Processing

A number of morphological operators have been performed by applying a single 3×3 pixel mask. There are others, such as shrinking, thinning, and skeletonization (discussed next), for which 3×3 will not suffice. A 5×5 mask is needed to perform these functions—but that mask size creates over 33 million conditional patterns that must be checked for each pixel! A very efficient method described by Pratt (in *Digital Image Processing*) is to use a two-stage pipeline processing technique, with both stages using 3×3 masks.

The first stage of the procedure is to process an image, checking for pixels that might be operated upon. This first stage of the pipeline generates a new binary image that marks the likely candidates. The second stage of the pipeline then uses the original binary image and the marked image to determine whether each pixel is a hit or a miss for the desired function. The look-up table method of processing is used, so these checks become very fast. The result is performing the equivalent of 33 million checks per pixel in two passes of a look-up table.

Program 25 is an implementation of this two-stage pipeline processing technique. It uses data files to define the conditions from which the look-up tables are built. These data files, which are read by the program during execution, also are listed. They define the conditions for performing the shrinking, thinning, and skeletonization operations that are defined in the following sections. Each of these processes are performed repetitively until a final result has been achieved.

```
/****************************************************************/
/*    program 25: pipelined morphological operations       */
/****************************************************************/

#include <stdio.h>
#define  XSIZE   640
#define  YSIZE   480

long int interp();

main()
   {
   FILE   *fp;
   char   line[256];
   unsigned char *ip;
   unsigned char *op;
   unsigned char *mp;
   unsigned char *i1,*i2,*i3;
   unsigned char *o1,*o2,*o3;
   unsigned char *m1,*m2,*m3;
   unsigned char lutm[512];
   unsigned char lutu[512];
   long   int   eof,m,u;
   long   int   x,y;
   long   int   diff;
   long   int   xx,x0,x1,x2,x3,x4,x5,x6,x7;
   long   int   l;

/****************************************************************/
/*    part 1: read in conditionals file and set up luts    */
/****************************************************************/

   /* open conditionals file */
   fp = fopen("cshrink","r");

   /****************************************************************
       file format (first token):
          #       - comment line, ignored
          uncond - start of unconditional conditions
          mark   - start of mark conditions
          0 / 1  - 9-pixel condition (NE,N,NW,E,X,W,SE,S,SW)
          end     - end of conditions
       ****************************************************************/

   /* initialize processing variables */
   eof = 0;
   m = 0;
   u = 0;
   for (x = 0; x < 512; x++) lutm[x] = 0x00;
   for (x = 0; x < 512; x++) lutu[x] = 0x00;

   /* read and process all lines of file,
        build look-up tables ('lutu' and 'lutm') */
   while (eof == 0)
      {
      if (fgets(line,255,fp) == NULL)
         {
         eof = 1;
         }
```

```
else
  {
  if (line[0] != '#')
    {
    switch (m)
      {
      case 0:
        if (strncmp(line,"mark",4) == 0)
          {
          m = 1;
          }
        break;
      case 1:
        if (strncmp(line,"end",3) == 0)
          {
          m = 2;
          }
        else
          {
          x = interp(line);
          lutm[x] = 0xff;
          }
        break;

      case 2:
        switch (u)
          {
          case 0:
            if (strncmp(line,"uncond",6) == 0)
              {
              u = 1;
              }
            break;
          case 1:
            if (strncmp(line,"end",3) == 0)
              {
              u = 2;
              }
            else
              {
              x = interp(line);
              lutu[x] = 0xff;
              }
            break;
          default:
            printf("unknown: u=%d\n",u);
            break;
          }
        break;              default:
        printf("unknown: m=%d\n",m);
        break;
      }
    }
  }
}
```

```
/*******************************************************************/
/*    part 2: process the image until final conclusions    */
/*******************************************************************/

  ip = (unsigned char *) malloc (XSIZE*YSIZE);
  op = (unsigned char *) malloc (XSIZE*YSIZE);
  mp = (unsigned char *) malloc (XSIZE*YSIZE);

  /* read the input image (note: read into OUTPUT buffer) */
  read_image("input",op);

  /* repetitively process the image until not changes are made */
  diff = 1;
  while (diff > 0)
    {
    /* move last pass result (output) into input buffer */
    for (x = 0; x < (XSIZE*YSIZE); x++)
      {
      *(ip+x) = *(op+x);
      *(mp+x) = 0x00;
      }

    /**** pipeline stage 1:                                    ****/
    /**** update undisputed pixels and mark potential pixels ****/

    /* initialize pointers into buffers */
    i2 = ip;
    i3 = ip + XSIZE;
    o2 = op;
    o3 = op + XSIZE;
    m2 = mp;
    m3 = mp + XSIZE;

    /* process all lines of image */
    for (y = 1; y < (YSIZE-1); y++)
      {
      i1 = i2;
      i2 = i3;
      i3 = i3 + XSIZE;
      o1 = o2;
      o2 = o3;
      o3 = o3 + XSIZE;
      m1 = m2;
      m2 = m3;
      m3 = m3 + XSIZE;
      for (x = 1; x < (XSIZE-1); x++)
        {
        /* generate index into lut from binary pixels */
        l = ((*(i2+x+0) & 0x01) << 8) +
            ((*(i2+x+1) & 0x01) << 7) +
            ((*(i1+x+1) & 0x01) << 6) +
            ((*(i1+x+0) & 0x01) << 5) +
            ((*(i1+x-1) & 0x01) << 4) +
            ((*(i2+x-1) & 0x01) << 3) +
            ((*(i3+x-1) & 0x01) << 2) +
            ((*(i3+x+0) & 0x01) << 1) +
             (*(i3+x+1) & 0x01);
```

```
        /* mark this pixel as a potential for change */
        *(m2+x) = lutm[l];

        /* if not a marked pixel, copy as-is to output buffer */
        if (*(m2+x) == 0x00) *(o2+x) = *(i2+x);
        }
    }

/**** pipeline stage 2:                              ****/
/**** revisit marked pixels and update accordingly ****/

/* re-initialize pointers into buffers */
i2 = ip;
i3 = ip + XSIZE;
o2 = op;
o3 = op + XSIZE;
m2 = mp;
m3 = mp + XSIZE;

/* process all lines of image */
for (y = 1; y < (YSIZE-1); y++)
  {
  i1 = i2;
  i2 = i3;
  i3 = i3 + XSIZE;
  o1 = o2;
  o2 = o3;
  o3 = o3 + XSIZE;
  m1 = m2;
  m2 = m3;
  m3 = m3 + XSIZE;
  for (x = 1; x < (XSIZE-1); x++)
    {
    /* check to see if this pixel is marked */
    if (*(m2+x) == 0xff)
      {
      /* generate index into lut from binary pixels */
      l = ((*(m2+x)   & 0x01) << 8) +
          ((*(m2+x+1) & 0x01) << 7) +
          ((*(m1+x+1) & 0x01) << 6) +
          ((*(m1+x)   & 0x01) << 5) +
          ((*(m1+x-1) & 0x01) << 4) +
          ((*(m2+x-1) & 0x01) << 3) +
          ((*(m3+x-1) & 0x01) << 2) +
          ((*(m3+x)   & 0x01) << 1) +
           (*(m3+x+1) & 0x01);

      /* update output image for marked pixels */
      *(o2+x) = lutu[l];
      }
    }
  }

/* determine if any pixels were changed during this pass */
diff = 0;
for (x = 0; x < (XSIZE*YSIZE); x++)
  if (*(ip+x) != *(op+x))
    diff++;
```

```
        printf("different pixel count: %d\n",diff);
        }

    /* write the output image */
    write_image("output",op);

    /* free memory buffers */
    free(ip);
    free(op);
    free(mp);
    }

/******  interpret 9-pixel group  ******/
long int interp(s)
    char *s;
    {
    long int z,z0,z1,z2,z3,z4,z5,z6,z7;
    long int i;

    sscanf(s,"%d %d %d  %d %d %d  %d %d %d",
                &z3,&z2,&z1,&z4,&z,&z0,&z5,&z6,&z7);
    i = ((z  & 0x01) << 8) +
        ((z0 & 0x01) << 7) +
        ((z1 & 0x01) << 6) +
        ((z2 & 0x01) << 5) +
        ((z3 & 0x01) << 4) +
        ((z4 & 0x01) << 3) +
        ((z5 & 0x01) << 2) +
        ((z6 & 0x01) << 1) +
         (z7 & 0x01);

    return i;
    }


#
#  cshrink: shrinking conditions file
#  (see W. Pratt, Digital Image Processing, pp 462-465)
#
#  x3 x2 x1
#  x4 x  x0
#  x5 x6 x7#
#  mask pattern: x3 x2 x1  x4 x x0  x5 x6 x7
#
# mark conditional pixels:
#
mark
#
0 0 1  0 1 0  0 0 0
1 0 0  0 1 0  0 0 0
0 0 0  0 1 0  1 0 0
0 0 0  0 1 0  0 0 1
#
0 0 0  0 1 1  0 0 0
0 1 0  0 1 0  0 0 0
0 0 0  1 1 0  0 0 0
0 0 0  0 1 0  0 1 0
#
```

```
0 0 1    0 1 1    0 0 0
0 1 1    0 1 0    0 0 0
1 1 0    0 1 0    0 0 0
1 0 0    1 1 0    0 0 0
0 0 0    1 1 0    1 0 0
0 0 0    0 1 0    1 1 0
0 0 0    0 1 0    0 1 1
0 0 0    0 1 1    0 0 1
#
0 0 1    0 1 1    0 0 1
1 1 1    0 1 0    0 0 0
1 0 0    1 1 0    1 0 0
0 0 0    0 1 0    1 1 1
#
1 1 0    0 1 1    0 0 0
0 1 0    0 1 1    0 0 1
0 1 1    1 1 0    0 0 0
0 0 1    0 1 1    0 1 0
#
0 1 1    0 1 1    0 0 0
1 1 0    1 1 0    0 0 0
0 0 0    1 1 0    1 1 0
0 0 0    0 1 1    0 1 1
#
1 1 0    0 1 1    0 0 1
0 1 1    1 1 0    1 0 0
#
1 1 1    0 1 1    0 0 0
0 1 1    0 1 1    0 0 1
1 1 1    1 1 0    0 0 0
1 1 0    1 1 0    1 0 0
1 0 0    1 1 0    1 1 0
0 0 0    1 1 0    1 1 1
0 0 0    0 1 1    1 1 1
0 0 1    0 1 1    0 1 1
#
1 1 1    0 1 1    0 0 1
1 1 1    1 1 0    1 0 0
1 0 0    1 1 0    1 1 1
0 0 1    0 1 1    1 1 1
#
0 1 1    0 1 1    0 1 1
1 1 1    1 1 1    0 0 0
1 1 0    1 1 0    1 1 0
0 0 0    1 1 1    1 1 1
#
1 1 1    0 1 1    0 1 1
0 1 1    0 1 1    1 1 1
1 1 1    1 1 1    1 0 0
1 1 1    1 1 1    0 0 1
1 1 1    1 1 0    1 1 0
1 1 0    1 1 0    1 1 1
1 0 0    1 1 1    1 1 1
0 0 1    1 1 1    1 1 1
#
1 1 1    0 1 1    1 1 1
1 1 1    1 1 1    1 0 1
1 1 1    1 1 0    1 1 1
```

```
1 0 1  1 1 1  1 1 1
#
end
#
# unconditional conditions for marked pixels:
#
unconditional
#
0 0 1  0 1 0  0 0 0
1 0 0  0 1 0  0 0 0
#
0 0 0  0 1 0  0 1 0
0 0 0  0 1 1  0 0 0
#
0 1 1  1 1 0  0 0 0
1 1 0  0 1 1  0 0 0
0 1 0  0 1 1  0 0 1
0 0 1  0 1 1  0 1 0
#
0 1 1  0 1 1  1 0 0
1 1 0  1 1 0  0 0 1
0 0 1  1 1 0  1 1 0
1 0 0  0 1 1  0 1 1
#
1 1 0  1 1 0  0 0 0
1 1 1  1 1 0  0 0 0
1 1 0  1 1 1  0 0 0
1 1 1  1 1 1  0 0 0
1 1 0  1 1 0  1 0 0
1 1 1  1 1 0  1 0 0
1 1 0  1 1 1  1 0 0
1 1 1  1 1 1  1 0 0
1 1 0  1 1 0  0 1 0
1 1 1  1 1 0  0 1 0
1 1 0  1 1 1  0 1 0
1 1 1  1 1 1  0 1 0
1 1 0  1 1 0  1 1 0
1 1 1  1 1 0  1 1 0
1 1 0  1 1 1  1 1 0
1 1 1  1 1 1  1 1 0
1 1 0  1 1 0  0 0 1
1 1 1  1 1 0  0 0 1
1 1 0  1 1 1  0 0 1
1 1 1  1 1 1  0 0 1
1 1 0  1 1 0  1 0 1
1 1 1  1 1 0  1 0 1
1 1 0  1 1 1  1 0 1
1 1 1  1 1 1  1 0 1
1 1 0  1 1 0  0 1 1
1 1 1  1 1 0  0 1 1
1 1 0  1 1 1  0 1 1
1 1 1  1 1 1  0 1 1
1 1 0  1 1 0  1 1 1
1 1 1  1 1 0  1 1 1
1 1 0  1 1 1  1 1 1
1 1 1  1 1 1  1 1 1
```

```
#
0 1 0   1 1 1   0 0 0
1 1 0   1 1 1   0 0 0
0 1 0   1 1 1   1 0 0
1 1 0   1 1 1   1 0 0
##
0 1 0   1 1 1   0 0 0
0 1 1   1 1 1   0 0 0
0 1 0   1 1 1   0 0 1
0 1 1   1 1 1   0 0 1
##
0 0 0   1 1 1   0 1 0
0 0 1   1 1 1   0 1 0
0 0 0   1 1 1   0 1 1
0 0 1   1 1 1   0 1 1
##
0 0 0   1 1 0   0 1 0
1 0 0   1 1 0   0 1 0
0 0 0   1 1 0   1 1 0
1 0 0   1 1 0   1 1 0
##
0 1 0   1 1 0   0 1 0
1 1 0   1 1 0   0 1 0
0 1 1   1 1 0   0 1 0
1 1 1   1 1 0   0 1 0
0 1 0   1 1 0   1 1 0
1 1 0   1 1 0   1 1 0
0 1 1   1 1 0   1 1 0
1 1 1   1 1 0   1 1 0
##
0 1 0   1 1 0   0 1 0
0 1 0   1 1 0   1 1 0
0 1 0   1 1 0   0 1 1
0 1 0   1 1 0   1 1 1
##
0 1 0   0 1 1   0 1 0
0 1 0   0 1 1   1 1 0
0 1 0   0 1 1   0 1 1
0 1 0   0 1 1   1 1 1
##
0 1 0   0 1 1   0 1 0
1 1 0   0 1 1   0 1 0
0 1 1   0 1 1   0 1 0
1 1 1   0 1 1   0 1 0
#
1 0 1   0 1 0   1 0 0
1 1 1   0 1 0   1 0 0
1 0 1   1 1 0   1 0 0
1 1 1   1 1 0   1 0 0
1 0 1   0 1 1   1 0 0
1 1 1   0 1 1   1 0 0
1 0 1   1 1 1   1 0 0
1 1 1   1 1 1   1 0 0
##
1 0 1   0 1 0   0 1 0
1 1 1   0 1 0   0 1 0
1 0 1   1 1 0   0 1 0
1 1 1   1 1 0   0 1 0
```

```
1 0 1   0 1 1   0 1 0
1 1 1   0 1 1   0 1 0
1 0 1   1 1 1   0 1 0
1 1 1   1 1 1   0 1 0
##
1 0 1   0 1 0   0 0 1
1 1 1   0 1 0   0 0 1
1 0 1   1 1 0   0 0 1
1 1 1   1 1 0   0 0 1
1 0 1   0 1 1   0 0 1
1 1 1   0 1 1   0 0 1
1 0 1   1 1 1   0 0 1
1 1 1   1 1 1   0 0 1
##
1 0 0   0 1 0   1 0 1
1 1 0   0 1 0   1 0 1
1 0 0   1 1 0   1 0 1
1 1 0   1 1 0   1 0 1
1 0 0   0 1 0   1 1 1
1 1 0   0 1 0   1 1 1
1 0 0   1 1 0   1 1 1
1 1 0   1 1 0   1 1 1
##
1 0 0   0 1 1   1 0 0
1 1 0   0 1 1   1 0 0
1 0 0   1 1 1   1 0 0
1 1 0   1 1 1   1 0 0
1 0 0   0 1 1   1 1 0
1 1 0   0 1 1   1 1 0
1 0 0   1 1 1   1 1 0
1 1 0   1 1 1   1 1 0
##
1 0 1   0 1 0   1 0 0
1 1 1   0 1 0   1 0 0
1 0 1   1 1 0   1 0 0
1 1 1   1 1 0   1 0 0
1 0 1   0 1 0   1 1 0
1 1 1   0 1 0   1 1 0
1 0 1   1 1 0   1 1 0
1 1 1   1 1 0   1 1 0
##
0 0 1   0 1 0   1 0 1
0 0 1   1 1 0   1 0 1
0 0 1   0 1 1   1 0 1
0 0 1   1 1 1   1 0 1
0 0 1   0 1 0   1 1 1
0 0 1   1 1 0   1 1 1
0 0 1   0 1 1   1 1 1
0 0 1   1 1 1   1 1 1
##
0 1 0   0 1 0   1 0 1
0 1 0   1 1 0   1 0 1
0 1 0   0 1 1   1 0 1
0 1 0   1 1 1   1 0 1
0 1 0   0 1 0   1 1 1
0 1 0   1 1 0   1 1 1
0 1 0   0 1 1   1 1 1
0 1 0   1 1 1   1 1 1
```

```
##
1 0 0    0 1 0    1 0 1
1 0 0    1 1 0    1 0 1
1 0 0    0 1 1    1 0 1
1 0 0    1 1 1    1 0 1
1 0 0    0 1 0    1 1 1
1 0 0    1 1 0    1 1 1
1 0 0    0 1 1    1 1 1
1 0 0    1 1 1    1 1 1
##
1 0 1    0 1 0    0 0 1
1 1 1    0 1 0    0 0 1
1 0 1    0 1 1    0 0 1
1 1 1    0 1 1    0 0 1
1 0 1    0 1 0    0 1 1
1 1 1    0 1 0    0 1 1
1 0 1    0 1 1    0 1 1
1 1 1    0 1 1    0 1 1
##
0 0 1    1 1 0    0 0 1
0 1 1    1 1 0    0 0 1
0 0 1    1 1 1    0 0 1
0 1 1    1 1 1    0 0 1
0 0 1    1 1 0    0 1 1
0 1 1    1 1 0    0 1 1
0 0 1    1 1 1    0 1 1
0 1 1    1 1 1    0 1 1
##
0 0 1    0 1 0    1 0 1
0 1 1    0 1 0    1 0 1
0 0 1    0 1 1    1 0 1
0 1 1    0 1 1    1 0 1
0 0 1    0 1 0    1 1 1
0 1 1    0 1 0    1 1 1
0 0 1    0 1 1    1 1 1
0 1 1    0 1 1    1 1 1
#
0 1 0    0 1 1    1 0 0
1 1 0    0 1 1    1 0 0
0 1 0    0 1 1    1 0 1
1 1 0    0 1 1    1 0 1
##
0 1 0    1 1 0    0 0 1
0 1 1    1 1 0    0 0 1
0 1 0    1 1 0    1 0 1
0 1 1    1 1 0    1 0 1
##
0 0 1    1 1 0    0 1 0
1 0 1    1 1 0    0 1 0
0 0 1    1 1 0    0 1 1
1 0 1    1 1 0    0 1 1
##
1 0 0    0 1 1    0 1 0
1 0 1    0 1 1    0 1 0
1 0 0    0 1 1    1 1 0
1 0 1    0 1 1    1 1 0
#
end
```

```
#
#   cthin: thinning conditions file
#   (see W. Pratt, Digital Image Processing, pp 462-465)
#
#   x3 x2 x1
#   x4 x  x0
#   x5 x6 x7
#
#   mask pattern: x3 x2 x1  x4 x x0  x5 x6 x7
#
# mark conditional pixels:
#
mark
#
0 1 0   0 1 1   0 0 0
0 1 0   1 1 0   0 0 0
0 0 0   1 1 0   0 1 0
0 0 0   0 1 1   0 1 0
#
0 0 1   0 1 1   0 0 1
1 1 1   0 1 0   0 0 0
1 0 0   1 1 0   1 0 0
0 0 0   0 1 0   1 1 1
#
1 1 0   0 1 1   0 0 0
0 1 0   0 1 1   0 0 1
0 1 1   1 1 0   0 0 0
0 0 1   0 1 1   0 1 0
#
0 1 1   0 1 1   0 0 0
1 1 0   1 1 0   0 0 0
0 0 0   1 1 0   1 1 0
0 0 0   0 1 1   0 1 1
#
1 1 0   0 1 1   0 0 1
0 1 1   1 1 0   1 0 0
#
1 1 1   0 1 1   0 0 0
0 1 1   0 1 1   0 0 1
1 1 1   1 1 0   0 0 0
1 1 0   1 1 0   1 0 0
1 0 0   1 1 0   1 1 0
0 0 0   1 1 0   1 1 1
0 0 0   0 1 1   1 1 1
0 0 1   0 1 1   0 1 1
#
1 1 1   0 1 1   0 0 1
1 1 1   1 1 0   1 0 0
1 0 0   1 1 0   1 1 1
0 0 1   0 1 1   1 1 1
#
0 1 1   0 1 1   0 1 1
1 1 1   1 1 1   0 0 0
1 1 0   1 1 0   1 1 0
0 0 0   1 1 1   1 1 1
#
1 1 1   0 1 1   0 1 1
0 1 1   0 1 1   1 1 1
```

```
1 1 1   1 1 1   1 0 0
1 1 1   1 1 1   0 0 1
1 1 1   1 1 0   1 1 0
1 1 0   1 1 0   1 1 1
1 0 0   1 1 1   1 1 1
0 0 1   1 1 1   1 1 1
#
1 1 1   0 1 1   1 1 1
1 1 1   1 1 1   1 0 1
1 1 1   1 1 0   1 1 1
1 0 1   1 1 1   1 1 1
#
end         .
#
# unconditional conditions for marked pixels:
#
unconditional
#
0 0 1   0 1 0   0 0 0
1 0 0   0 1 0   0 0 0
#
0 0 0   0 1 0   0 1 0
0 0 0   0 1 1   0 0 0
#
0 1 1   1 1 0   0 0 0
1 1 0   0 1 1   0 0 0
0 1 0   0 1 1   0 0 1
0 0 1   0 1 1   0 1 0
#
0 1 1   0 1 1   1 0 0
1 1 0   1 1 0   0 0 1
0 0 1   1 1 0   1 1 0
1 0 0   0 1 1   0 1 1
#
1 1 0   1 1 0   0 0 0
1 1 1   1 1 0   0 0 0
1 1 0   1 1 1   0 0 0
1 1 1   1 1 1   0 0 0
1 1 0   1 1 0   1 0 0
1 1 1   1 1 0   1 0 0
1 1 0   1 1 1   1 0 0
1 1 1   1 1 1   1 0 0
1 1 0   1 1 0   0 1 0
1 1 1   1 1 0   0 1 0
1 1 0   1 1 1   0 1 0
1 1 1   1 1 1   0 1 0
1 1 0   1 1 0   1 1 0
1 1 1   1 1 0   1 1 0
1 1 0   1 1 1   1 1 0
1 1 1   1 1 1   1 1 0
1 1 0   1 1 0   0 0 1
1 1 1   1 1 0   0 0 1
1 1 0   1 1 1   0 0 1
1 1 1   1 1 1   0 0 1
1 1 0   1 1 0   1 0 1
1 1 1   1 1 0   1 0 1
1 1 0   1 1 1   1 0 1
1 1 1   1 1 1   1 0 1
1 1 0   1 1 0   0 1 1
1 1 1   1 1 0   0 1 1
```

```
1 1 0   1 1 1   0 1 1
1 1 1   1 1 1   0 1 1
1 1 0   1 1 0   1 1 1
1 1 1   1 1 0   1 1 1
1 1 0   1 1 1   1 1 1
1 1 1   1 1 1   1 1 1
#
0 1 0   1 1 1   0 0 0
1 1 0   1 1 1   0 0 0
0 1 0   1 1 1   1 0 0
1 1 0   1 1 1   1 0 0
##
0 1 0   1 1 1   0 0 0
0 1 1   1 1 1   0 0 0
0 1 0   1 1 1   0 0 1
0 1 1   1 1 1   0 0 1
##
0 0 0   1 1 1   0 1 0
0 0 1   1 1 1   0 1 0
0 0 0   1 1 1   0 1 1
0 0 1   1 1 1   0 1 1
##
0 0 0   1 1 0   0 1 0
1 0 0   1 1 0   0 1 0
0 0 0   1 1 0   1 1 0
1 0 0   1 1 0   1 1 0
##
0 1 0   1 1 0   0 1 0
1 1 0   1 1 0   0 1 0
0 1 1   1 1 0   0 1 0
1 1 1   1 1 0   0 1 0
0 1 0   1 1 0   1 1 0
1 1 0   1 1 0   1 1 0
0 1 1   1 1 0   1 1 0
1 1 1   1 1 0   1 1 0
##
0 1 0   1 1 0   0 1 0
0 1 0   1 1 0   1 1 0
0 1 0   1 1 0   0 1 1
0 1 0   1 1 0   1 1 1
##
0 1 0   0 1 1   0 1 0
0 1 0   0 1 1   1 1 0
0 1 0   0 1 1   0 1 1
0 1 0   0 1 1   1 1 1
##
0 1 0   0 1 1   0 1 0
1 1 0   0 1 1   0 1 0
0 1 1   0 1 1   0 1 0
1 1 1   0 1 1   0 1 0
#
1 0 1   0 1 0   1 0 0
1 1 1   0 1 0   1 0 0
1 0 1   1 1 0   1 0 0
1 1 1   1 1 0   1 0 0
1 0 1   0 1 1   1 0 0
1 1 1   0 1 1   1 0 0
1 0 1   1 1 1   1 0 0
1 1 1   1 1 1   1 0 0
##
```

```
1 0 1   0 1 0   0 1 0
1 1 1   0 1 0   0 1 0
1 0 1   1 1 0   0 1 0
1 1 1   1 1 0   0 1 0
1 0 1   0 1 1   0 1 0
1 1 1   0 1 1   0 1 0
1 0 1   1 1 1   0 1 0
1 1 1   1 1 1   0 1 0
##
1 0 1   0 1 0   0 0 1
1 1 1   0 1 0   0 0 1
1 0 1   1 1 0   0 0 1
1 1 1   1 1 0   0 0 1
1 0 1   0 1 1   0 0 1
1 1 1   0 1 1   0 0 1
1 0 1   1 1 1   0 0 1
1 1 1   1 1 1   0 0 1
##
1 0 0   0 1 0   1 0 1
1 1 0   0 1 0   1 0 1
1 0 0   1 1 0   1 0 1
1 1 0   1 1 0   1 0 1
1 0 0   0 1 0   1 1 1
1 1 0   0 1 0   1 1 1
1 0 0   1 1 0   1 1 1
1 1 0   1 1 0   1 1 1
##
1 0 0   0 1 1   1 0 0
1 1 0   0 1 1   1 0 0
1 0 0   1 1 1   1 0 0
1 1 0   1 1 1   1 0 0
1 0 0   0 1 1   1 1 0
1 1 0   0 1 1   1 1 0
1 0 0   1 1 1   1 1 0
1 1 0   1 1 1   1 1 0
##
1 0 1   0 1 0   1 0 0
1 1 1   0 1 0   1 0 0
1 0 1   1 1 0   1 0 0
1 1 1   1 1 0   1 0 0
1 0 1   0 1 0   1 1 0
1 1 1   0 1 0   1 1 0
1 0 1   1 1 0   1 1 0
1 1 1   1 1 0   1 1 0
##
0 0 1   0 1 0   1 0 1
0 0 1   1 1 0   1 0 1
0 0 1   0 1 1   1 0 1
0 0 1   1 1 1   1 0 1
0 0 1   0 1 0   1 1 1
0 0 1   1 1 0   1 1 1
0 0 1   0 1 1   1 1 1
0 0 1   1 1 1   1 1 1
##
0 1 0   0 1 0   1 0 1
0 1 0   1 1 0   1 0 1
0 1 0   0 1 1   1 0 1
```

```
0 1 0    1 1 1    1 0 1
0 1 0    0 1 0    1 1 1
0 1 0    1 1 0    1 1 1
0 1 0    0 1 1    1 1 1
0 1 0    1 1 1    1 1 1
##
1 0 0    0 1 0    1 0 1
1 0 0    1 1 0    1 0 1
1 0 0    0 1 1    1 0 1
1 0 0    1 1 1    1 0 1
1 0 0    0 1 0    1 1 1
1 0 0    1 1 0    1 1 1
1 0 0    0 1 1    1 1 1
1 0 0    1 1 1    1 1 1
##
1 0 1    0 1 0    0 0 1
1 1 1    0 1 0    0 0 1
1 0 1    0 1 1    0 0 1
1 1 1    0 1 1    0 0 1
1 0 1    0 1 0    0 1 1
1 1 1    0 1 0    0 1 1
1 0 1    0 1 1    0 1 1
1 1 1    0 1 1    0 1 1
##
0 0 1    1 1 0    0 0 1
0 1 1    1 1 0    0 0 1
0 0 1    1 1 1    0 0 1
0 1 1    1 1 1    0 0 1
0 0 1    1 1 0    0 1 1
0 1 1    1 1 0    0 1 1
0 0 1    1 1 1    0 1 1
0 1 1    1 1 1    0 1 1
##
0 0 1    0 1 0    1 0 1
0 1 1    0 1 0    1 0 1
0 0 1    0 1 1    1 0 1
0 1 1    0 1 1    1 0 1
0 0 1    0 1 0    1 1 1
0 1 1    0 1 0    1 1 1
0 0 1    0 1 1    1 1 1
0 1 1    0 1 1    1 1 1
#
0 1 0    0 1 1    1 0 0
1 1 0    0 1 1    1 0 0
0 1 0    0 1 1    1 0 1
1 1 0    0 1 1    1 0 1
##
0 1 0    1 1 0    0 0 1
0 1 1    1 1 0    0 0 1
0 1 0    1 1 0    1 0 1
0 1 1    1 1 0    1 0 1
##
0 0 1    1 1 0    0 1 0
1 0 1    1 1 0    0 1 0
0 0 1    1 1 0    0 1 1
1 0 1    1 1 0    0 1 1
##
```

```
1 0 0   0 1 1   0 1 0
1 0 1   0 1 1   0 1 0
1 0 0   0 1 1   1 1 0
1 0 1   0 1 1   1 1 0
#
end


#
#   cskel: skeltonization conditions file
#   (see W. Pratt, Digital Image Processing, pp 462-465)
#
#   x3 x2 x1
#   x4 x  x0
#   x5 x6 x7
#
#   mask pattern: x3 x2 x1   x4 x x0   x5 x6 x7
#
# mark conditional pixels:
#
mark
#
0 1 0   0 1 1   0 0 0
0 1 0   1 1 0   0 0 0
0 0 0   1 1 0   0 1 0
0 0 0   0 1 1   0 1 0
#
0 0 1   0 1 1   0 0 1
1 1 1   0 1 0   0 0 0
1 0 0   1 1 0   1 0 0
0 0 0   0 1 0   1 1 1
#
1 1 1   0 1 1   0 0 0
0 1 1   0 1 1   0 0 1
1 1 1   1 1 0   0 0 0
1 1 0   1 1 0   1 0 0
1 0 0   1 1 0   1 1 0
0 0 0   1 1 0   1 1 1
0 0 0   0 1 1   1 1 1
0 0 1   0 1 1   0 1 1
#
1 1 1   0 1 1   0 0 1
1 1 1   1 1 0   1 0 0
1 0 0   1 1 0   1 1 1
0 0 1   0 1 1   1 1 1
#
0 1 1   0 1 1   0 1 1
1 1 1   1 1 1   0 0 0
1 1 0   1 1 0   1 1 0
0 0 0   1 1 1   1 1 1
#
1 1 1   0 1 1   0 1 1
0 1 1   0 1 1   1 1 1
1 1 1   1 1 1   1 0 0
1 1 1   1 1 1   0 0 1
1 1 1   1 1 0   1 1 0
1 1 0   1 1 0   1 1 1
1 0 0   1 1 1   1 1 1
0 0 1   1 1 1   1 1 1
```

```
#
1 1 1   0 1 1   1 1 1
1 1 1   1 1 1   1 0 1
1 1 1   1 1 0   1 1 1
1 0 1   1 1 1   1 1 1
#
1 1 1   1 1 1   0 1 1
1 1 1   1 1 1   1 1 0
1 1 0   1 1 1   1 1 1
0 1 1   1 1 1   1 1 1
#
end
#
# unconditional conditions for marked pixels:
#
unconditional
#
0 0 0   0 1 0   0 0 1
0 0 0   0 1 0   1 0 0
0 0 1   0 1 0   0 0 0
1 0 0   0 1 0   0 0 0
#
0 0 0   0 1 0   0 1 0
0 0 0   0 1 1   0 0 0
0 0 0   1 1 0   0 0 0
0 1 0   0 1 0   0 0 0
#
0 1 0   0 1 1   0 0 0
0 1 0   1 1 0   0 0 0
0 0 0   0 1 1   0 1 0
0 0 0   1 1 0   0 1 0
#
0 1 1   0 1 1   0 0 0
1 1 1   0 1 1   0 0 0
0 1 1   1 1 1   0 0 0
1 1 1   1 1 1   0 0 0
0 1 1   0 1 1   1 0 0
1 1 1   0 1 1   1 0 0
0 1 1   1 1 1   1 0 0
1 1 1   1 1 1   1 0 0
0 1 1   0 1 1   0 1 0
1 1 1   0 1 1   0 1 0
0 1 1   1 1 1   0 1 0
1 1 1   1 1 1   0 1 0
0 1 1   0 1 1   1 1 0
1 1 1   0 1 1   1 1 0
0 1 1   1 1 1   1 1 0
1 1 1   1 1 1   1 1 0
0 1 1   0 1 1   0 0 1
1 1 1   0 1 1   0 0 1
0 1 1   1 1 1   0 0 1
1 1 1   1 1 1   0 0 1
0 1 1   0 1 1   1 0 1
1 1 1   0 1 1   1 0 1
0 1 1   1 1 1   1 0 1
1 1 1   1 1 1   1 0 1
0 1 1   0 1 1   0 1 1
1 1 1   0 1 1   0 1 1
0 1 1   1 1 1   0 1 1
```

```
1 1 1   1 1 1   0 1 1
0 1 1   0 1 1   1 1 1
1 1 1   0 1 1   1 1 1
0 1 1   1 1 1   1 1 1
1 1 1   1 1 1   1 1 1
#
0 0 0   1 1 0   1 1 0
1 0 0   1 1 0   1 1 0
0 1 0   1 1 0   1 1 0
1 1 0   1 1 0   1 1 0
0 0 1   1 1 0   1 1 0
1 0 1   1 1 0   1 1 0
0 1 1   1 1 0   1 1 0
1 1 1   1 1 0   1 1 0
0 0 0   1 1 1   1 1 0
1 0 0   1 1 1   1 1 0
0 1 0   1 1 1   1 1 0
1 1 0   1 1 1   1 1 0
0 0 1   1 1 1   1 1 0
1 0 1   1 1 1   1 1 0
0 1 1   1 1 1   1 1 0
1 1 1   1 1 1   1 1 0
0 0 0   1 1 0   1 1 1
1 0 0   1 1 0   1 1 1
0 1 0   1 1 0   1 1 1
1 1 0   1 1 0   1 1 1
0 0 1   1 1 0   1 1 1
1 0 1   1 1 0   1 1 1
0 1 1   1 1 0   1 1 1
1 1 1   1 1 0   1 1 1
0 0 0   1 1 1   1 1 1
1 0 0   1 1 1   1 1 1
0 1 0   1 1 1   1 1 1
1 1 0   1 1 1   1 1 1
0 0 1   1 1 1   1 1 1
1 0 1   1 1 1   1 1 1
0 1 1   1 1 1   1 1 1
1 1 1   1 1 1   1 1 1
#
1 1 0   1 1 0   0 0 0
1 1 1   1 1 0   0 0 0
1 1 0   1 1 1   0 0 0
1 1 1   1 1 1   0 0 0
1 1 0   1 1 0   1 0 0
1 1 1   1 1 0   1 0 0
1 1 0   1 1 1   1 0 0
1 1 1   1 1 1   1 0 0
1 1 0   1 1 0   0 1 0
1 1 1   1 1 0   0 1 0
1 1 0   1 1 1   0 1 0
1 1 1   1 1 1   0 1 0
1 1 0   1 1 0   1 1 0
1 1 1   1 1 0   1 1 0
1 1 0   1 1 1   1 1 0
1 1 1   1 1 1   1 1 0
1 1 0   1 1 0   0 0 1
1 1 1   1 1 0   0 0 1
1 1 0   1 1 1   0 0 1
```

```
1 1 1   1 1 1   0 0 1
1 1 0   1 1 0   1 0 1
1 1 1   1 1 0   1 0 1
1 1 0   1 1 1   1 0 1
1 1 1   1 1 1   1 0 1
1 1 0   1 1 0   0 1 1
1 1 1   1 1 0   0 1 1
1 1 0   1 1 1   0 1 1
1 1 1   1 1 1   0 1 1
1 1 0   1 1 0   1 1 1
1 1 1   1 1 0   1 1 1
1 1 0   1 1 1   1 1 1
1 1 1   1 1 1   1 1 1
#
0 0 0   0 1 1   0 1 1
1 0 0   0 1 1   0 1 1
0 1 0   0 1 1   0 1 1
1 1 0   0 1 1   0 1 1
0 0 1   0 1 1   0 1 1
1 0 1   0 1 1   0 1 1
0 1 1   0 1 1   0 1 1
1 1 1   0 1 1   0 1 1
0 0 0   1 1 1   0 1 1
1 0 0   1 1 1   0 1 1
0 1 0   1 1 1   0 1 1
1 1 0   1 1 1   0 1 1
0 0 1   1 1 1   0 1 1
1 0 1   1 1 1   0 1 1
0 1 1   1 1 1   0 1 1
1 1 1   1 1 1   0 1 1
0 0 0   0 1 1   1 1 1
1 0 0   0 1 1   1 1 1
0 1 0   0 1 1   1 1 1
1 1 0   0 1 1   1 1 1
0 0 1   0 1 1   1 1 1
1 0 1   0 1 1   1 1 1
0 1 1   0 1 1   1 1 1
1 1 1   0 1 1   1 1 1
0 0 0   1 1 1   1 1 1
1 0 0   1 1 1   1 1 1
0 1 0   1 1 1   1 1 1
1 1 0   1 1 1   1 1 1
0 0 1   1 1 1   1 1 1
1 0 1   1 1 1   1 1 1
0 1 1   1 1 1   1 1 1
1 1 1   1 1 1   1 1 1
#
0 1 0   1 1 1   0 0 0
1 1 0   1 1 1   0 0 0
0 1 1   1 1 1   0 0 0
1 1 1   1 1 1   0 0 0
0 1 0   1 1 1   1 0 0
1 1 0   1 1 1   1 0 0
0 1 1   1 1 1   1 0 0
1 1 1   1 1 1   1 0 0
#
0 1 0   1 1 0   0 1 0
1 1 0   1 1 0   0 1 0
```

```
0 1 1   1 1 0   0 1 0
1 1 1   1 1 0   0 1 0
0 1 0   1 1 1   0 1 0
1 1 0   1 1 1   0 1 0
0 1 1   1 1 1   0 1 0
1 1 1   1 1 1   0 1 0
0 1 0   1 1 0   1 1 0
1 1 0   1 1 0   1 1 0
0 1 1   1 1 0   1 1 0
1 1 1   1 1 0   1 1 0
0 1 0   1 1 1   1 1 0
1 1 0   1 1 1   1 1 0
0 1 1   1 1 1   1 1 0
1 1 1   1 1 1   1 1 0
0 1 0   1 1 0   0 1 1
1 1 0   1 1 0   0 1 1
0 1 1   1 1 0   0 1 1
1 1 1   1 1 0   0 1 1
0 1 0   1 1 1   0 1 1
1 1 0   1 1 1   0 1 1
0 1 1   1 1 1   0 1 1
1 1 1   1 1 1   0 1 1
0 1 0   1 1 0   1 1 1
1 1 0   1 1 0   1 1 1
0 1 1   1 1 0   1 1 1
1 1 1   1 1 0   1 1 1
0 1 0   1 1 1   1 1 1
1 1 0   1 1 1   1 1 1
0 1 1   1 1 1   1 1 1
1 1 1   1 1 1   1 1 1
#
0 0 0   1 1 1   0 1 0
1 0 0   1 1 1   0 1 0
0 1 0   1 1 1   0 1 0
1 1 0   1 1 1   0 1 0
0 0 1   1 1 1   0 1 0
1 0 1   1 1 1   0 1 0
0 1 1   1 1 1   0 1 0
1 1 1   1 1 1   0 1 0
0 0 0   1 1 1   1 1 0
1 0 0   1 1 1   1 1 0
0 1 0   1 1 1   1 1 0
1 1 0   1 1 1   1 1 0
0 0 1   1 1 1   1 1 0
1 0 1   1 1 1   1 1 0
0 1 1   1 1 1   1 1 0
1 1 1   1 1 1   1 1 0
0 0 0   1 1 1   0 1 1
1 0 0   1 1 1   0 1 1
0 1 0   1 1 1   0 1 1
1 1 0   1 1 1   0 1 1
0 0 1   1 1 1   0 1 1
1 0 1   1 1 1   0 1 1
0 1 1   1 1 1   0 1 1
1 1 1   1 1 1   0 1 1
0 0 0   1 1 1   1 1 1
1 0 0   1 1 1   1 1 1
0 1 0   1 1 1   1 1 1
```

```
1 1 0   1 1 1   1 1 1
0 0 1   1 1 1   1 1 1
1 0 1   1 1 1   1 1 1
0 1 1   1 1 1   1 1 1
1 1 1   1 1 1   1 1 1
#
0 1 0   0 1 1   0 1 0
1 1 0   0 1 1   0 1 0
0 1 1   0 1 1   0 1 0
1 1 1   0 1 1   0 1 0
0 1 0   1 1 1   0 1 0
1 1 0   1 1 1   0 1 0
0 1 1   1 1 1   0 1 0
1 1 1   1 1 1   0 1 0
0 1 0   0 1 1   1 1 0
1 1 0   0 1 1   1 1 0
0 1 1   0 1 1   1 1 0
1 1 1   0 1 1   1 1 0
0 1 0   1 1 1   1 1 0
1 1 0   1 1 1   1 1 0
0 1 1   1 1 1   1 1 0
1 1 1   1 1 1   1 1 0
0 1 0   0 1 1   0 1 1
1 1 0   0 1 1   0 1 1
0 1 1   0 1 1   0 1 1
1 1 1   0 1 1   0 1 1
0 1 0   1 1 1   0 1 1
1 1 0   1 1 1   0 1 1
0 1 1   1 1 1   0 1 1
1 1 1   1 1 1   0 1 1
0 1 0   0 1 1   1 1 1
1 1 0   0 1 1   1 1 1
0 1 1   0 1 1   1 1 1
1 1 1   0 1 1   1 1 1
0 1 0   1 1 1   1 1 1
1 1 0   1 1 1   1 1 1
0 1 1   1 1 1   1 1 1
1 1 1   1 1 1   1 1 1
#
1 0 1   0 1 0   1 0 0
1 1 1   0 1 0   1 0 0
1 0 1   1 1 0   1 0 0
1 1 1   1 1 0   1 0 0
1 0 1   0 1 1   1 0 0
1 1 1   0 1 1   1 0 0
1 0 1   1 1 1   1 0 0
1 1 1   1 1 1   1 0 0
#
1 0 0   0 1 0   1 0 1
1 1 0   0 1 0   1 0 1
1 0 0   1 1 0   1 0 1
1 1 0   1 1 0   1 0 1
1 0 0   0 1 0   1 1 1
1 1 0   0 1 0   1 1 1
1 0 0   1 1 0   1 1 1
1 1 0   1 1 0   1 1 1
#
0 0 1   0 1 0   1 0 1
```

```
0 0 1   1 1 0   1 0 1
0 0 1   0 1 1   1 0 1
0 0 1   1 1 1   1 0 1
0 0 1   0 1 0   1 1 1
0 0 1   1 1 0   1 1 1
0 0 1   0 1 1   1 1 1
0 0 1   1 1 1   1 1 1
#
1 0 1   0 1 0   0 0 1
1 1 1   0 1 0   0 0 1
1 0 1   0 1 1   0 0 1
1 1 1   0 1 1   0 0 1
1 0 1   0 1 0   0 1 1
1 1 1   0 1 0   0 1 1
1 0 1   0 1 1   0 1 1
1 1 1   0 1 1   0 1 1
#
1 0 1   0 1 0   0 1 0
1 1 1   0 1 0   0 1 0
1 0 1   1 1 0   0 1 0
1 1 1   1 1 0   0 1 0
1 0 1   0 1 1   0 1 0
1 1 1   0 1 1   0 1 0
1 0 1   1 1 1   0 1 0
1 1 1   1 1 1   0 1 0
#
1 0 0   0 1 1   1 0 0
1 1 0   0 1 1   1 0 0
1 0 0   1 1 1   1 0 0
1 1 0   1 1 1   1 0 0
1 0 0   0 1 1   1 1 0
1 1 0   0 1 1   1 1 0
1 0 0   1 1 1   1 1 0
1 1 0   1 1 1   1 1 0
#
0 1 0   0 1 0   1 0 1
0 1 0   1 1 0   1 0 1
0 1 0   0 1 1   1 0 1
0 1 0   1 1 1   1 0 1
0 1 0   0 1 0   1 1 1
0 1 0   1 1 0   1 1 1
0 1 0   0 1 1   1 1 1
0 1 0   1 1 1   1 1 1
#
0 0 1   1 1 0   0 0 1
0 1 1   1 1 0   0 0 1
0 0 1   1 1 1   0 0 1
0 1 1   1 1 1   0 0 1
0 0 1   1 1 0   0 1 1
0 1 1   1 1 0   0 1 1
0 0 1   1 1 1   0 1 1
0 1 1   1 1 1   0 1 1
#
1 0 1   0 1 0   0 0 1
1 1 1   0 1 0   0 0 1
1 0 1   1 1 0   0 0 1
```

```
1 1 1   1 1 0   0 0 1
1 0 1   0 1 1   0 0 1
1 1 1   0 1 1   0 0 1
1 0 1   1 1 1   0 0 1
1 1 1   1 1 1   0 0 1
#
1 0 1   0 1 0   1 0 0
1 1 1   0 1 0   1 0 0
1 0 1   1 1 0   1 0 0
1 1 1   1 1 0   1 0 0
1 0 1   0 1 0   1 1 0
1 1 1   0 1 0   1 1 0
1 0 1   1 1 0   1 1 0
1 1 1   1 1 0   1 1 0
#
1 0 0   0 1 0   1 0 1
1 0 0   1 1 0   1 0 1
1 0 0   0 1 1   1 0 1
1 0 0   1 1 1   1 0 1
1 0 0   0 1 0   1 1 1
1 0 0   1 1 0   1 1 1
1 0 0   0 1 1   1 1 1
1 0 0   1 1 1   1 1 1
#
0 0 1   0 1 0   1 0 1
0 1 1   0 1 0   1 0 1
0 0 1   0 1 1   1 0 1
0 1 1   0 1 1   1 0 1
0 0 1   0 1 0   1 1 1
0 1 1   0 1 0   1 1 1
0 0 1   0 1 1   1 1 1
0 1 1   0 1 1   1 1 1
#
0 1 0   0 1 1   1 0 0
1 1 0   0 1 1   1 0 0
0 1 0   0 1 1   1 0 1
1 1 0   0 1 1   1 0 1
#
0 1 0   1 1 0   0 0 1
0 1 1   1 1 0   0 0 1
0 1 0   1 1 0   1 0 1
0 1 1   1 1 0   1 0 1
#
0 0 1   1 1 0   0 1 0
1 0 1   1 1 0   0 1 0
0 0 1   1 1 0   0 1 1
1 0 1   1 1 0   0 1 1
#
1 0 0   0 1 1   0 1 0
1 0 0   0 1 1   0 1 0
1 0 1   0 1 1   1 1 0
1 0 1   0 1 1   1 1 0
#
end
```

Program 25 Pipelined morphological operations.

Shrinking

Shrinking will reduce objects in an image to a single point located at the geometric center. This can be thought of as finding the center of mass of an object. For objects that do not have holes in them, a single point is generated. If there is a hole, the process will produce a ring of pixels that surrounds the hole and is equidistant from the nearest boundary. Figure 6.10(b) shows the original image midway through the shrinking process, and Fig. 6.10(c) shows the result. Objects from the original image are shown as gray pixels.

Thinning

The thinning function is similar to shrinking, except that instead of finding a center of mass, thinning generates a minimally connected line that is equidistant from the boundaries. Figure 6.11(b) shows the results of this operation. Note how it differs from shrinking in that some of the structure of the object is maintained. Thinning also is useful when the binary sense of the image is reversed, creating black objects on a white background, as shown in Fig. 6.11(c). If the thinning function is used on this image, the results, shown in Fig. 6.11(d), are minimally connected lines that form equidistant boundaries between the objects.

Skeletonization

Skeletonization also is similar to thinning, except that it maintains more information about the internal structure of objects. The classic way to think about skeletonization is to set fire (mentally, of course) to pixels around the outer edge of an object simultaneously. As the fire burns inward toward the center of the object, eventually it will meet burning pixels from the opposite direction. When two opposing fires meet they extinguish one another, leaving behind a single (or double) pixel boundary, or skeleton, of the object. Figure 6.12(b) shows the results of this process when applied to the image in Fig. 6.12(a).

An example of a practical application of skeletonization is locating paths in a printed circuit board. The image in Fig. 6.12(c) shows a thresholded image of a circuit board. Figure 6.12(d) is the same image after this skeletonization function has been performed. It would be much easier for automated software to verify the paths of these circuits than in the original.

Grayscale Morphological Operations

As stated at the beginning of this chapter, morphological operations usually are performed on binary images, but some processing tech-

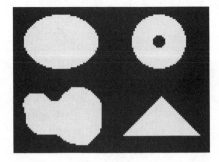

(a) Original Image

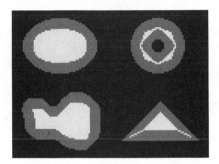

(b) Partial Shrinking

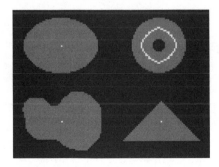

(c) After Shrinking

Figure 6.10 Shrinking.

niques also apply to grayscale images. These operations are for the most part limited to erosion and dilation. Grayscale erosions and dilations produce results identical to the nonlinear minimum and maximum filters that were discussed in the preceding chapter.

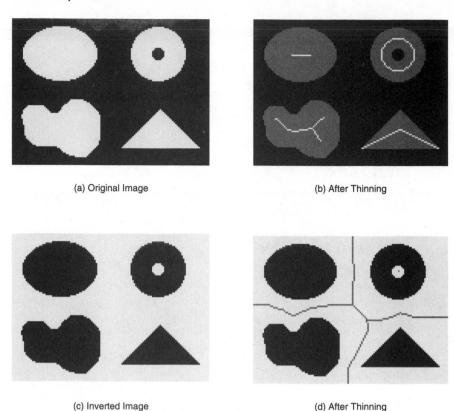

(a) Original Image   (b) After Thinning

(c) Inverted Image   (d) After Thinning

Figure 6.11 Thinning.

The minimum operator will interrogate a 3×3 (or any other size) neighborhood and select the smallest pixel value to become the output value. This has the effect of causing the bright areas of an image to shrink, or erode. Similarly, grayscale dilation is performed by using the maximum operator to select the greatest value in a neighborhood. The results of these operations are shown in Fig. 6.13.

Functions based on dilation or erosion, such as opening and closing, can be migrated to grayscale imagery. Other morphological functions that are based on hit-or-miss processing, such as thinning and skeletonization, do not translate well to grayscale images.

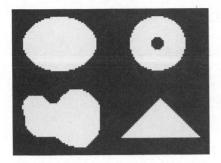

(a) Original Image

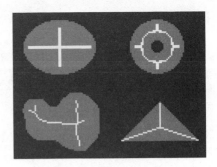

(b) After Skeletonization

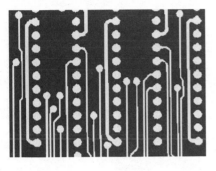

(c) Original Image

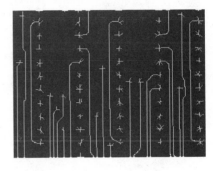

(d) After Skeletonization

Figure 6.12 Skeletonization.

(a) Original Image

(b) After Erode

(c) After Dilate

Figure 6.13 Grayscale erosion and dilation.

7

Miscellaneous Operations

Some image operations do not fit into the well-defined categories of point, neighborhood, or morphological. They are nonetheless important and, in fact, include some of the most exciting areas of research in the field of digital image processing. This chapter will discuss them at an introductory level and show examples of their use.

Fast Fourier Transform (FFT)

Images can be thought of as a collection of pixels of varying brightness that are arranged in a fixed, two-dimensional pattern. It is this *spatial* positioning of pixel intensities that forms a digital image. From preceding chapters, it has been shown that images also contain patterns of intensity change, or *frequencies*, that define things such as the sharp edges of objects and slowly changing color hues.

An image also can be thought of as a collection of signals. From signal processing, we know that any signal can be reduced, or *decomposed*, into a series of simple sinusoidal components, each of which has a frequency, amplitude, and phase. As such, it is possible to change, or transform, an image from the spatial domain into the frequency domain, where information is represented as signals having various characteristics.

As it turns out, some frequency-based operations, such as high-, low-, and bandpass filtering, can be performed quite easily on a frequency domain image, while the equivalent operation in the spatial domain involves cumbersome and time-consuming convolutions. In addition (and not surprisingly), the accuracies of frequency-oriented operations, such as the aforementioned filters, are much higher than if they were performed in the spatial domain.

Several mathematical transforms can be used to convert an image from the spatial to the frequency domain. The discrete Fourier transform, or DFT, is a well-known and popular method. A related and more commonly used procedure, tailored to the needs of digital imagery, is the *fast Fourier transform*, or FFT. The *inverse FFT* is the corresponding procedure used to transform from the frequency domain to the spatial domain.

The FFT is a one-dimensional process. It is therefore performed first on each row of pixels and then on the columns. The result is a two-dimensional array of values, called the *power spectra*, that represents the frequency components of each pixel in the original image. The power spectra can be displayed as a two-dimensional frequency distribution map, as shown in Fig. 7.1.

The first thing to realize is that the frequencies will appear as mirror images of one another around the center point, since each frequency will be matched with a corresponding negative component. The center of the transformed image is the *zero frequency,* also known as the *dc offset* (a term used in signal processing to indicate "direct current"). As the distance from the center increases, the frequency becomes higher. The brightness of the "pixels" in the power spectra corresponds to the magnitude of the signal.

As an example, consider the use of frequency domain processing for filtering. In the image shown in Fig. 7.2(a) there is a distinct repetitive diagonal noise pattern that runs primarily from the upper right to lower left. In addition, there is a more subtle pattern running from the upper left to lower right. This type of noise can be injected into an image easily by a faulty sensor or a weak trans-

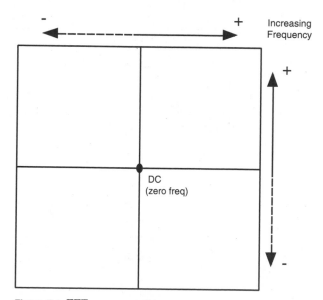

Figure 7.1 FFT power spectra.

(a) Original Image

(b) Power Spectra

(c) Modified Power Spectra

(d) Filtered Image

Figure 7.2 Filtering with FFTs. *(Image courtesy of Media Cybernetics.)*

mitted video signal (as anyone who has tried to watch television in a fringe reception area can attest). The FFT of this image was generated by using the Media Cybernetics ImagePro Plus software, and is shown in Fig. 7.2(b). This is a typical example of an image's power spectra and the four over-bright, off-axis spots represent the unwanted noise. (Remember, each frequency has an identical but negative component.)

At this point, the power of filtering in the frequency domain becomes apparent: The noise can be eliminated by simply removing the unwanted data from the power spectra. Figure 7.2(c) shows the necessary modification that eliminates the noise. Now all that is needed is to perform the inverse FFT, returning the image to the spatial domain where our vision system can comprehend it as an image. Figure 7.2(d) is the result and, as can be seen, nearly all of the noise is gone.

This same procedure can be invoked to perform high-pass filtering (eliminating the low frequencies clustered near the center of the power spectra) or low-pass filtering (eliminating all but the central low frequencies). It might seem as if it is a lot of trouble to perform frequency operations that could be performed in the spatial domain with convolution, but operating in the frequency domain affords much more control, which might be required for certain applications.

Perspective Terrain Reconstruction

It is likely that you already have seen artificially reconstructed terrains. Television newscasts of recent military conflicts have shown simulated flights into hostile territory. Spacecraft circling distant planets have sent back image data that have been turned into perspective views of the alien landscape. Terrain reconstruction is one of the most useful techniques available today to users of digital images. What is even more amazing is that perspective views are generated by using only two overhead images of the same area, taken from slightly different angles. The process is called *digital elevation mapping* (DEM), and it has application in many disciplines.

Consider the exaggerated view of a mountainous area as seen from the side, shown in Fig. 7.3. If an image of this area were captured from each of two viewpoints, such as from an orbiting satellite, the views will be nearly identical; there will be only slight differences due to the relative distances between the satellite and points on the surface. For instance, the high point near the center of the area will appear shifted to the right when viewed from satellite position 1 and will appear slightly to the left when viewed from position 2. These offsets are so slight that a person looking at the images probably wouldn't notice the difference. But the images are different, and if the resolution of the images is high enough, even small differences in elevation will produce a displacement in position.

If the resolution of the image and the satellite's elevation are known, and if matching reference points can be identified precisely in both images, a relative elevation for each pixel can be computed. Given these parameters and using triangulation, positional differences in the two images that correspond to elevations can be calculated (Fig. 7.4).

This creates a new image wherein pixel intensity is a representation of elevation. The higher the value of a pixel, the higher the elevation at that point. Now that this digital elevation map has been generated, the next task is to use it to create a perspective view of the terrain. The DEM can be thought of as a collection of solid square pegs rising from a flat surface, as shown in Fig. 7.5. The height of each peg is proportional to the intensity of the pixel at that location. As this figure shows, the DEM is viewed from some angle, or perspective, which gives it a three-dimensional look.

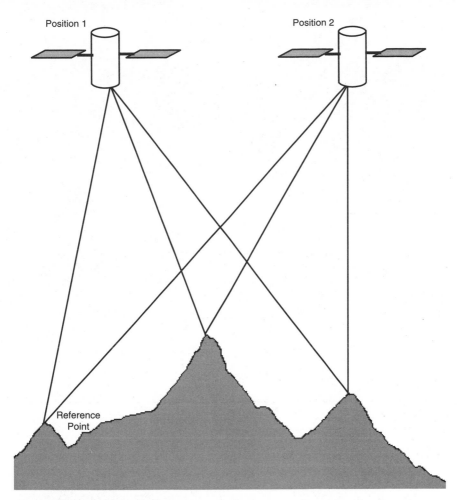

Position 1

Position 2

Reference
Point

Figure 7.3 Terrain image capture.

Now it is necessary to create a surface. One method is called *inverse ray tracing*, which mathematically draws lines from an imaginary viewpoint in space until contact is made with some point in the DEM. Techniques borrowed from computer graphics also can aid in image construction. A fast method for generating perspective views is with a *wire frame*, which is nothing more that a series of straight lines connecting equally spaced points. The image in Fig. 7.6(a) shows a wire frame before any elevation information is entered. The view is simply a flat surface as seen from some point in space. If some elevation information is introduced, as shown in Fig. 7.6(b), an extrusion forms that rises above the plane. If the entire area is filled with elevation

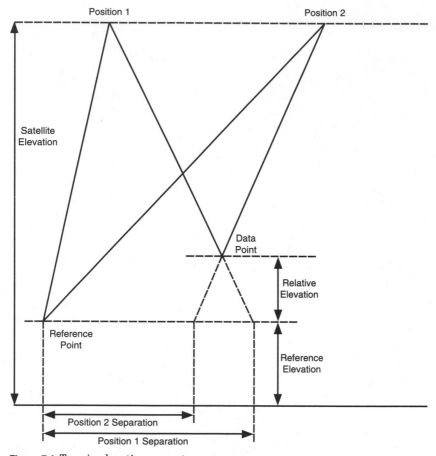

Figure 7.4 Terrain elevation geometry.

information (i.e., the DEM), the wire frame becomes a complex image of rolling hills and valleys. For realism, a shaded texture can replace the grid of lines, giving the appearance of terrain, which is illustrated in Fig. 7.6(d). Note that higher areas in the foreground obscure the view of lower areas further back. It is possible to view this digital terrain from any given angle or elevation; sequences of images can be generated to create animations that simulate flight.

The final step in achieving realistic perspective terrain images is to use actual imagery, instead of a simulated graphical texture, to overlay the DEM. One of the original images that was captured to create the elevation information usually is used for this purpose, and is called the *reflective data*. Figure 7.7 shows two views of the mountainous Ovda Regio region of Venus that were created in this fashion. NASA's Magellan spacecraft transmitted different radar images of the same area on the planet's surface; from these a DEM was generated. Then one of the images was used as the reflective data to create these views.

Three-Dimensional Volumetrics

All of the imaging operations discussed so far have occurred in two dimensions. Even terrain reconstruction, which appears to have a three-dimensional quality, is really the manipulation of two-dimensional images. But there is a branch of digital image processing that is truly three-dimensional in nature and is one of the most exciting areas of research.

The best way to think of a three-dimensional image is to consider a deck of ordinary playing cards. Each card has a definite thickness and each can be viewed by cutting the deck. Figure 7.8 extends this analogy to digital images. A series of images can be "stacked" one atop the other, each producing a plane in the resultant volume. (For the sake of simplicity, consider each image in the stack to be a single-plane grayscale image, but realize that each "plane" of the volume could be a "three-plane" color image.) Recall that a two-dimensional image is an array of picture elements, or pixels, and each element can be thought of as having a length and width of one unit. You can consider a three-dimensional image to be an array of volume elements, or *voxels,* that

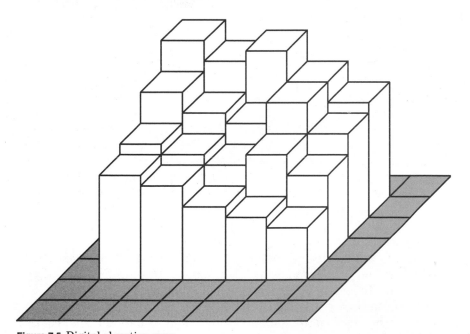

Figure 7.5 Digital elevation map.

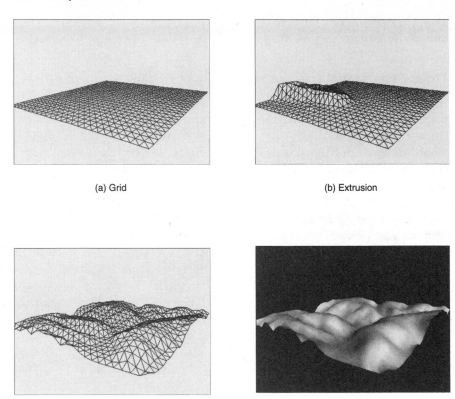

(a) Grid

(b) Extrusion

(c) Terrain Grid

(d) Terrain Surface

Figure 7.6 Wire frame perspective view.

have a length, width, and height of one unit. The image no longer occupies an area, but is now a volume.

Until technology progresses somewhat further, a 3D image cannot be viewed directly; it must be reduced to a 2D image suitable for display. This can be viewed in one of two ways: The volume can be sliced to generate an arbitrary plane through its interior, or the data can be *rendered* so that the entire volume can be seen at once. In the future, true three-dimensional display monitors might make it possible to view the volume data in its native form, but until then we will have to live with today's technology.

Slicing is a straightforward operation. Figure 7.9 shows a 3D image; it is composed of 2D images stacked one atop another. What if this object actually existed and were sliced at some arbitrary angle? The result would be a newly exposed flat portion of the interior, which, if viewed perpendicular to the cut, would be a two-dimensional plane. Mathematically we can slice through the digital volume and acquire an image of the interior.

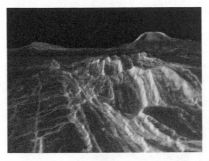

Figure 7.7 Venus perspective views. *(Image courtesy of NASA-JPL.)*

This has tremendous ramifications in several application areas, but especially in the field of medicine. Using a Computerized Axial Tomography (CAT) or Magnetic Resonance Imagery (MRI) scanner, cross-sections of human patients can be acquired via nonintrusive means. These scans become the two-dimensional images that are then stacked into a 3D image volume and arbitrarily sliced to gain different views of the patient's interior. Figure 7.10 illustrates an example of how this works.

A series of axial images is obtained from a patient, as shown in Fig. 7.10(a). Application software then allows the operator to cut the

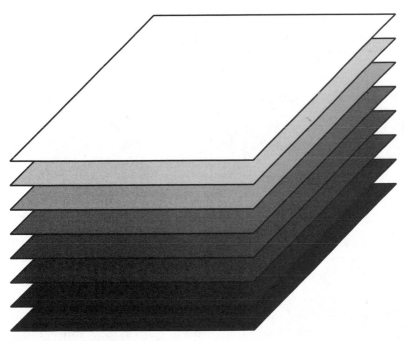

Figure 7.8 Stack of 2D images.

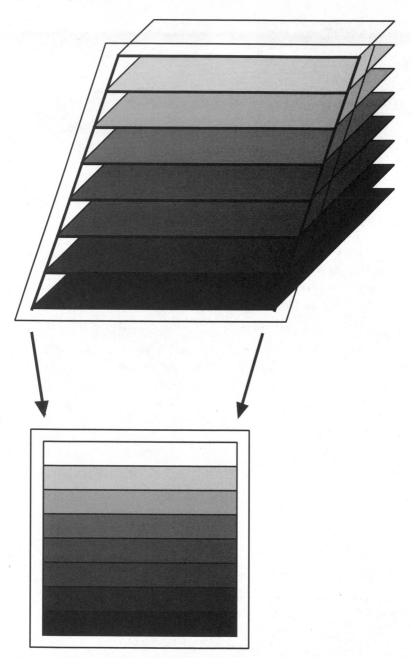

Figure 7.9 Slicing of 3D images.

volume along any given plane. The three images shown provide orthogonal views of the brain along the axial, sagital, and coronal axes. These images were generated by a program called BrainImage and are provided courtesy of the Behavioral Neurogenetics and Neuroimaging Research Center of the Kennedy Krieger Institute, located in Baltimore, Md. This software is available free of charge from the Institute's Internet page (*http://sol.med.jhu.edu/welcome.html*).

Another application of this operation is in nondestructive testing of production parts. Devices similar to those that probe the body can be used to take cross-section views of critically manufactured parts, such as the nose cones of aircraft. Allowing quality control engineers to

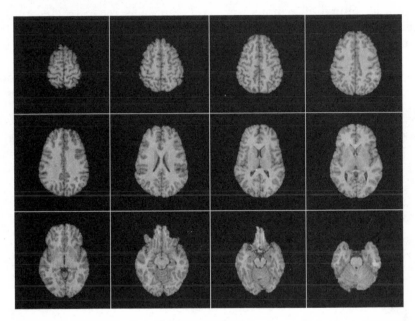

(a) Image Stack

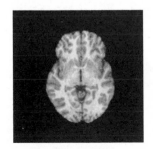

(b) Axial

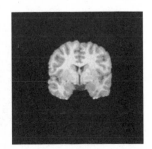

(d) Coronal

(c) Sagital

Figure 7.10 Orthogonal views of a 3D image. *(Image courtesy of Kennedy Kreiger Institute.)*

look inside the part without destroying it has obvious beneficial consequences. Programs of this sort usually have a graphical interface to indicate to the user how the volume is being sliced, and provide appropriate control handles for moving the viewing plane within the volume.

Another technique used to view 3D image data is called *rendering*. Here again, a primary application of this is in medicine. There are well-defined graphics algorithms that allow a computer-generated object, such as an airplane or a chair, to be viewed realistically in three dimensions. The same principle can be applied to 3D image data. Figure 7.11 shows a volume of a human cadaver that was reconstructed by the General Electric Corporate Research and Development Center. The outer border of each axial slice (which is the subject's skin) forms a useful surface for generating a solid 3D view, as seen in Fig. 7.11(a).

There is much more that can be done than reconstruct the surface, however. Through a process called *segmentation*, different tissues of

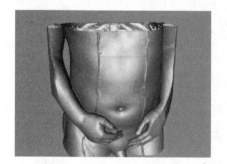
(a) Opaque Surface

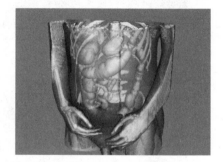
(b) Translucent Surface

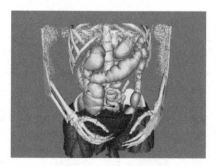
(c) Transparent Surface

Figure 7.11 Three-dimensional volumetric rendering. *(Image courtesy of General Electric Corporate Research and Development.)*

the body can be assigned different values of translucency. Voxels that represent bone typically are opaque, and soft tissues such as skin and fat might be assigned values that make them nearly transparent. Figure 7.11(b) assigns a partial transparency to the skin, thereby revealing the internal organs. The last image shows even more transparency, so that only the bones and deeper internal organs are visible.

Visualization

The last class of image processing techniques to be discussed is visualization. An underlying theme of this book is that digital image processing allows us to extend the range of human vision beyond the world we perceive with our eyes. We have seen already how this can be accomplished by processing real-world data in ways not possible just a few years ago. It is also possible to create images from real-world data that have nothing to do with the visible spectrum of light.

Because images are nothing more than collections of pixel intensities, it doesn't matter where those data come from. For example, data can be collected as sound waves that are reflected from the ocean bottom (or from boundaries between different layers of sea water, for that matter). The data can be used in the same fashion as digital elevation values, allowing us to generate perspective views of the ocean floor, where no light has ever shone.

Another example is sensing pressure differences that surround objects placed in a wind tunnel. Flow patterns can be assigned different colors that provide better visualization of the objects in question. Figure 7.12 is a simulation of a fluid in a vibrating tank, generated by the Aerospace Engineering and Mechanical Finite Element Group at the Army HPC Research Center in Minneapolis, Minn. It would be difficult, if not impossible, to capture this information in a real-life environment. Visualizations of abstract data sets have no limits, and new uses are being found for them every day.

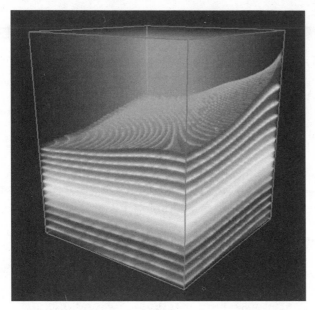

Figure 7.12 Scientific visualization. *(Image courtesy of Army HPC Research Center.)*

Chapter

8

File Storage and Formats

Up to this point in the book, nothing has been mentioned about how digital images are stored or what formats image files can take. The massive size of digital images has been discussed, so it would follow that the storage and format of all that information is the subject of much thought among programmers and software engineers. It is. No other discipline in computer science has to deal with the sheer number of bytes that come naturally with digital image processing.

The typical home computer system might have a few hundred megabytes, or a few gigabytes, of disk storage capacity. A minimal-resolution digital image for the motion picture industry, in full color at 2048×1536 pixels, requires 9MB of disk storage. Now consider that there are 24 of these images for each second of film, and it becomes clear that even a well-outfitted home computer can hold no more than a few seconds of what we see passing across the movie screen. To store a typical two-hour movie requires about 1.5 *terabytes* of disk space. The situation is no better in other applications: A single high-resolution, multispectral satellite image can contain several hundred megabytes of information, and a three-dimensional 1K pixel data set is, by definition, one gigabyte in size.

It is reasonable to believe that disk and tape storage capacity and performance will continue to grow at the exponential rate of the last 30 years, so in the not-too-distant future everyone will have the capacity to keep a favorite movie in the desktop computer. But it is also reasonable to believe that demand for data, and especially a demand for image data, will find a way to use all up of this expanded capacity. Research will have to continue finding better ways to store and access this huge volume of information.

Digital images are always stored as pixel-by-pixel representations of the rectangular area (or volume) they occupy. There are techniques that can compress this so-called *raster data*; unlike computer vector graphics (drawing and CAD programs, for example), digital images cannot be saved as a series of parameters and mathematical equations that allow later reconstruction, or rendering, of the scene. This is why images require so much storage space. Luckily, this also means that there are very few basic *storage techniques* that can be employed with them.

Unfortunately, however, there are many different *file formats*, developed by a multitude of companies that implement not-always- compatible variations of these basic techniques. This has caused a great deal of confusion and has stifled interchangeability between competing systems. This chapter will first describe the possible ways that image data can be stored, then present some of the most popular file formats used in today's digital imaging environment. Finally, there will be a discussion of some of the ways that image data can be compressed to use less storage space.

Storage Techniques

Figure 8-1 shows a typical conceptual view of a color digital image. There are three planes of information, one each for red, green, and blue. Each of these color planes is composed of rows of pixels, which forms a matrix of information. As has been shown in preceding chapters, the origin of the image is usually the top-left corner, with x signifying the horizontal dimension and y the vertical. Sometimes the number of planes is referred to as z, but this can cause confusion when working with three-dimensional imagery. For this reason the number of planes usually is

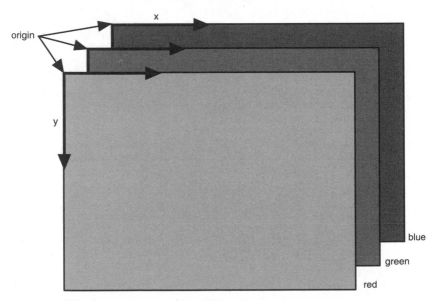

Figure 8.1 Color image conceptual structure.

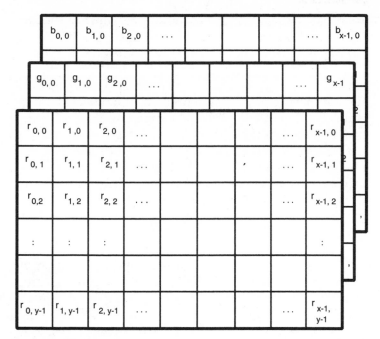

Figure 8.2 Pixel structure.

stated simply in words or digits: one for grayscale and three for color. There can be more planes than this, however. If there is a matte (or mattes) associated with the image, this produces two planes for grayscale images and four for color. When dealing with multispectral sensor imagery, typically received from orbiting satellites, there might be four, seven, nine, or more individual planes of information.

For now, the discussion of image planes will be limited to three planes, which will be assumed to be red, green and blue for color images. Each plane will contain 8-bit pixel values. There are only three methods in which this image data can be saved. They are generically referred to as *plane sequential*, *line sequential*, and *point sequential*. Figure 8.2 is a more detailed representation of an image showing individual pixels that are labeled according to their horizontal and vertical position. The diagram has been drawn so that the red, green, and blue pixels align with one another, as they would in an actual color image.

Any data can be thought of as a one-dimensional array, where each element is one byte long; that is how it is saved on tape or disk. Digital image data is, therefore, a contiguous string of bytes in which each byte holds a pixel value. If the plane sequential method of data storage is used, all data for one plane (usually red) is saved first, followed by all data for the second (green) plane and, finally, all for the third (blue) plane. Within the data for a color plane, pixels are arranged as they appear in lines, starting from the top and proceeding to the bottom. Pixels within each line are arranged from left to right. This structure is shown in Fig. 8.3. (Note that the very beginning of the file is a header, which contains information such as file size, organization, and other parameters. Headers will be discussed shortly.) Plane sequential storage is common among film and three-pass flatbed scanners because the data are acquired one plane at a time.

Line sequential storage is shown in Fig. 8.4. In this situation, the first line of red data is followed immediately by the first line of green data, which is followed by the first blue. Each successive line is stored in the same fashion until the entire image is saved. This type of storage technique is common with multispectral sensors or one-pass flatbed scanners, since the data for all color or spectral planes for a single line are captured in unison.

Figure 8.5 shows the third technique, known as point sequential or sometimes as *pixel sequential*. In this situation, color information for a single pixel is stored adjacent to the other color plane values for that pixel, sometimes expressed with the nomenclature: *rgb rgb rgb* .... This storage technique is not conducive to any given sensor operation but, for logical reasons, is common in certain software packages.

There is no one best way to store image data; each has its merits and drawbacks. Plane sequential is very popular because, in operating on entire images, data can be transferred very efficiently from disk files to memory buffers, and vice versa. Once the pointer for the disk file is positioned correctly, an entire plane of data can be read with a single instruction. To accomplish the same operation with a line or — even worse — a point sequential file, the pointer must be repositioned continually to access the desired data.

The major drawback of a plane sequential file structure becomes evident if only a portion of an image is to be retrieved from disk. Selective reading of the file is required in this situation, whereas in a point sequential structure all of the data for a section of an image is grouped more closely together and can be accessed more rapidly.

Engineers and programmers therefore must choose the data storage method with great care, lest a system be created that does not have good performance because of this seemingly simple limitation. Some file formats limit the storage technique to just one of those described above, while others permit data to be saved with more than one method.

File Formats

One of the unfortunate realities of digital image processing is that there is no common file format in which to save data. Not that this

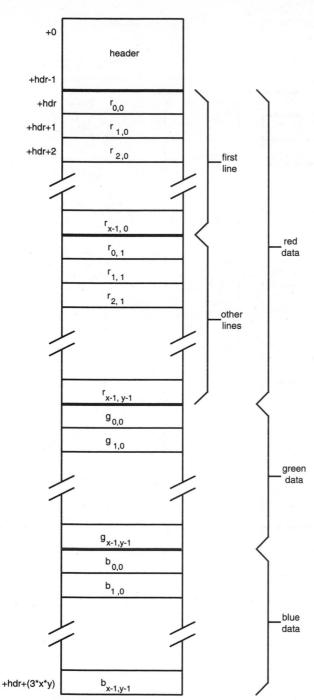

Figure 8.3 Plane sequential file structure.

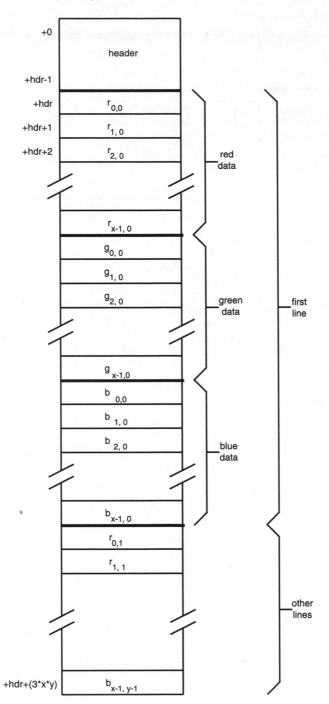

Figure 8.4 Line sequential file structure.

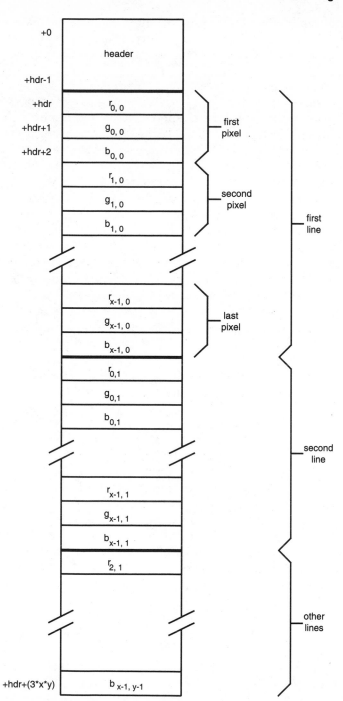

Figure 8.5 Point sequential file structure.

field is the only discipline faced with this problem. Competing manufacturers of word processing software use different formats, as do different drawing packages and database managers. Because there are so few ways to save the bytes of a digital image in a file, however, programmers find it disheartening to have to deal with so many formats. A bright spot on this subject, though, is that of compressed images, which will be discussed later in this chapter. There has been much research in the subject of compression; the Joint Photographic Experts Group (JPEG) has defined a standard that is becoming widely accepted.

Until the day when all images are JPEG — which, of course, might never come to pass — programmers will be required to deal with the smorgasbord of what the world has to offer in the way of bitmap storage formats. Figure 8.6 is a partial list of image file formats available today. It is not the intent of this book to describe each of these formats; there already are excellent texts of that sort available. What this book will show is a few sample programs that read and write some common image files. The hope is that when you are confronted with one of the many formats that exist, you will feel more comfortable knowing that they all have the same basic structure. After all, they're just bits and bytes.

There are a few basic steps that you, as a programmer, should take before tackling an image storage task. First, if you feel a great compulsion to create yet another file format, please don't. From Fig. 8.6 one can see that there are already more than enough file formats in the world; creating yet another one will only make the situation worse. If you think that your application has special needs not covered by any existing format, do some research into what's already out there. The chances are good that your situation has been encountered before, and existing formats will provide what you need.

Many times the software engineer or programmer will not even have a choice in the matter, because the image file type will be dictated by the application specification or by the user environment. For instance, a government contract might require NITF files, or the developer of a Mac application would know that PICT must be used. It also might be desirable to allow the application to read and write multiple formats, based on user selection. Not only will this make more existing images available to the application, it also will make the application more robust and therefore more likely to find a wider audience. Some sophisticated applications will interrogate a file to determine its format so that the user need not even tell the program what it is.

Usually there is a file format native to the computer system being used and any applications that run on that machine are required to read and write that type. For example, applications running on Sun Microsystems workstations usually can read and write Sun Raster files. If a PC system uses Truevision image capture hardware, the Targa

Abekas A60 Digital Video

Adobe Postscript

Aldus/Microsoft TIFF

Amiga IFF

ANSI CGM

CompuServe GIF

International Astronomical Union FITS

JPEG (Joint Photographic Experts Group)

Kodak Cineon

Macintosh MacPaint

Macintosh PICT

Microsoft BMP

Microsoft WMF

MPEG (Motion Picture Experts Group)

NITF (National Information Transfer Format)

Novell GEM

PhotoCD

Pixar PIC

Scitex

SGI Raster Files

Sun Microsystems Rasterfiles

Truvision Targa

X Window Bitmap

Zsoft PCX

Figure 8.6 Popular file formats.

format is a given. For every file format there is a specification that defines all possible nuances of the data structure. Specifications are available from the particular company or organization that created the file format or from books on the subject. There also is a wealth of information available on the Internet that can be found with a little searching.

All image files, regardless of format, have some kind of header. This occurs at the beginning of the file, hence the name "header" used to describe it. Headers might be just a few bytes long, containing nothing more than some type of identifier and the image size, or they might contain thousands of bytes that define a multitude of parameters about the data.

Any program designed to read image files of a given type will know the structure of the header and how to extract information from it; this type of program is called a *reader*. A *writer* is a program that will generate an image file with the correct data structure that satisfies the specification of that format. It usually is easier for a programmer to create a writer, because only minimal adherence to a specification is needed—some formats can be quite complex—to create an acceptable file. Conversely, readers must be able to interpret all possible configurations defined in a specification, which can make the task much more daunting for something like the many "flavors" of TIFF files.

Regardless of the format, a programmer's most useful tool for working with image files is a simple hexadecimal dump program; most computer systems have them. On Unix systems it is the *od*, or octal dump command (which, with the –x option, can be forced into hexadecimal mode); the DEBUG program in MS-DOS is much the same. A dump program simply reads a file and creates a listing of each sequential byte in the file. If your computer system does not have a dump feature, you can implement the one shown in Program 26 (which is superior to *od* because it provides an ASCII character listing down the right side of the display).

Following are some examples of reading and writing different image file formats. As noted earlier, no attempt is made to cover all possible formats; the intent is to provide you with enough information so that you will feel comfortable tackling others on your own. The first format is the Silicon Graphics, Inc., RGB format. The Tag Image File Format (TIFF) is presented next. The last section explains different compression techniques, specifically JPEG compression and SGI's RLE format.

Silicon Graphics RGB

Silicon Graphics, Inc., supports a proprietary image file format that most software running on those machines can read and write. It was chosen to be examined here because it is one of the simplest and most straightforward formats that exists today. It also has the ability to contain a simple compression technique, which will be discussed later; for now, only uncompressed files will be considered.

The RGB format has a 512-byte header whose structure is shown in Fig. 8.7. The first word contains something common to many formats: a *magic number*. The magic number is a constant value that usually is the very first item in the header and is used to identify the file. In SGI files this number is 2 bytes long and always has a value of 474 (0x1DA). Following the magic number is a 2-byte type field which, if equal to 1, indicates an uncompressed raster file. Next is a 2-byte field that holds the dimension of the file, which for a color image is 3. Then there are the *x, y,* and *z* sizes for the image. (The *z* here is the number of planes, 3 for color.) Optionally, there also may be fields for minimum and maximum values in the image, and 80 characters for a name.

The actual image data is stored in plane sequential mode, with the red plane first followed by the green and blue planes. An oddity of the SGI format is that the origin is considered to be the lower-left corner of the image instead of the upper-left corner; for normal viewing, the

```
/****************************************************************/
/*    program 26: hexadecimal dump                           */
/****************************************************************/
#include "sys/file.h"
main (argc,argv)
  long    argc;
  char **argv;
  {
  long fp;
  long addr,cnt,m,n;
  unsigned char buf[20];
  unsigned char *b;
  if (argc < 2)
    {
    printf ("Usage: dumpit <file>\n");
    }
  else
    {
    printf("Dump file: %s\n",argv[1]);
    fp = open(argv[1],O_RDONLY);
    if (fp <= 0)
      {
      printf("Cannot open file %s\n",argv[1]);
      }
    else
      {
      addr = 0;
      cnt = 1;
      while (cnt > 0)
        {
        cnt = read(fp,buf,16);
        b = buf;
        printf ("%5d (%08lx)   ",addr,addr);
        addr = addr + 16;
        for (m = 0; m < 4; m++)
          {
          for (n = 0; n < 4; n++)
            {
            printf ("%02x",*b++);
            }
          printf (" ");
          }
        printf("   ");
        for (n = 0; n < 16; n++)
          {
          if ((buf[n] < 32) || (buf[n] > 126))
            printf("%c",'.');
          else
            printf("%c",buf[n]);
          }
        printf("\n");
        }
      close(fp);
      printf ("End of dump\n");        }
    }
  }
```

Program 26 Hexadecimal dump.

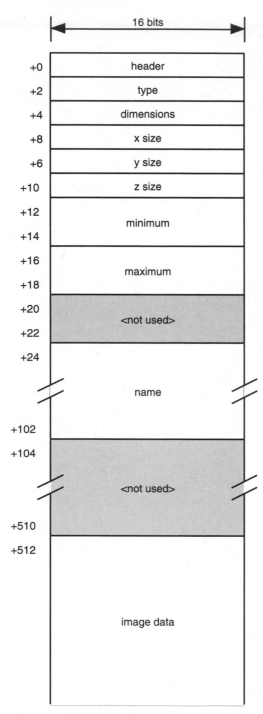

Figure 8.7 SGI RGB file format.

image must be flipped top-to-bottom. This is not a remarkable oddity, since SGI computers are heavily used for computer graphics processing, which discipline generally maintains the origin in the lower-left corner.

Another common feature of image files is that the name of the file usually includes a descriptive extension or suffix. For SGI RGB files a .rgb extension is used. Figure 8.8 is a hexadecimal dump of the beginning of an RGB file. The elements of the header are identified, and the red data can be seen to begin at byte location

The recommended way of programming readers and writers for image files is to create a group of functions, or subroutines, that can reside in a precompiled library and then can be accessed when the application is linked. For each format, four subroutines should be generated that perform the following tasks: read the file header, read the file data, write the file header, and write the file data. Program 27 contains these four routines for reading and writing SGI files; they are called read_sgi_header, read_sgi_data, write_sgi_header, and write_sgi_data.

In the sample programs that have been presented so far, each one has invoked two mysterious functions called read_image and write_image, with no explanation of what they are or how they work. This was intentional, so that attention could be focused on the image processing concept and not on the mechanics of creating an operational program. But to create a correctly functioning program, the issue of reading and writing image files must be addressed. The read_image routine is a simple intermediate function that invokes read_sgi_header and read_sgi_data (assuming, of course, that SGI RGB format files were being read), and write_image simply calls write_sgi_header and write_sgi_data.

It is important to separate the reading of a file header from reading the file data. In nearly all situations, the size of the digital image is kept in the header. Note that read_sgi_header returns this image size in variables which, in an actual application, can be used to allocate the correctly sized memory buffers that the read_sgi_data function will fill with pixel data.

Program 28 is a new version of Program 1, with the "generic" read_image and write_image calls replaced by those for reading and writing SGI RGB files. Note how the structure of the program is slightly different in that it is no longer necessary to "hard code" the size of the image being processed. Instead, the image size is determined when the file header is read, with memory buffer allocations and loop indices adjusted accordingly. Now it also is possible to verify that the file is of the correct format and, if not, to generate an error message and terminate the processing. Also note that the name of the existing input file and the desired output file are passed to the program as command-line

```
dimensions ─────────+       +─────── x size
       type ──────+  |       |     +──── y size
magic number ─+   |  |       |     |    +─ z size
              |   |  |       |     |    |
              v   v  v       v     v    v
     0 (00000000) 01da0001 00030140 00f00003 00000000  ....@...........
    16 (00000010) 000000ff 00000000 00000000 00000000  ................
    32 (00000020) 00000000 00000000 00000000 00000000  ................
    48 (00000030) 00000000 00000000 00000000 00000000  ................
     :
   480 (000001e0) 00000000 00000000 00000000 00000000  ................
   496 (000001f0) 00000000 00000000 00000000 00000000  ................
   512 (00000200) 4b4c4e4f 4f525556 52505051 5153514a  KLNOORUVRPPQQSQJ
   528 (00000210) 41383234 3f484957 8aafaba2 9e9d9d9d  A824?HIW........
   544 (00000220) 9b989184 77727475 76796e69 71767b80  ....wrtuvyniqv{.
   560 (00000230) 82878c8d 90919292 93939293 93939393  ................
   576 (00000240) 91908f8e 8e8f8f8f 8e8c8c8b 8a898989  ................
   592 (00000250) 89888888 87868585 87868686 85858483  ................
   608 (00000260) 82848585 86868686 86858585 84848585  ................
   624 (00000270) 85848382 82828383 83828383 82838382  ................
   640 (00000280) 83838282 83858686 888b8c8b 8b8c8d8d  ................
     :
```

Figure 8.8 Hexadecimal dump of an SGI RGB file.

```
/*************************************************************/
/*    program 27: SGI RGB read/write functions              */
/*************************************************************/

typedef struct          /* SGI RGB header structure */
  {
  short int  magic;
  short int  type;
  short int  dim;
  short int  xsize;
  short int  ysize;
  short int  zsize;
  long  int  min;
  long  int  max;
  long  int  waste;
  char       name[80];
  long  int  space[102];
  }  SGI_HEADER;

/*************************************************************/
/*    function: read_sgi_header                             */
/*************************************************************/

void read_sgi_header (fp,xs,ys,pl,type)
  long  int  fp;           /* file pointer */
  long  int  *xs,*ys;      /* x,y size */
  long  int  *pl;          /* plane count */
  long  int  *type;        /* file type */
  {
  SGI_HEADER header;

  read(fp,&header,sizeof(header));
  if (header.magic != 474)
    {
    printf("INVALID SGI MAGIC NUMBER: %d\n",header.magic);
    }
  else
    {
    *xs = (long)header.xsize;
    *ys = (long)header.ysize;
    *pl = (long)header.zsize;
    *type = (long)header.type;
    if (*type != 1)
      {
      printf("SGI TYPE NOT 1: %d\n",header.type);
      }
    }
  return;
  }

/*************************************************************/
/*    function: read_sgi_data                               */
/*************************************************************/
void read_sgi_data(fp,xs,ys,pl,type,r,g,b)
  long  int  fp;           /* file pointer */
  long  int  xs,ys;        /* x,y size */
  long  int  pl;           /* plane count */
```

```
long  int  type;          /* file type */
unsigned char *r,*g,*b; /* data buffer pointers */
{
long  int  x,y,c;
unsigned char *d;

for (c = 0; c < pl; c++)
  {
  if (c == 0) d = r;
  if (c == 1) d = g;
  if (c == 2) d = b;
  d = d + ((ys - 1) * xs);
  for (y = 0; y < ys; y++)
    {
    read(fp,d,xs);
    d = d - xs;
    }
  }
return;
}
```

```
/************************************************************/
/*    function: write_sgi_header                            */
/************************************************************/

void write_sgi_header (fp,xs,ys,pl,type)
  long  int  fp;           /* file pointer */
  long  int  xs,ys;        /* x,y size */
  long  int  pl;           /* plane count */
  long  int  type;         /* file type */
  {
  SGI_HEADER header;
  long  int  i;

  header.magic = 474;
  header.type  = type;
  header.dim   = 3;
  header.xsize = xs;
  header.ysize = ys;
  header.zsize = pl;
  header.min   = 0;
  header.max   = 255;
  header.waste = 0;

  for (i = 0; i <  80; i++) header.name[i] = 0;
  for (i = 0; i < 102; i++) header.space[i] = 0;

  write(fp,&header,sizeof(header));

  return;  }
```

```
/************************************************************/
/*    function: write_sgi_data                              */
/************************************************************/

void write_sgi_data(fp,xs,ys,pl,r,g,b,type)
  long  int  fp;           /* file pointer */
```

```
long  int  xs,ys;        /* x,y size */
long  int  pl;           /* plane count */
unsigned char *r,*g,*b;  /* data buffer pointers */
long  int  type;         /* file type */
{
long  int  x,y,c;
unsigned char *o;
unsigned char *d;

for (c = 0; c < pl; c++)
  {
  if (c == 0) d = r;
  if (c == 1) d = g;
  if (c == 2) d = b;
  d = d + ((ys - 1) * xs);
  for (y = 0; y < ys; y++)
    {
    write(fp,d,xs);
    d = d - xs;
    }
  }
return;
}
```

Program 27 SGI RGB read/write functions.

parameters, along with the number of bits per pixel that will be present in the output file. Following is a sample command line invocation of this program:

```
prog28 input.rgb output.rgb 3
```

With this type of structure, the program is more flexible because it now will operate on any size image. No recompilation is needed; its operation is driven by the data presented to it.

Simply by using a collection of image read and write functions, a very powerful application program that does nothing but convert an image of one format into another can be constructed. In fact, there are several software products available today that do just this.

Tag Image File Format (TIFF)

TIFF was developed jointly by Aldus and Microsoft for use in desktop publishing. It has grown in popularity since its introduction, and is one of the most common and universally accepted formats available today. It is more complex than SGI's format but not as complicated as, for instance, Kodak's Cineon format. This is one of the formats for which it is easier to create a writer but more difficult to build a reader.

Because of its almost universal acceptance, TIFF is an excellent choice for a wide range of applications. It can be used on MS-DOS personal computers, Macintosh computers, and Unix computers.

```
/*************************************************************/
/*     program 28: program 1 rewrite                        */
/*************************************************************/

#include "sys/file.h"
#include "math.h"

main(argc,argv)
short int argc;                      /* number of arguments */
char      *argv[];                   /* argument values */
  {
  unsigned char *ir,*ig,*ib;
  unsigned char *or,*og,*ob;
  long  int  x,y;
  long  int  fpi,fpo;
  long  int  xsize,ysize;
  long  int  planes;
  long  int  sgi_type;
  long  int  depth;
  float      scale;
  char       in_file[256],out_file[256];

  if (argc < 4)
    {
    printf("Usage: prog28 <in_file> <out_file> <depth>\n");
    }
  else
    {
    sscanf(argv[1],"%s",in_file);
    sscanf(argv[2],"%s",out_file);
    sscanf(argv[3],"%d",&depth);

    if ((depth < 1) || (depth > 7))
      {
      printf("invalid depth request: %d\n",depth);
      }
    else
      {
      /* open the input image file */
      fpi = open(in_file,O_RDONLY);
      if (fpi <= 0)
        {
        printf("cannot open input file: %s\n",in_file);
        }
      else
        {
        /* read the input image file header */
        read_sgi_header(fpi,&xsize,&ysize,&planes,&sgi_type);

        /* allocate input and output memory buffers */
        ir = (unsigned char *) malloc (xsize*ysize);
        ig = (unsigned char *) malloc (xsize*ysize);
        ib = (unsigned char *) malloc (xsize*ysize);
        or = (unsigned char *) malloc (xsize*ysize);
        og = (unsigned char *) malloc (xsize*ysize);
        ob = (unsigned char *) malloc (xsize*ysize);

        /* read the input image data */
```

```
read_sgi_data(fpi,xsize,ysize,planes,sgi_type,ir,ig,ib);
close(fpi);

/* calculate the scale factor that will reduce 8-bit values
       (0-255, inclusive) to evenly spaced values of 0-255 for
       the requested depth resolution. */
/* example: if depth = 2, values are 0, 85, 171, and 255 */
scale = 255.0 / (powf (2.0, (float)depth) - 1.0);

/* reduce depth res by generating new 8-bit pixel values */
for (y = 0; y < ysize; y = y++)
  {
  for (x = 0; x < xsize; x = x++)
    {
    or[(y*xsize)+x] = (ir[(y*xsize)+x] >>
    (8 - depth)) * scale;
    og[(y*xsize)+x] = (ig[(y*xsize)+x] >>
    (8 - depth)) * scale;
    ob[(y*xsize)+x] = (ib[(y*xsize)+x] >>
    (8 - depth)) * scale;
    }
  }

/* create and open the output image file */
fpo = open(out_file,O_WRONLY|O_CREAT|O_TRUNC,0666);
if (fpo <= 0)
  {
  printf("cannot open input file: %s\n",in_file);
  }
else
  {
  /* write the output image */
  write_sgi_header(fpo,xsize,ysize,planes,sgi_type);
  write_sgi_data(fpo,xsize,ysize,planes,or,og,ob,sgi_type);
  close(fpo);
  }

/* free memory buffers */
free (ir);
free (ig);
free (ib);
free (or);
free (og);
free (ob);
  }
  }
  }
```

Program 28 Program 1 rewrite.

With this flexibility also comes complexity, however. The TIFF specification is very large and, analogous to a spoken language, most program readers and writers speak the common words but very few know the entire language. In addition, proprietary fields can be registered with Aldus (now owned by Adobe), which spawns "flavors" of TIFF and can hinder data exchange. As long as application programs stick with the basics, however, few if any problems should be experienced.

TIFF-format files contain three primary structures: a header, one or more image file directories or IFDs, and data. As with other formats, the header is always the very first entry in the file, the contents of which are shown in Fig. 8.9. The first two bytes contain the ASCII characters MM or II, which in hexadecimal notation are 0x4D4D or 0x4949, respectively. The MM indicates that data is stored in Motorola (Unix or Macintosh) format, and the II indicates Intel (PC), or byte-swapped format.

The next two bytes contain the decimal value 42 (hex 0x002A, or 0x2A00 if byte-swapped). This word acts as the magic number, even though it is labeled "version" in the TIFF specification. The next four bytes are a pointer to the first IFD. (In TIFF, all pointers are byte offsets from the start of the file.) The term "first IFD" is used because it is possible to have multiple images inside a single TIFF file, each of which would have its own IFD. This is one more indication that TIFF files can become quite complex, though most of the time only a single image will appear in one file.

Usually, but not necessarily, the first IFD will follow the header directly, but this should not be assumed to be true. Pointers must be followed with TIFF, because data can reside anywhere. The structure of an IFD is shown in Fig. 8.10. The first two bytes contain the number of tagged pointers, also called *tag fields*, which are 12-byte fields within the IFD that describe the image parameters. The final tagged pointer in the IFD is followed by the terminating field. This 4-byte field is either a pointer to the next IFD (if multiple images reside in this file), or zeros if this is the last image in the chain.

TIFF format has been rather straightforward so far, but that is about to change. The tagged pointers or tag fields are themselves structures, as described in Fig. 8.11. The first two bytes of the 12-byte structure comprise a numerical value called the *tag code*. The tag code indicates what

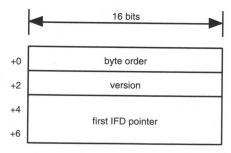

Figure 8.9 TIFF Header structure.

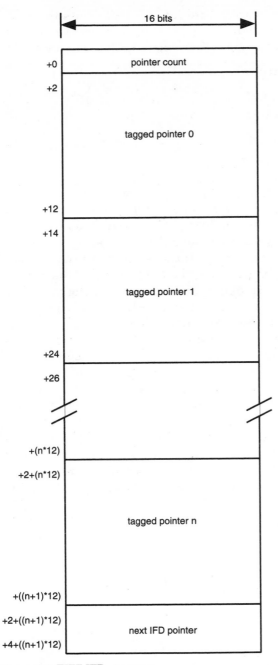

16 bits

+0   pointer count

+2

tagged pointer 0

+12

+14

tagged pointer 1

+24

+26

+(n*12)

+2+(n*12)

tagged pointer n

+((n+1)*12)

+2+((n+1)*12)   next IFD pointer

+4+((n+1)*12)

Figure 8.10 TIFF IFD structure.

the following data delineates, such as the image width, image height, samples per pixel, etc. Codes above 32768 (or 0x8000 hex) indicate the proprietary fields mentioned earlier. After the tag code comes the 2-byte *data type* indicating the type of data that this tagged pointer uses. There are five data type codes, numbered 1 to 5, that have the following meanings:

1. 1-byte integer (type BYTE)
2. 1-byte ASCII (type ASCII)
3. 2-byte integer (type SHORT)
4. 4-byte integer (type LONG)
5. 8-byte fraction (type RATIONAL)

The next 4-byte field of the tagged pointer is the *field length* , which is the number of values of the type indicated by the data type code. Note that this is not the number of bytes of data contained in this tag field, but is the number of values, or items. The last four bytes contain either the *data field* or a *data pointer.* If the length of the data is four bytes or less (computed by multiplying the field length by the number of bytes per value of the given data type), the data are stored directly in this field. If the length of the data is greater than four, this field is a pointer to where the data reside within the file.

Figure 8.12 is a summary of the most common TIFF tagged pointers, indicating the tag code and meaning. For a complete reference and explanation of all tagged pointers, refer to the TIFF specification or to one of appropriate books on this subject. Figure 8.12 can be used as a quick-reference guide once these fields are more thoroughly understood. Figure 8.13 is a hexadecimal dump of the start of a TIFF file.

The first four bytes identify this as a TIFF file in Motorola format. The next four bytes point to the first IFD, which is located at byte offset 10 (0x0000000a). There are 11 (0x000b) tagged pointers in this IFD; the tagged code of each data structure has been highlighted. The

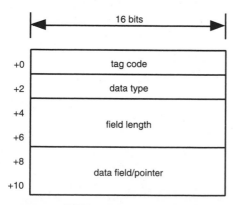

Figure 8.11 TIFF tagged pointer structure.

Code	Meaning
256 (x0100)	Image Width
257 (x0101)	Image Length
258 (x0102)	Bits per Sample
259 (x0103)	Compression Type
262 (x0106)	Photometric Interpretation
271 (x010f)	Image Description
273 (x0111)	Strip Offsets
277 (x0115)	Samples per Pixel
278 (x0116)	Rows per Strip
279 (x0117)	Strip Byte Counts
282 (x011a)	X Resolution
283 (x011b)	Y Resolution
284 (x011c)	Planar Configuration
296 (x0128)	Resolution Unit
306 (x0132)	Date/Time
316 (x013c)	Host Computer
320 (x0140)	Color Map

Figure 8.12 Common TIFF tagged pointers.

pointer to the next IFD (byte offset 144) is zero, indicating this is the last image in the chain. Note that the Strip Offset field (tagged code 0x0111) indicates the pixel data starts at byte offset 512 (0x0200).

Program 29 contains the routines read_tiff_header, read_tiff_data, write_tiff_header, and write_tiff_data. Like the similar routines that read SGI format, these can be substituted for the read_image and write_image that have been used in preceding examples. Note that the lengths of these routines, especially read_tiff_data, are greater than other programs presented so far; this is because the processing of most tagged pointers has to be covered. This implementation of a TIFF reader and writer is not complete, but the structure is such that it can be expanded easily. The TIFF writer will generate files that meet the specification; most files can be processed with the TIFF reader, unless the file contains esoteric and less-used features of the format.

Image Compression Techniques

One of the functions not covered by the TIFF reader and writer described above is the ability to save compressed data in a file. Compression is a subject that has been the subject of much research and debate for many years within the image processing community. Many computer systems employ data compression techniques that can reduce storage requirements substantially.

```
    0 (00000000)  4d4d002a 0000000a 0000000b 00fe0004   MM.*............
   16 (00000010)  00000001 00000000 01000003 00000001   ................
   32 (00000020)  00500000 01010003 00000001 003c0000   .P...........<..
   48 (00000030)  01020003 00000003 00000100 01030003   ................
   64 (00000040)  00000001 00010000 01060003 00000001   ................
   80 (00000050)  00020000 01110004 00000001 00000200   ................
   96 (00000060)  01150003 00000001 00030000 01160003   ................
  112 (00000070)  00000001 003c0000 01170004 00000001   ...........<....
  128 (00000080)  00003840 011c0003 00000001 00010000   ..8@............
  144 (00000090)  00000000 00000000 00000000 00000000   ................
  160 (000000a0)  00000000 00000000 00000000 00000000   ................
  176 (000000b0)  00000000 00000000 00000000 00000000   ................
  192 (000000c0)  00000000 00000000 00000000 00000000   ................
    :
  480 (000001e0)  00000000 00000000 00000000 00000000   ................
  496 (000001f0)  00000000 00000000 00000000 00000000   ................
  512 (00000200)  2416011b 0e002a20 0b463417 59432264   $.....*..F4.YC"d
  528 (00000210)  551f5a58 18413f13 1a110725 2017655d   U.ZX.A?....% .e]
  544 (00000220)  54514b3c 403a2955 4c3a3c31 0e41320b   TQK<@:)UL:<1.A2.
  560 (00000230)  5443164d 3d1e322a 1c2e2817 39331d3b   TC.M=.2*..(.93.;
  576 (00000240)  331f5445 1a3b3210 30310939 3b0b2d2b   3.TE.;2.01.9;.-+
  592 (00000250)  0c473f27 80714d91 763b9872 2d816022   .G?'.qM.v;.r-.`"
  608 (00000260)  3f402527 39272337 20263e19 313f213f   ?@%'9'#7 &>.1?1?
  624 (00000270)  38263f31 1d4d3e28 403a3050 4e496c64   8&?1.M>(@:0PNIld
  640 (00000280)  5d8d7670 8d706975 6863645f 5c635e5b   ].vp.piuhcd_\c^[
    :
```

Figure 8.13 Hexadecimal dump of a TIFF file.

```
/**********************************************************/
/*    program 29: TIFF read/write functions              */
/**********************************************************/

#include <stdio.h>
#define II       1        /* intel byte order */
#define MM       2        /* motorola byte order */
#define BYTE     1        /* tag IFD field types */
#define ASCII    2
#define SHORT    3
#define LONG     4
#define RATIONAL 5

typedef struct             /* header structure */
  {
  short int byte_order;
  short int version;
  long  int ifd_offset;
  } TIFF_HEADER;

typedef struct             /* pointer structure */
  {
  short {{TAB}}int tag;
  short {{TAB}}int type;
  long  {{TAB}}int length;
  long  {{TAB}}int voff;
  } TIFF_POINTER;

typedef struct             /* file information structure */
  {
  long  int  iimm;
  long  int  subfile_flags;
  long  int  photo_interp;
  long  int  planar_config;
  short int  bits_sample[3];
  short int  sample_pixel;
  long  int  rows_strip;
  long  int  strip_cnt_length;
  long  int  strip_cnt_offset;
  long  int  strip_off_length;
  long  int  strip_off_offset;
  } TIFF_DATA;

unsigned char *make_tag();
short int ii2mms();
long  int ii2mml();
long  int strip_read();


/**********************************************************/
/*    function: read_tiff_header                         */
/**********************************************************/

void read_tiff_header(fp,xs,ys,pl,td)
```

```
long   int   fp;          /* file pointer */
long   int   *xs,*ys;     /* x,y size */
long   int   *pl;         /* plane count */
TIFF_DATA  *td;           /* file information */
{
TIFF_HEADER  header;
TIFF_POINTER pointer;
long   int   error;
short  int   n,c,cnt;
long   int   next_ifd;
long   int   next_pointer;
char         *pbyte;
short  int   *pshort;
long   int   *plong;

/* initialize variables */
*xs = 0;
*ys = 0;
*pl = 0;
td->iimm = 0;
td->planar_config = 1;
td->rows_strip = 0;
td->bits_sample[0] = 0;
td->bits_sample[1] = 0;
td->bits_sample[2] = 0;

/* read file header */
read(fp,&header,sizeof(header));
if (header.byte_order == 0x4d4d)
  td->iimm = MM;
else
  if (header.byte_order == 0x4949)
    td->iimm = II;
  else
    printf("!! INVALID TIFF BYTE ORDER: 0x%04x\n",
      header.byte_order);

/* verify header information */
if (td->iimm == II) ii2mms(&header.version);
if (header.version != 42)
  printf("!! INVALID TIFF VERSION: %d\n",header.version);

/* get pointer to first IFD */
if (td->iimm == II) ii2mml(&header.ifd_offset);
next_ifd = header.ifd_offset;

/* process all IFDs */
while (next_ifd != 0)
  {
  lseek(fp,next_ifd,SEEK_SET);
  next_pointer = next_ifd;
  read(fp,&cnt,2);
  next_pointer = next_pointer + 2;
  if (td->iimm == II) ii2mms(&cnt);
```

```
/* process all tagged pointers in this IFD */
for (c = 1; c <= cnt; c++)
  {
  read(fp,&pointer,sizeof(pointer));
  next_pointer = next_pointer + sizeof(pointer);
  if (td->iimm == II)
    {
    ii2mms(&pointer.tag);
    ii2mms(&pointer.type);
    ii2mml(&pointer.length);
    ii2mml(&pointer.voff);
    if (pointer.type == SHORT) pointer.voff = pointer.voff << 16;
    }
  switch(pointer.type)
    {
    case BYTE:
    case ASCII:
      pbyte  = (char *)&pointer.voff;
      break;
    case SHORT:
      pshort = (short int *)&pointer.voff;
      break;
    case LONG:
    case RATIONAL:
      plong  = (long int *)&pointer.voff;
      break;
    default:
      printf("!! UNKNOWN TIFF POINTER TYPE: %d\n",pointer.type);
      break;
    }

  error = NULL;
  switch(pointer.tag)
    {
    case 254: /* new subfile type */
      if ((pointer.type == LONG) && (pointer.length == 1))
        td->subfile_flags = pointer.voff;
      else
        error++;
      break;
    case 256: /* image width */
      if (pointer.length == 1)
        if (pointer.type == LONG)
          *xs = *plong;
        else
          if (pointer.type == SHORT)
            *xs = (long int)*pshort;
          else
            error++;
      else
        error++;
      break;

    case 257: /* image length */
```

```
      if (pointer.length == 1)
        if (pointer.type == LONG)
          *ys = *plong;
        else
          if (pointer.type == SHORT)
            *ys = (long int)*pshort;
          else
            error++;
      else
        error++;
      break;
case 258: /* bits per sample */
  if (pointer.type == SHORT)
    {
    if (pointer.length == 1)
      {
      td->bits_sample[0] = *pshort;
      }
    else
      {
      lseek(fp,pointer.voff,SEEK_SET);
      for (n = 0; n < pointer.length; n++)
        {
        read(fp,&td->bits_sample[n],2);
        if (td->iimm == II) ii2mms(&td->bits_sample[n]);
        }
      lseek(fp,next_pointer,SEEK_SET);
      }
    }
  else
    {
    error++;
    }
  break;
case 259: /* compression */
  if ((pointer.type == SHORT) && (pointer.length == 1))
    {
    if ((pointer.voff >> 16) != 1)
      printf("!! CANNOT DECODE TIFF COMPRESION: %d\n",
        pointer.voff);
    }
  else
    {
    error++;
    }
  break;
case 262: /* photometric interpretation */
  td->photo_interp = pointer.voff >> 16;
  if ((pointer.type == SHORT) && (pointer.length == 1))
    if ((td->photo_interp == 0) || (td->photo_interp == 1))
      *pl = 1;
    else
      if (td->photo_interp == 2)
        *pl = 3;
```

```
            else
              printf("!! CANNOT DECODE PHOTOMETRIC INTERP: %d\n",
                td->photo_interp);
      else
        error++;
      break;
    case 273: /* strip offsets */
      td->strip_off_length = pointer.length;
      if (td->strip_off_length == 1)
        {
        td->strip_off_offset = next_pointer - 4;
        }
      else
        {
        if (pointer.type == SHORT)
          td->strip_off_offset = (long int)*pshort;
        else
          td->strip_off_offset = *plong;
        }
      if (pointer.type == SHORT)
        td->strip_off_offset = -td->strip_off_offset;
      break;
    case 277: /* samples per pixel */
      if (pointer.length == 1)
        if (pointer.type == SHORT)
          td->sample_pixel = *pshort;
        else
          error++;
      else
        error++;
      break;
    case 278: /* rows per strip */
      if (pointer.length == 1)
        if (pointer.type == LONG)
          td->rows_strip = *plong;
        else
          if (pointer.type == SHORT)
            td->rows_strip = (long int)*pshort;
          else
            error++;
      else
        error++;
      break;
    case 279: /* strip byte counts */
      td->strip_cnt_length = pointer.length;
      if (td->strip_cnt_length == 1)
        {
        td->strip_cnt_offset = next_pointer - 4;
        }
      else
        {
        if (pointer.type == SHORT)
          td->strip_cnt_offset = (long int)*pshort;
        else
```

```
                td->strip_cnt_offset = *plong;
            }              if (pointer.type == SHORT)
              td->strip_cnt_offset = -td->strip_cnt_offset;
          break;
        case 284: /* planar configuration */
          if ((pointer.type == SHORT) && (pointer.length == 1))
            td->planar_config = pointer.voff >> 16;
          else
            error++;
          break;

        /* the following tags are ignored */
        case 282: /* x resolution */
        case 283: /* y resolution */
        case 290: /* grey response unit */
        case 291: /* grey response curve */
        case 296: /* resolution unit */
        case 301: /* color response curves */
        case 317: /* predictor */
        case 318: /* white point */
        case 319: /* primary chromaticities */
        case 320: /* color map */
        case 270: /* image description */
        case 271: /* make */
        case 272: /* model */
        case 305: /* software */
        case 306: /* date time */
        case 315: /* artist */
        case 316: /* host computer */
        case 292: /* group 3 options */
        case 293: /* group 4 options */
        case 269: /* document name */
        case 285: /* page name */
        case 286: /* x position */
        case 287: /* y position */
        case 297: /* page number */
          break;

        default:
          printf("!! UNKNOWN TIFF POINTER TAG: %d\n",pointer.tag);
          break;
        }
    if (error != NULL)
      printf("!! INVALID TIFF POINTER STRUCTURE: %d %d %d %d\n",
        pointer.tag,pointer.type,pointer.length,pointer.voff);
    }
  read(fp,&next_ifd,4);
  if (td->iimm == II) ii2mml(&next_ifd);
  }

if (td->rows_strip == 0) td->rows_strip = *ys;

return;
}
```

```
/**********************************************************/
/*   function: read_tiff_data                             */
/**********************************************************/

void read_tiff_data(fp,xs,ys,pl,td,r,g,b)
  long   int   fp;          /* file pointer */
  long   int   xs,ys;       /* x,y size */
  long   int   pl;          /* plane count */
  TIFF_DATA   td;           /* file information */
  unsigned char *r,*g,*b;   /* data buffer pointers */
  {
  unsigned char *dr,*dg,*db;
  unsigned char *line;
  long   int   sco,scf;
  long   int   soo,sof;
  long   int   c,l;

  /* verify information for this file */
  if ((td.photo_interp == 0) ||
      (td.photo_interp == 1) ||
      (td.photo_interp == 2))
    {
    if (td.planar_config == 1)
      {
      if (td.bits_sample[0] == 8)
        {
        if (td.strip_cnt_length == td.strip_off_length)
          {
          line = (unsigned char *)malloc(xs*pl);
          dr = r;
          dg = g;
          db = b;

          sco = td.strip_cnt_offset;
          if (sco >= 0)
            {
            scf = LONG;
            }
          else
            {
            sco = -sco;
            scf = SHORT;
            }
          soo = td.strip_off_offset;
          if (soo >= 0)
            {
            sof = LONG;
            }
          else
            {
            soo = -sco;
            sof = SHORT;
            }
```

```
            /* read all strips */
            for (c = 0; c < td.strip_cnt_length; c++)
              {
              strip_read(fp,td.iimm,xs,pl,sco,scf,soo,sof,line,
                dr,dg,db,&l);
              dr = dr + (l / pl);
              dg = dg + (l / pl);
              db = db + (l / pl);
              if (scf == SHORT)
                sco = sco + 2;
              else
                sco = sco + 4;
              if (sof == SHORT)
                soo = soo + 2;
              else
                soo = soo + 4;
              }
            free(line);
            }
          else
            {
            printf("!! ERROR, TIFF strip count/offset
              mismatch=%d,%d\n",
              td.strip_cnt_length,td.strip_off_length);
            }
          }
        else
          {
          printf("!! ERROR, TIFF bits/sample = %d\n",
            td.bits_sample[0]);
          }
        }
      else
        {
        printf("!! ERROR, TIFF planar config = %d\n",
          td.planar_config);
        }
      }
    else
      {
      printf("!! ERROR, TIFF photometric interp = %d\n",
        td.photo_interp);
      }

  return;
  }

/*********************************************************/
/*    function: write_tiff_header                        */
/*********************************************************/

void write_tiff_header(fp,xs,ys,pl)
  long  int  fp;            /* file pointer */
  long  int  xs,ys;         /* x,y size */
```

```
  long  int  pl;            /* plane count */
  {
  char       cnt;
  unsigned char  buf[512];  unsigned char *b;
  long  int    n;

  for (n = 0; n < 512; n++) buf[n] = 0;

  buf[0] = 0x4d;    /* tiff file header */
  buf[1] = 0x4d;
  buf[3] = 42;
  buf[7] = 10;

  cnt = 0;
  b = buf + 12;
  b = make_tag(254,LONG, 1,0,b,&cnt);          /* new subfile type */
  b = make_tag(256,SHORT,1,(xs<<16),b,&cnt);   /* image width */
  b = make_tag(257,SHORT,1,(ys<<16),b,&cnt);   /* image length */
  if (pl == 3)                                 /* bits per sample */
     b = make_tag(258,SHORT,3,256,b,&cnt);
  else
     b = make_tag(258,SHORT,1,(8<<16),b,&cnt);
  b = make_tag(259,SHORT,1,(1<<16),b,&cnt);    /* compression */
  if (pl == 3)                                 /* photo interp */
     b = make_tag(262,SHORT,1,(2<<16),b,&cnt);
  else
     b = make_tag(262,SHORT,1,(1<<16),b,&cnt);
  b = make_tag(273,LONG, 1,512,b,&cnt);        /* strip offset */
  b = make_tag(277,SHORT,1,(pl<<16),b,&cnt);   /* samples per pixel
*/
  b = make_tag(278,SHORT,1,(ys<<16),b,&cnt);   /* rows per strip */
  b = make_tag(279,LONG, 1,(ys*xs*pl),b,&cnt); /* strip byte count */
  b = make_tag(284,SHORT,1,(1<<16),b,&cnt);    /* planar config */
  b = make_tag(0,0,0,0,b,&cnt);                /* next IFD */
  cnt—;

  buf[11] = cnt;

  if (pl == 3)
     {
     buf[257] = 8;
     buf[259] = 8;
     buf[261] = 8;
     }
  write(fp,buf,512);

  return;
  }


/**********************************************************/
/*    function: write_tiff_data                           */
/**********************************************************/

void write_tiff_data(fp,xs,ys,pl,r,g,b)
```

```
long  int  fp;              /* file pointer */
long  int  xs,ys;           /* x,y size */
long  int  pl;              /* plane count */
unsigned char *r,*g,*b;  /* data buffer pointers */
{
long  int  x,y,z;
unsigned char *dr,*dg,*db;
int error;
long  int  *p,*s;
unsigned char *l,*line;

line = (unsigned char *)malloc(xs*pl);
for (y = 0; y < ys; y++)
   {
   dr = r + (y * xs);
   dg = g + (y * xs);
   db = b + (y * xs);
   l = line;
   for (x = 0; x < xs; x++)
      {
      *l++ = *dr++;
      if (pl > 1)
         {
         *l++ = *dg++;
         *l++ = *db++;
         }
      }
   write(fp,line,(xs*pl));
   }
free(line);

return;
}


/**********************************************************/
/*    utility functions                                 */
/**********************************************************/

unsigned char *make_tag(tag,type,lng,fld,b,cnt)
  short int  tag;
  short int  type;
  long  int  lng;
  long  int  fld;
  unsigned char *b;
  char          *cnt;
  {
  *b++ = (unsigned char)((tag  >> 8)  & 0xff);
  *b++ = (unsigned char)( tag         & 0xff);
  *b++ = (unsigned char)((type >> 8)  & 0xff);
  *b++ = (unsigned char)( type        & 0xff);
  *b++ = (unsigned char)((lng  >> 24) & 0xff);
  *b++ = (unsigned char)((lng  >> 16) & 0xff);
  *b++ = (unsigned char)((lng  >>  8) & 0xff);
```

```
  *b++ = (unsigned char)( lng          & 0xff);
  *b++ = (unsigned char)((fld  >> 24) & 0xff);
  *b++ = (unsigned char)((fld  >> 16) & 0xff);
  *b++ = (unsigned char)((fld  >>  8) & 0xff);
  *b++ = (unsigned char)( fld          & 0xff);
  *cnt = *cnt + 1;
  return(b);
  }

short ii2mms(value)
short int *value;
  {
  short temp;
  temp = *value;
  *value = ((temp >> 8) & 0x00ff) +
           ((temp << 8) & 0xff00);
  return;
  }

long ii2mml(value)
long  int *value;
  {
  long temp;
  temp = *value;
  *value = ((temp >> 24) & 0x000000ff) +
           ((temp >>  8) & 0x0000ff00) +
           ((temp <<  8) & 0x00ff0000) +
           ((temp << 24) & 0xff000000);
  return;
  }


long strip_read(fp,im,xs,pl,sco,scf,soo,sof,line,r,g,b,lng)
  long  int  fp;
  long  int  im;
  long  int  xs,pl;
  long  int  sco,scf;
  long  int  soo,sof;
  unsigned char *line;
  unsigned char *r,*g,*b;
  long  int *lng;
  {
  long  int  lcnt,loff;
  short int  scnt,soff;
  long  int  x;
  unsigned char *l;

  lseek(fp,sco,SEEK_SET);
  if (scf == LONG)
    {
    read(fp,&lcnt,4);
    if (im == II) ii2mml(&lcnt);
    }
  else
```

```
      {
      read(fp,&scnt,2);
      if (im == II) ii2mms(&scnt);
      lcnt = (long int)scnt;
      }
    *lng = lcnt;
    lseek(fp,soo,SEEK_SET);
    if (sof == LONG)
      {
      read(fp,&loff,4);
      if (im == II) ii2mml(&loff);
      }
    else
      {
      read(fp,&soff,2);
      if (im == II) ii2mms(&soff);
      loff = (long int)soff;
      }

    lseek(fp,loff,SEEK_SET);
    while (lcnt > 0)
      {
      read(fp,line,(xs*pl));
      l = line;
      for (x = 0; x < xs; x++)
        {
        *r++ = *l++;
        if (pl == 3)
          {
          *g++ = *l++;
          *b++ = *l++;
          }
        }
      lcnt = lcnt - (xs * pl);
      }
    return;
```

Program 29 TIFF read/write functions.

Strings of blank characters, for example, occur regularly in ASCII text files and can be compressed to reduce file size. Graphical systems routinely store images not as arrays of pixels, but as parameters for mathematical formulae that can recreate the image when needed. This process is called rendering, and can it save large amounts of storage space — with the trade-off being the time required to perform the rendering. Digital images, such as scanned photographs, are much more difficult to compress, but there are ways to do it. Before presenting those methods, however, first it is necessary to define some terms.

Compression can take one of two forms. It is either *lossless* or it is *lossy*. Lossless compression means just that: An image that is compressed for storage and then decompressed for processing suffers no loss of data. In other words, a pixel-by-pixel comparison of the original image and the compressed/decompressed one will show that not a single pixel value has been changed. Lossy compression techniques, on the other hand, sacrifice some pixels by allowing their values to differ from the original image in order to achieve more data storage savings.

In many cases, the amount of loss in lossy compression is negligible and undetectable by the human eye when the image is viewed on a monitor. Nonetheless, care must be taken when using these techniques. If an image is compressed only once and then decompressed for viewing, such as in teleconferencing applications, the amount of loss may be acceptable. If an image is repeatedly compressed and decompressed during processing, however, any amount of data loss, no matter how small, could be amplified and thereby destroy image quality. In applications where that might occur, it is prudent to either not use any compression techniques, or to use only those that provide lossless results, even if the savings are not as great.

The amount of storage space saved by compression is called the *compression ratio*. If an image consumes 10 megabytes of space before compression and 5 megabytes after compression, the compression ratio is said to be 2:1 (pronounced "2-to-1"). The original image size divided by compressed image size equals the compression ratio. If the same image were compressed to 1 megabyte, the compression ratio is 10:1, that is, 10/1 = 10. Because of the nature of lossless compression, ratios greater than 2:1 usually are not achieved, but (as will soon be shown) higher-contrast images can produce greater compression with these techniques. Lossy algorithms have much greater ability to compress images: Ratios of 20:1 are common and, depending on how much data loss can be tolerated, ratios as high as 100:1 can be achieved.

The first compression scheme to be investigated is one that has been used for many years and is lossless. It is called *run-length encoding*, or RLE. Remember that pixels are generally saved in files as a contiguous string of values. Figure 8.14 shows such a string of 16 pixels. Notice that in several places there are adjacent pixels with the same value: three pixels with the value 0x61, four with value 0x5b, and five with value 0x54. It seems inherently wasteful to save the same pixel value over and over again, when instead it is possible to save the value only once, along with the count of how many adjacent pixels have that value. Thus, a run of identical pixels of a given length is encoded. The are many ways to perform run-length encoding; the SGI system provides a simple and straightforward implementation.

Figure 8.15 shows how the pixels in Fig. 8.14 would be encoded with this RLE method. Here the first byte encountered contains the count, and the most significant bit (MSB) of the count indicates if the run is of different (0) or identical (1) pixels. The original string of 16 pixels is

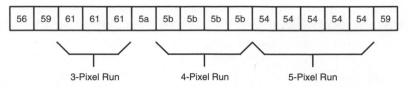

Figure 8.14 Uncompressed pixel string.

reduced to 13. This is not a very high compression ratio, only 1.23:1, but on large image files even this small compression can mean many megabytes are saved. Program 30 is a re-implementation of the read_sgi_data and write_sgi_data routines that now incorporates run-length encoding.

If the type field of the an SGI file header is 257 (0x0101), the file is run-length encoded. The 512-byte header is the same as that described earlier, but now following this structure are two tables. One table contains pointers, or byte offsets into the file, where the encoded data for each line of the image begins. Each pointer is four bytes long and there is one entry in the table for each line in the image. This is necessary since the lines are of variable length. In addition, there is a table is for the red, green, and blue data. The second table, also with four bytes per entry and an entry for every line, provides the length of run-length encoded data stream, in bytes, for each line of the image. Thus, the total length of the header can be calculated as follows:

$$\text{length} = 512 + (((y\_size \times 4) \times 3) \times 2)$$

The factor of 4 accounts for each table entry being a long integer, the factor of 3 assumes a color image, and the final factor of 2 allows space for the data pointer and line length tables.

The dump in Fig. 8.16 shows the header and beginning initial data of an RLE SGI file. The y dimension of the 80×60-pixel image size indicates that the data pointer and line length tables are 60 entries long; they begin at byte offsets 512 and 1232, respectively. The run-length encoded data begins at location 1952; the first byte of the first few lines have been highlighted.

Each run of identical pixels is reduced to two bytes: The first byte contains the number of pixels and the second pixel contains the value. For a run of pixels where each one is different from its neighbor, the count indicates how many pixels there are, and is followed by the string of values.

Run-length encoding can provide significant savings for computer-generated graphics files that tend to have long strings of identical values. Images obtained from the real world via various sensors generally do not have these characteristics, however, because they are burdened with things like electronic noise and film grain. These characteristics tend to give every pixel a slightly different value, making it a not-good candidate for run-length encoding. In fact, sometimes an image will be compressed with this technique and the resulting file actually is larger than the original!

One class of image that does compress well using this technique consists of those that have been processed for higher contrast. Under these circumstances, much of the noise and other localized variations have been "squeezed out" and the image becomes a better candidate for run-length encoding.

Another run-length compression technique, commonly used with 1-bit images such as those used in morphological processing, is called *Huffman encoding*, named after the person who created the technique in 1952. Huffman encoding assigns set bit patterns for strings of white and black binary pixels, based on the probable frequency of their occurrence.

There are many variations of the codings, but the most common is that instituted by the International Telegraph and Telephone Consultative Committee, or CCITT. The CCITT Group 3 and Group 4 schemes, also called One-Dimensional Modified Huffman Run-Length Encodings, are used for transmitting the binary images most typically generated by facsimile machines. For example, a string of three white pixels has the unique binary code 1000, while three black pixels has the code 10. By following the prescribed coding, very high compression ratios can be achieved; an entire line of white or black pixels is reduced to less that 20 bits of transmitted information. This is why a fax machine operates much more quickly on pages of text, which happen to be mostly white.

A modification of Huffman encoding is called *LZW compression*, named after the Sperry Corporation researchers who developed it: Lempel, Zev, and Welch. This compression technique resembles Huffman encoding in that it builds a table of bit streams that take the place of successive pixel values. This method is generally applied to graphics images, or to color images that have been reduced to 8-bit color depth (called *pseudocolor* images). LZW compression is employed in the Graphic Interchange Format (GIF) images that are prevalent on

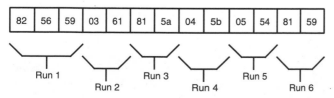

Figure 8.15 SGI run-length encoding.

```
/*********************************************************/
/*    program 30: SGI RLE read/write functions           */
/*********************************************************/

typedef struct        /* SGI RGB header structure */
  {
  short int  magic;
  short int  type;
  short int  dim;
  short int  xsize;
  short int  ysize;
  short int  zsize;
  long  int  min;
  long  int  max;
  long  int  waste;
  char       name[80];
  long  int  space[102];
  } SGI_HEADER;

/*********************************************************/
/*    function: read_sgi_header                          */
/*********************************************************/

void read_sgi_header (fp,xs,ys,pl,type)
  long  int  fp;          /* file pointer */
  long  int  *xs,*ys;     /* x,y size */
  long  int  *pl;         /* plane count */
  long  int  *type;       /* file type */
  {
  SGI_HEADER header;

  read(fp,&header,sizeof(header));
  if (header.magic != 474)
    {
    printf("INVALID SGI MAGIC NUMBER: %d\n",header.magic);
    }
  else
    {
    *xs = (long)header.xsize;
    *ys = (long)header.ysize;
    *pl = (long)header.zsize;
    *type = (long)header.type;
    if ((*type != 1) && (*type != 257))
      {
      printf("SGI TYPE NOT 1 OR 257: %d\n",header.type);
      }
    }
  return;
  }

/*********************************************************/
/*    function: read_sgi_data                            */
*//*********************************************************/

void read_sgi_data(fp,xs,ys,pl,type,r,g,b)
  long  int  fp;          /* file pointer */
  long  int  xs,ys;       /* x,y size */
```

```
long  int  pl;             /* plane count */
long  int  type;           /* file type */
unsigned char *r,*g,*b;  /* data buffer pointers */
{
long  int  x,y,c;
unsigned char pixel;
unsigned char *d,*si,*in,*out;
long  int  count,s2;
long  int  *p,*s;
long  int  *pr,*pg,*pb,*po,*sr,*sg,*sb,*so;

if (type == 1)
  {
  /* non-rle data */
  for (c = 0; c < pl; c++)
    {
    if (c == 0) d = r;
    if (c == 1) d = g;
    if (c == 2) d = b;
    d = d + ((ys - 1) * xs);
    for (y = 0; y < ys; y++)
      {
      read(fp,d,xs);
      d = d - xs;
      }
    }
  }
else
  {
  /* run-length encoded data */

  /* allocate buffers for pointer and size tables */
  pr = (long int *) malloc (ys*4);
  pg = (long int *) malloc (ys*4);
  pb = (long int *) malloc (ys*4);
  po = (long int *) malloc (ys*4);
  sr = (long int *) malloc (ys*4);
  sg = (long int *) malloc (ys*4);
  sb = (long int *) malloc (ys*4);
  so = (long int *) malloc (ys*4);
  si = (unsigned char *) malloc (xs*4);


  /* position file past basic header,
       then read pointer and size tables */
  lseek(fp,512,0);
  read(fp,pr,(ys*4));     /* pointer tables */
  if (pl >= 3)
    {
    read(fp,pg,(ys*4));        read(fp,pb,(ys*4));
    }
  if (pl == 4)
    {
    read(fp,po,(ys*4));
    }
  read(fp,sr,(ys*4));     /* size tables */
  if (pl >= 3)
```

```
      {
  read(fp,sg,(ys*4));
  read(fp,sb,(ys*4));
  }
if (pl == 4)
  {
  read(fp,so,(ys*4));
  }

/* process each plane */
for (c = 0; c < pl; c++)
  {
  /* initialize buffer pointers */
  switch (c)
    {
    case 0:
      d = r;
      p = pr;
      s = sr;
      break;
    case 1:
      d = g;
      p = pg;
      s = sg;
      break;
    case 2:
      d = b;
      p = pb;
      s = sb;
      break;
    }

  /* process all lines */
  for (y = 0; y < ys; y++)
    {
    out = d + ((ys - y - 1) * xs);
    lseek(fp,p[y],0);
    read(fp,si,s[y]);
    in = si;
    s2 = 0;

    /* process all runs in current line */
    while (s2 < s[y])
      {
      pixel = in[s2++];
      count = ((long)pixel & 0x0000007f);
      if (count != 0)                    {
        if ((pixel & 0x80) == 0)
          {
          pixel = in[s2++];
          while (count > 0)
            {
            *out++ = pixel;
            count-;
            }
          }
        else
```

```
                      {
                      while (count > 0)
                        {
                        *out++ = in[s2++];
                        count-;
                        }
                      }
                  }
              else
                {
                s2 = s[y] + 1;
                }
              }
          }
      }
    }

  /* free pointer and size tables */
  free(pr);
  free(pg);
  free(pb);
  free(po);
  free(sr);
  free(sg);
  free(sb);
  free(si);
  free(so);
  }

return;
}


/*************************************************************/
/*    function: write_sgi_header                          */
/*************************************************************/

void write_sgi_header (fp,xs,ys,pl,type)
  long  int  fp;            /* file pointer */
  long  int  xs,ys;         /* x,y size */
  long  int  pl;            /* plane count */
  long  int  type;          /* file type */
  {
  SGI_HEADER header;
  long  int  i;
  header.magic = 474;
  header.type  = type;
  header.dim   = 3;
  header.xsize = xs;
  header.ysize = ys;
  header.zsize = pl;
  header.min   = 0;
  header.max   = 255;
  header.waste = 0;

  for (i = 0; i < 80; i++) header.name[i] = 0;
  for (i = 0; i < 102; i++) header.space[i] = 0;
```

```
    write(fp,&header,sizeof(header));

    return;
    }


/***********************************************************/
/*    function: write_sgi_data                            */
/***********************************************************/
void write_sgi_data(fp,xs,ys,pl,r,g,b,type)
  long  int  fp;            /* file pointer */
  long  int  xs,ys;         /* x,y size */
  long  int  pl;            /* plane count */
  unsigned char *r,*g,*b;   /* data buffer pointers */
  long  int  type;          /* file type */
  {
  long  int  x,y,cc,f;
  unsigned char *c,*d,*so,*o;
  long  int  *p,*s;
  long  int  *pr,*pg,*pb,*sr,*sg,*sb;
  long  int  cnt,scnt;
  char       bcnt;

  if (type == 1)
    {
    /* non-rle data */
    for (cc = 0; cc < pl; cc++)
      {
      if (cc == 0) d = r;
      if (cc == 1) d = g;
      if (cc == 2) d = b;
      d = d + ((ys - 1) * xs);
      for (y = 0; y < ys; y++)
        {
        write(fp,d,xs);
        d = d - xs;
        }
      }
    }
  else
    {
    /* run-length encoded data */

    /* allocate buffers for pointer and size tables */
    pr = (long int *) malloc (ys*4);
    pg = (long int *) malloc (ys*4);
    pb = (long int *) malloc (ys*4);
    sr = (long int *) malloc (ys*4);
    sg = (long int *) malloc (ys*4);
    sb = (long int *) malloc (ys*4);
    so = (unsigned char *) malloc (xs*4);

    /* set pointer and size buffers to zero */
    for (y = 0; y < ys; y++)
      {
      pr[y] = 0;
```

```
    pg[y] = 0;
    pb[y] = 0;
    sr[y] = 0;
    sg[y] = 0;
    sb[y] = 0;
    }


/* write pointer and size buffers to file to save space for them
*/
    lseek(fp,512,0);
    write(fp,pr,(ys*4));
    write(fp,sr,(ys*4));
    if (pl == 3)
      {
      write(fp,pg,(ys*4));
      write(fp,pb,(ys*4));
      write(fp,sg,(ys*4));
      write(fp,sb,(ys*4));
      }

/* process each plane,
       run-length encode all lines,
       updating pointer and size buffers */
    f = 512 + (((ys*4) * pl) * 2);
    for (cc = 0; cc < pl; cc++)
      {
      /* initialize buffer pointers */
      switch (cc)
        {
        case 0:
          c = r;
          p = pr;
          s = sr;
          break;
        case 1:
          c = g;
          p = pg;
          s = sg;
          break;
        case 2:
          c = b;
          p = pb;
          s = sb;
          break;
        }

      /* process all lines */
      for (y = 0; y < ys; y++)
        {
        d = c + ((ys - y - 1) * xs);
        p[y] = f;
        x = 0;
        scnt = 0;
        /* process all pixels in current line */
        while (x < xs)
          {
```

```
            o = so + 1;
            if (x == (xs-1))
              {
              /* special case! last pixel in line */
              x++;
              *o = *d;
              *so = (unsigned char)1;
              scnt = scnt + 2;
              write(fp,so,2);
              }
            else
              {
              if (((*d == *(d+1)) && (*d == *(d+2))))
                {
                /* run of identical pixels */
                *o = *d;
                cnt = 1;
                x++;
                while ((*d == *(d+1)) && (x < xs) && (cnt < 126))
                  {
                  d++;
                  cnt++;
                  x++;
                  }
                d++;
                *so = (unsigned char)cnt;
                scnt = scnt + 2;
                write(fp,so,2);
                }
              else
                {
                /* run of different pixels */
                cnt = 0;
                while (((*d != *(d+1)) ||
                        ((*d == *(d+1)) && (*d != *(d+2)))) &&
                        (x < xs) && (cnt < 126))
                  {
                  *o++ = *d++;                    cnt++;
                  x++;
                  }
                *so = (unsigned char)cnt + 0x80;
                scnt = scnt + cnt + 1;
                write(fp,so,(cnt+1));
                }
              }
            }
        /* this last byte must be 0 for compatibility
              with SGI utilities */
        bcnt = 0;
        write(fp,&bcnt,1);
        scnt++;

        s[y] = scnt;
        f = f + scnt;
        }
    }
```

```
/* write out completed pointer and size buffers */
lseek(fp,512,0);
write(fp,pr,(ys*4));
if (pl == 3)
   {
   write(fp,pg,(ys*4));
   write(fp,pb,(ys*4));
   }
write(fp,sr,(ys*4));
if (pl == 3)
   {
   write(fp,sg,(ys*4));
   write(fp,sb,(ys*4));
   }

/* free pointer and size buffers */
free(pr);
free(pg);
free(pb);
free(sr);
free(sg);
free(sb);
free(so);
   }

   return;
```

Program 30 SGI RLE read/write functions.

the Internet. Like Huffman encoding, LZW is lossless and generates acceptable compression ratios of about 2:1.

JPEG

The Joint Photographic Experts Group, known as JPEG and pronounced "jay-peg," is a technical committee formed between the ISO and CCITT. Its purpose is to develop a general-purpose international standard for the compression of digital images. Three categories of processes have been defined: the baseline sequential process, the extended DCT-based processes, and the lossless process. Any hardware or software readers or writers must support the first process, but support of the other two is optional. Though the JPEG baseline sequential process is rather complex, it has become more widespread because of VLSI chips, developed by C-Cube Microsystems, that perform the compression and decompression.

The JPEG standard does not define a file format, only the technique for compression. Because of this oversight, many vendors have developed proprietary formats that incorporate the standard. Two of these have become dominant: the C-Cube JFIF and the Aldus/Adobe TIFF/JPEG. JFIF is a minimal implementation of JPEG and has been

```
   0  (00000000)   01da0101  00030050  003c0003  00000000    ......P.<.....
  16  (00000010)   000000ff  00000000  6e6f206e  616d6500    ........no name.
  32  (00000020)   00000000  00000000  00000000  00000000    ................
  48  (00000030)   00000000  00000000  00000000  00000000    ................
  :
 480  (000001e0)   00000000  00000000  00000000  00000000    ................
 496  (000001f0)   00000000  00000000  00000000  00000000    ................
 512  (00000200)   000007a0  000007f3  00000847  00000899    ..........G.....
 528  (00000210)   000008ec  00000940  00000994  000009e8    .......@........
 544  (00000220)   00000a3c  00000a90  00000ae3  00000b36    ..<.........6
  :
1200  (000004b0)   00003fe3  00004037  0000408b  000040df    .?...@7.|@...@.
1216  (000004c0)   00004133  00004187  000041db  0000422f    ..A3..A...A...B/
1232  (000004d0)   00000053  00000054  00000052  00000053    ...S...T...R...S
1248  (000004e0)   00000054  00000054  00000054  00000054    ...T...T...T...T
1264  (000004f0)   00000054  00000054  00000053  00000054    ...T...S...S...T
  :
1920  (00000780)   00000054  00000054  00000054  00000054    ...T...T...T...T
1936  (00000790)   00000054  00000054  00000054  00000054    ...T...T...T...T
1952  (000007a0)   98484c46  352f4986  a1957b74  798a9395    .HLF5/I...{ty...
1968  (000007b0)   94908e8d  8a888687  860485b2  84838384    ................
1984  (000007c0)   85888b8d  8e8b847f  7d80838d  8d888483    .............}...
2000  (000007d0)   83848389  8e90908f  8e898488  8f8e8b8d    ................
2016  (000007e0)   9da9adaa  a2a0a09f  9ba0bb9b  54540143    ...........TT.C
2032  (000007f0)   013e00ad  272a201a  2a405999  9b85777c    >..'*.*@Y...w|
2048  (00000800)   90989794  928f8d8b  89888886  86858484    ................
2064  (00000810)   85868586  8a8b8c8d  8d89827b  797f848d    ...........{y...
2080  (00000820)   8c03879e  86848387  8d90918f  8f8d8b8d    ................
2096  (00000830)   8f8f8c88  8a9ba8ac  a6a1a09f  9ea7bd6d    ...............m
2112  (00000840)   564c0134  01330097  1e435a5d  4f3c3a71    VL.4.3...CZ]O<:q
2128  (00000850)   9e8d7781  94a9a995  93308d8a  89866605    ..w.............
  :
```

Figure 8.16 Hexadecimal dump of a run-length encoded SGI file.

agreed upon by several major vendors, thus becoming the de facto standard. TIFF/JPEG is a newer implementation but, because of the acceptance of TIFF and the format's inherent ability to store a multitude of parameters about an image, it may become more widely supported.

The JPEG committee has defined an official standard called SPIFF. It is yet unclear whether SPIFF will replace JFIF or TIFF/JPEG, but it has the advantage of being sanctioned by the ISO/CCITT.

There are many texts that describe JPEG implementations, and operational JPEG source code is available free of charge from the Internet. What is presented here is an overview of the baseline sequential process and some examples of what sort of quality can be expected from this type of compression.

JPEG is based on the relative inability of human vision to distinguish among small variations in color — as opposed to the well-documented ability to detect even minute changes in intensity. JPEG-compressed images will look good to human eyes because the loss of some original data is not noticeable. Digital processing operations, however, might well give false or unexpected results because of this missing data. The moral is the same one cited throughout this book: Application designers must be aware of the limitations of the tools, in this case JPEG, so as not to produce a product that does not meet expectations.

The baseline sequential process has three stages:

1. Removing redundant data with a DCT

2. Quantizing the remaining data, optimized for human vision

3. Encoding the result to minimize storage requirements

Sometimes there is a preliminary stage that converts images from the RGB color space into one like YIQ or YUV, where the intensity component is separated from the color components. By doing this, greater compression of the color components can be achieved, with less perceivable loss of overall image quality.

The first step in the process is to divide the image into blocks of 8×8 pixels, because data values typically change very little over this small an area. Each block is then operated on separately. The first operation performed is a *discrete cosine transform* (DCT). A DCT is similar to a Fourier transform except that only the real, or cosine, part is retained. The transformed output, performed in two dimensions, is ordered so that the mean value (known as the *dc coefficient*) is in the upper-left corner of the 8×8 block. Higher frequencies progress in rows and columns towards the lower right. The other values in the block are called *ac coefficients*.

The next stage, called *quantization,* reduces the magnitude of the frequency coefficients and increases the number of coefficients that are equal to zero. This step is accomplished by dividing each ac coefficient by a constant value based on the position of the 8×8 block. The position-dependent constants are located in a structure called a *quantization table* and are designed to optimize the resultant values for human vision. The results are then rounded to the nearest integer.

The first two stages, DCT and quantization, are where data are lost. The last stage of the process, encoding the data, is lossless. The 8×8 data block that is created from the quantization stage is scanned in the zigzag pattern shown in Fig. 8.17. Due to the processing done to the data thus far, the ac coefficients will tend to increase in value along this path. A Huffman coding is used to save the data within a block, which greatly reduces space. The difference between the dc coefficients of adjacent blocks is usually small, so a technique called *differential*

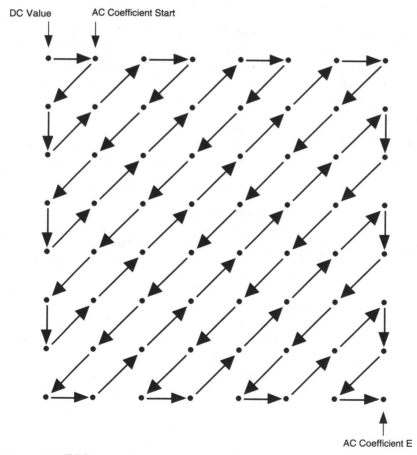

Figure 8.17 JPEG scan order.

(a) Original Image

(b) 20-to-1 Compression

(c) 40-to-1 Compression

(d) 80-to-1 Compression

Figure 8.18 JPEG compression ratios. *(Image courtesy of Eastman Kodak Co.).*

pulse code modulation (DPCM) is used to store only the differences, or *deltas*, between them; this usually will require fewer bits.

To decompress an image, the inverse of each process is performed. One benefit of JPEG compression is that its parameters can be altered to suit the particular needs of an application, allowing users to make size-versus-quality and quality-versus-speed tradeoffs. In other words, higher compression ratios can be achieved if the application can accept low-quality images. This might be the case when generating a sequence of images to be displayed for an online catalog of stock pictures, where transfer speed is of the utmost importance. Similarly, less compression (and higher quality) may be dictated when a high-resolution of a selected image is made from the catalog.

Considering the perceived loss of image quality, the compression ratios obtainable with JPEG are truly phenomenal. Figure 8.18(a) shows an image in RGB color space in its original, uncompressed form. Figure 8.18(b) is the same image, having been compressed at a ratio of about 20:1 and then decompressed. There is almost no visible loss of image quality, but if the actual pixel values were to be examined, differences would be immediately obvious.

Repetitive compression and decompression of an image, using even small compression ratios, can cause image quality to degrade rapidly and should be avoided at all costs. Figure 8.18(c) depicts the same image compressed to about 40:1. Now there are some noticeable flaws beginning to appear, but the image is still viewable. Finally, Fig. 8.18(d) shows an image compressed to about 80:1. Now the quality is quite degraded and the borders between the 8×8 pixel blocks are very noticeable. The image is still recognizable, however, even though it consumes slightly more than 1 percent of its original size!

Image Displays

Digital image processing is practically impossible to discuss without actually viewing images—it is nothing if not a visual experience. Many devices can be used to output processed images, but by far the most common means for viewing are computer displays. This chapter will discuss the use of displays and how they relate to digital image processing. Before the technical aspects of display technology can be appreciated, though, it is useful to have an understanding of human vision.

Human Vision

The faculty of human vision can be divided into three parts: the physical, the physiological, and the psychological. The process of sunlight striking a distant mountain scene, or an incandescent light filling a darkened room, are well-understood and quantifiable actions. We can measure the intensity of the light, we can determine its spectrum, and we can analyze the way in which it reflects off objects. There are numerous experiments that allow us to quantify the nature of light in a deterministic and objective fashion. This is the *physics* of light and it is independent of human interaction.

The physical nature, or physiology, of how our eyes work is also well known. Light enters through the cornea and is focused by the lens onto the retina. We know that the retina is composed of two type of light receptors, rods and cones. Nerves, their ends are connected to the rods and cones, exit the eyeball clustered together in the optic nerve and proceed into the brain. Rods are known to be more sensitive to light intensity, or *luminance*, than are the cones. But the cones, unlike rods, are sensitive to various light frequencies, or *hue*. Human vision thus operates in a realm of hue, saturation, and intensity.

There are a few million cone receptors distributed over the retina, but there are about 100 million rods. Figure 9-1 shows the absolute luminance of differently lit scenes. The human eye reacts to light over a tremendous dynamic range, from starlight to sunlight. In mathematical terms this is about seven decades. (It's a logarithmic scale.) In dark lighting conditions, no brighter than moonlight, the cone receptors are not stimulated but the rods are. This is why "night vision" is, for the most part, black and white and includes no color sensation.

Our eyes do not react to the entire possible range all at once, though. A process called *adaptation* limits us to seeing over only a small, two-decade range (a luminance range of 100:1) at any given time; it is governed by the total amount of light striking the retina. Luckily this is a sliding scale, as illustrated by the smaller graph on the right-hand side of Fig. 9.1. Each of us has experienced this phenomenon when, for example, we walk from a brightly lit room to the darkness of the outdoor night. At first we cannot see anything. Everything is black. This is because our eyes, more precisely the sensors in our retina, have adapted to the light indoors. Any absolute luminance that falls below

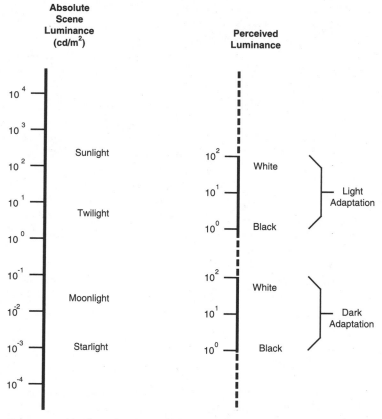

Figure 9.1 Absolute luminance scale. *(From Charles A. Poynton,* A Technical Introduction to Digital Video, *copyright 1996. Reprinted by permission of John Wiley & Sons.)*

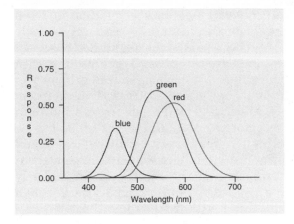

(a) Cone Receptors

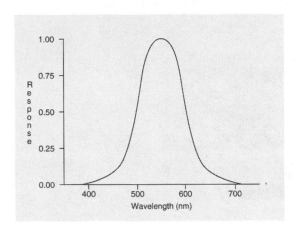

(b) Rod Receptors

Figure 9.2 Optical receptors response curves.

our currently sensory range of 1 is perceived as "black." In the presence of darkness, that is, less total light striking our retinas, the sliding scale moves downward and, after several minutes, we can see things that are only dimly illuminated. This is called *dark adaptation*.

The opposite effect, known as *light adaptation*, can be demonstrated by watching a Saturday matinee at the local theater. When we leave the dark theater, where our retinas have adapted to dark lighting conditions, we are suddenly thrust into bright sunlight. Nearly everything appears bright and washed out, because absolute luminance greater than our current sensory range of 100 appears "white." We instantly and uncontrollably squint to allow our vision systems time to adapt. Light adaptation occurs much more rapidly than dark adaptation and can cause pain until it is complete. The irises in our eyes react very quickly to changes in light, but are used only to aid in the adaptation process.

It has been determined that there are three basic types of cones, each of which respond to a different range of frequencies. This is known as the *tristimulus* nature of vision. The response curves of these receptors, usually classified as red, green, and blue receptors, are shown in Fig. 9.2(a); that of the rod receptors appears in Fig. 9.2(b). As can be seen from these graphs, the human eye is least sensitive to blue and most sensitive to green. In fact, the luminance we perceive gets about 30 percent of its power from red, about 59 percent from green, and only 11 percent from blue. This is why pure blue objects appear darker than red or green ones, even though they may have the same absolute luminance, and all white objects seem brighter still. It is interesting, and by no means a coincidence, that CRT display devices also operate in the RGB color realm; it is a natural choice given that humans perceive color that way.

(a) Linear Steps
(Appears Nonlinear)

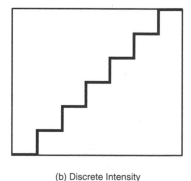

(b) Discrete Intensity

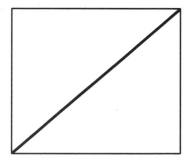

(c) Continuous Intensity

Figure 9.3 Linearly increasing luminance.

(a) Logarithmic Steps
(Appears Linear)

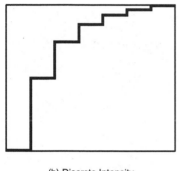

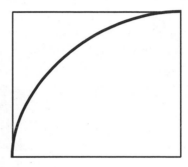

(b) Discrete Intensity

(c) Continuous Intensity

Figure 9.4 Logarithmically increasing luminance.

Another physiological aspect of human vision is its nonlinear response to luminance. For example, the vertical bars in Fig. 9.3(a) are increasing in luminance linearly from left to right, as shown in the graph printed beside the image. To our eyes, however, the intensities do not appear to increase in that fashion. Instead, the bars on the left appear dark and suddenly jump to being bright on the right-hand side. Figure 9.3(b) shows something more like what we would expect, where the bars appear to increase in intensity smoothly and equally as we move from left to right. But if we look at the graph of this image, we see that the actual intensity steps are not equal. This happens because our eyes react logarithmically, not linearly, to increases in intensity. Figure 9.4 shows the perceived brightness as a function of actual luminance.

So what happens after the nerves in our eyes react to various intensities and frequencies of light? How does our brain actually perceive objects and color and luminance? The psychology, or visual *perception*, of what happens within our brains is not as well understood as the physiology. What can be determined, though, are our reactions to different visual situations, even if we do not understand why we react that way. For example, consider the image and intensity graph in Fig. 9.5. There are only two levels of intensity in this image: the left side is dark and the right side is light.

When we look at the image, however, the dark area appears darker at the junction and the light area appears lighter. Our eyes see a graph like the one shown beside the true one. The series of intensity bands in Fig. 9.4 highlights the effect even better. This phenomenon is known as the *Mach band effect* and is caused by the spatial frequency response of our eyes. We are less sensitive to high and low spatial frequencies than we are to middle frequencies.

Figure 9.6 illustrates another phenomenon, called *simultaneous contrast*. At first glance, the small squares embedded in larger squares appear to decrease in brightness from left to right. All the small squares actually are of identical intensity, but our eyes tell us something different because of the background. Figure 9.7 shows other well-known visual illusions. In the first picture, do you see two faces

(a) Two Steps

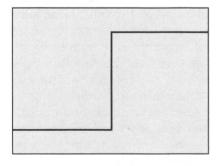

(b) Actual Intensity   (c) Perceived Intensity

Figure 9.5 Mach band phenomenon.

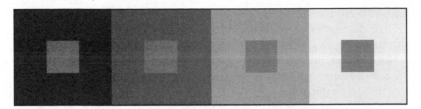

Figure 9.6 Simultaneous contrast phenomenon.

looking at one another, or do you see a vase? In the other, do you see a beautiful young woman or a crone?

Many such experiments can be performed. The point is that even if we cannot accurately say why these perceptions occur, we can be aware of their existence. Certain phenomena can hinder the users of image display systems and should be avoided.

CRT Displays

The Commission Internationale de L'Eclairage (International Commission on Illumination, or CIE for short), located in Vienna, is the organization chartered to set standards in the area of color perception.

In the 1920s a famous experiment was performed on many different human subjects. The experiment involved mixing different light wave (spectral) distributions so that the experiment subjects could try to match different colors. In 1931 the CIE standardized these values into a mathematical model based on the color matching experimental results. These curves, shown in Fig. 9.8, are called the CIE Color Matching Functions (CMFs) and are labeled X, Y, and Z. Note the

(a) Vase or Two Faces?   (b) Young Woman or Old Hag?

Figure 9.7 Visual illusions.

similarity, and complementary nature, of these graphs to those shown in Fig. 9.2(a), the response curves for the human cone receptors. These graphs define the *CIE XYZ Tristimulus* system for luminance. They provide the correct spectral composition for linear color matching in humans. Y is luminance in this system, and X and Z are spectral (or color) weighting curves.

The CIE also defined a model for representing pure color that is independent of brightness. By normalizing the XYZ tristimulus values, two color (or *chromaticity*) values called x and y can be calculated as follows:

$$x = X / (X + Y + Z)$$

$$y = Y / (X + Y + Z)$$

A third chrominance value, z, can be computed, but it is redundant if x and y are known. These equations define the *CIE x,y Chromaticity* model on which all color reproduction is based. Suppose an absolutely pure, monochromatic light source could be constructed, one that would smoothly change its wavelength from 400 nanometers to 700 nanometers (the accepted range that humans can "see" in the electromagnetic spectrum). If the X, Y, and Z values were measured, the result would be the graph of x,y chromaticity values shown in Fig. 9.9. The area within this curve contains all colors that the human eye can see.

One interesting and immediate finding of this chromaticity diagram is explanation of "the case of the missing purple." If you look at a rainbow or sunlight that has been passed through a prism and split into the visible spectrum, purple is nowhere to be found. It must be somewhere, however, because we see it all the time. The answer lies in the fact that purple is a mixture of red and blue frequencies. In fact, the straight line connecting the longer-wavelength (700 nm) red end of the

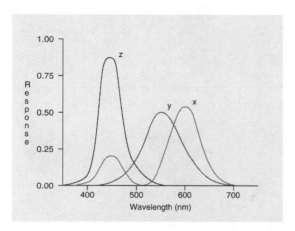

Figure 9.8 CIE color matching functions.

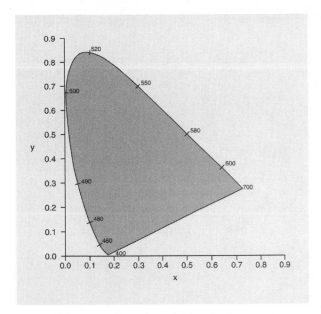

Figure 9.9 Human vision chromaticity graph.

chromaticity diagram to the shorter-wavelength (400 nm) blue end is called the *line of purples*, and it completes the otherwise open-ended line to form an area. If you think about it, most of the colors we see are not in the spectrum. Brown, cyan, mauve, pink, or any color apart from the few that are pure, single wavelengths (such as those generated by lasers) are mixtures. They can be located somewhere within the interior of this diagram.

So one might ask: What does all of this have to do with computer image displays? The answer is everything. Not only is this the basis for creating phosphors for CRT displays, it is also used to determine the color response of photographic film, printing inks, and just about any other technology that reproduces color. For now, however, the discussion will remain focused on cathode ray tubes.

Light from a CRT is the result of a high-energy beam of electrons striking a substance which, when so stimulated, emits photons of specific frequencies. There are three of these substances, called *phosphors*, lining the inside of the face of a CRT. One emits light primarily in the red range, one in the green, and the other in the blue. These colors can be charted on the CIE chromaticity diagram and, via color mixing, all other reproducible colors can be synthesized. But what "color" is red or green or blue—or white, for that matter? Where should these primary colors be located on the diagram?

There are several competing standards which, for all intents and purposes, are quite close to one another. Consider Fig. 9.10, which

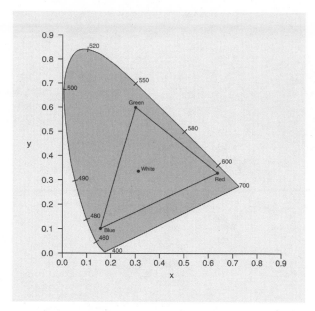

Figure 9.10 CCIR Rec. 709 chromaticity graph.

shows the internationally agreed-upon standard for high-definition television, known as CCIR Rec. 709. The red, green, blue, and white chromaticities are defined as follows:

Red:	$x = 0.6400$	$y = 0.3300$
Green:	$x = 0.3000$	$y = 0.6000$
Blue:	$x = 0.1500$	$y = 0.0600$
White:	$x = 0.3127$	$y = 0.3290$

The red, green, and blue points on this graph form the vertices of a triangle; when connected, they define an area (called a gamut) encompassing all possible colors that a display device can reproduce. Note that there are many colors falling outside of this reproducible range that are, nonetheless, detectable by humans. Similar graphs for film and print processing can be calculated, and might show a greater range of color—but they still will fall short of the outer curve. This is why, no matter how high the resolution or how accurate the medium, reproduced color can never compete with the experience of seeing something in person.

Gamma

The term *gamma* is often misunderstood and even more often used incorrectly. Unfortunately, it is one of those terms that means different things to different audiences. In a discussion of photographic film, gamma is the numerical value of the exponent of the power function in the straight-line region of the film's response curve. For movie film or 35mm slides designed to be viewed in a dark room, a gamma of about 1.5 is used. But gamma for film is not the same as gamma for CRTs.

CRT displays are governed by the physics of the device's electron guns. Light output on the face of the tube is proportional to the gun's voltage input raised to the power of 5/2 (five divided by two), which is also known as the *five-halves power law*. This numerical value of 2.5, which in reality can range from about 2.3 to 2.6, is known as gamma. A graph of voltage input versus light intensity output is shown in Fig. 9.11. This is an inherent function of all CRTs and cannot be avoided. The nonlinear response of CRTs can be compensated for by hardware, which is called *gamma correction*. This is done by applying a 0.45-power function, which is nearly a square root function, to the voltage input signal.

Something interesting is apparent if we compare this nonlinearity curve of CRTs to the nonlinear nature of human vision receptors shown in Fig. 9.4. They are nearly the inverse of one other! This means that CRTs compensate almost precisely for the way our eyes work, and this means that with very little additional modification, a scale of linearly increasing pixel values will appear to be correctly increasing linearly when viewed on a CRT. This is a wonderful coincidence. Because other output media such as film or ink do not operate in this

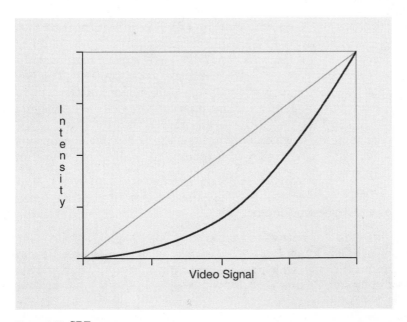

Figure 9.11 CRT gamma.

manner, however, a digital image might look fine on a display monitor but look terrible if transferred to film or paper. Similarly, images that look fine when printed on film or paper may look flat or washed-out on CRTs.

A new problem arises when one considers the incorporation of computer-generated elements into a scanned scene. Unlike scanned images, computer graphic images have no counterpart in the real world, and most application software packages allow the user to change various visual parameters such as lighting, contrast, and shading. These types of systems also allow modification of a term they call gamma. This gamma is independent of, but related to, the uses of the term described earlier. For these environments, a look-up table is constructed that modifies the voltage input signal in a prescribed manner that is usually a power function of the input pixel intensity:

$$m_{x,y} = p_{x,y}\text{gamma}$$

where p is the original pixel value and m is the modified "gamma-adjusted" pixel value. The term *gamma* can be any value greater or less than 1.0. If a gamma of 1.0 is selected, the output values are identical to the input values. A value greater than one will make everything appear darker on the screen while accentuating contrast in the mid- and high-intensity areas; this is sometimes referred to as "crushing the blacks." A gamma of less than one will increase apparent brightness and give the display a flatter look. A gamma of 2.2 often is recommended, which is approximately 1/0.45, and which will "undo" the gamma correction performed by most monitors. The ambient illumination in the user's physical environment also will affect the choice of gamma to use for best results: Bright rooms require higher gammas.

There is no doubt that the term gamma causes a great deal of confusion, with which engineers and programmers must contend. The best suggestion is to know your audience: Are they doctors, artists, photo technicians, or one of a growing number of people who are being exposed to digital images for the first time? It is also necessary to know the equipment for which applications are being developed; some operating systems do not allow for modification of display look-up tables, while others do.

True Color versus Pseudocolor

The piece of computer hardware that enables the display of color information on a CRT is known as a *frame buffer*. It is responsible for converting the pixel array, which represents information to be displayed, into the analog signals that the CRT requires as input. No matter what type of frame buffer is used, there are three analog signals that are fed into the CRT: the red, green, and blue information. Obviously, grayscale CRTs have only one input signal, but this discussion will be limited to color CRTs.

There are two types of frame buffers, *true color* and *pseudocolor*. All of the color digital image processing techniques discussed in this book have been geared primarily to images that are composed of three color planes (red, green, and blue), each of which contains eight bits of data per pixel. These images would be best suited for display with a true color frame buffer, because this type of hardware directly translates three color planes of information into three separate analog signals.

A very simple block diagram of this type of display system, referred to as a 24-bit frame buffer, is shown in Fig. 9.12. The application program writes pixel information to the red, green, and blue areas of the frame buffer's random access memory (RAM). As the timing of the raster scan demands it, the necessary information is extracted from RAM and passed through a look-up table (called a *display LUT*), which makes any last-minute adjustments to the data. If the system allows it, the contents of the display LUTs can be modified, making it possible for the application program to control the gamma of the display.

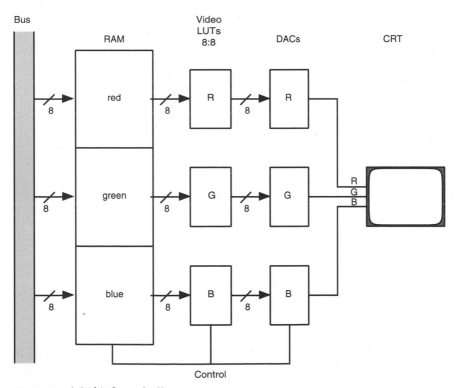

Figure 9.12 A 24-bit frame buffer.

The output from the display LUTs then passes through digital-to-analog converters (DACs) that generate the voltage input for the CRT.

Whether due to cost or other manufacturing constraints, some computer systems do not have this true color capability, yet are required to have a color display. Figure 9.13 illustrates a hardware system of this sort. Pseudocolor systems can use 8- or 16-bit RAM buffers; the one shown is 8-bit. Here the application places 8-bit information into the frame buffer RAM; it represents color information, but it is not the true color information described above.

The frame buffer accesses this data and passes it through a look-up table that is quite different from the LUTs that have been described so far. This LUT defines the color map of the digital image information. Because the data is only 8 bits deep, only 256 colors can be represented. The color map (sometimes referred to as the color *palette*) therefore expands the 8-bit data into 8 bits for each primary color, which then proceed into the DACs and eventually the display. The color map can be thought of as means for the operator to select and use 256 colors from the 16 million-plus true colors that are available. As such, this LUT is accessible to application programs for writing new color maps. There is an almost limitless number of possible color maps that can be

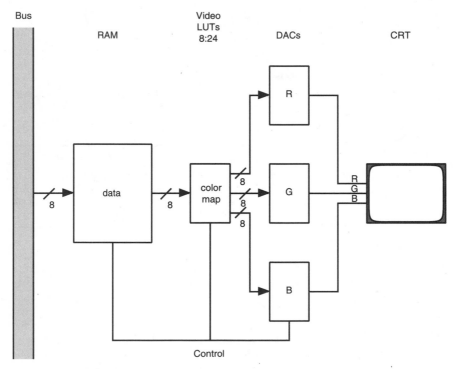

Figure 9.13 Pseudocolor frame buffer.

produced. Sometimes an image is interrogated to determine the 256 most frequently occurring true colors, which then become the entries in the LUT.

As an example of pseudocolor, consider the scheme shown in Fig. 9.14. Here the upper three bits of an 8-bit pixel will represent red intensity, the middle three bits are for green, and the lower two bits are for blue. The input 8-bit signal is split into three copies that are used as the indices for the red, green, and blue LUTs. The operation of these LUTs is the same as has been described earlier in this book, except the data in the tables now takes on a completely different look.

For the red look-up table, the three bits of relevant information mean that eight possible values for red intensity can be generated, as shown in the table next to the red LUT. Because the lower five bits of the data word are "don't cares," meaning that the same output value results whether they are 0 or 1, the eight possible red intensity values occur repetitively throughout the table. The same process occurs for the green and blue look-up tables, thus generating 24 bits of information for the DACs. The drawback in this example is, of course, that even though a full 24 bits of color are created, there are only eight discrete intensity levels of red and green, and only four of blue.

It should be obvious that true color display systems are desirable for most image processing applications. Due to the subtle color changes of digital images, pseudocolor systems (even 16-bit implementations that permit 65,536 colors instead of only 256) are not acceptable except for very low-cost environments. Sometimes grayscale image applications can use pseudocolor, since the color map translates the 8-bit pixel data value to identical signals for red, green, and blue, therefore providing for the greatest possible dynamic range of CRT intensities that the input data allows. Pseudocolor systems are most advantageous in low-end computer graphics applications where 256 or 65,536 colors are more than enough to create charts, diagrams, and simple objects.

Stereoscopic Displays

We all remember going to see a 3D movie at the local theater as a kid and wearing those funny red-and-green filter glasses. (Well, those of us who are old enough remember doing it!) The result was a poor but identifiable three-dimensional image that seemed to reach out at us from the screen. What was happening to us, thanks to the glasses, was that each of our eyes was seeing the same scene photographed from slightly different perspective angles. The effect was to trick our brains into seeing depth as well as width and height. Before 3D films, stereo photography was a rage throughout the world, and "stereoscopes" were common throughout parlors around the turn of the century.

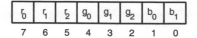

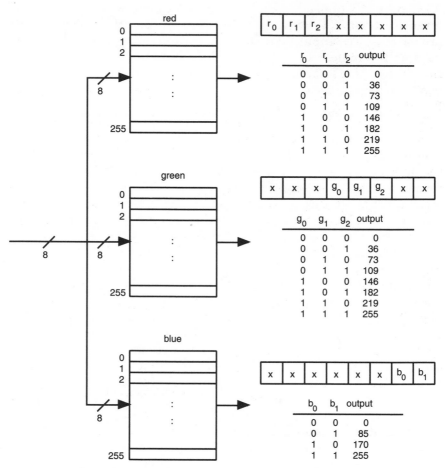

Figure 9.14 Pseudocolor implementation.

These devices, still available today in different formats, provide separate views for each eye and create the three-dimensional effect.

Figure 9.15 shows how human stereoscopic vision (from the Greek *stereopsis*, or "solid vision") works. An object in the foreground (closer to the viewer) will appear offset against the background when seen from different viewpoints. This displacement is called *parallax* and is the main reason we see in three dimensions. Since our eyes are separated by a horizontal distance, each one produces a cyclopean, "one-eyed" image from two slightly different angles. The visual cortex in the brain compares these two images and, primarily through differences between them, calculates their distance. There are other visual cues and clues that our vision system uses to perceive distance, such as shadows, shading, obscuring, and atmospheric density, or haze.

Just as the old stereoscopes and 3D movies artificially induce the perception of depth in our brains, the same techniques (albeit more refined) are used in display systems today. They are called stereoscopic displays, and they can provide realistic three-dimensional viewing. The three common methods used to do this are illustrated in Fig. 9.16. The first method, often seen in virtual reality applications, is to mount separate small display screens in front of each eye and display separate left- and right-eye information on the appropriate one. This usually requires the user to wear a headset that eliminates any peripheral vision that would destroy the illusion.

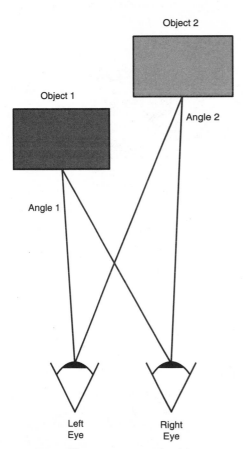

Figure 9.15 Human stereoscopic vision.

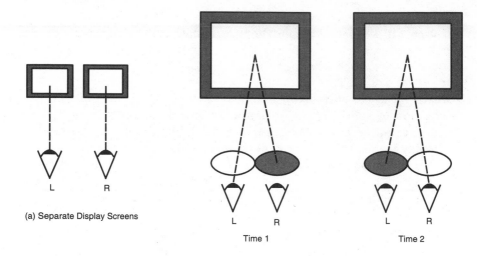

(a) Separate Display Screens

Time 1   Time 2

(b) One Display with Shutters

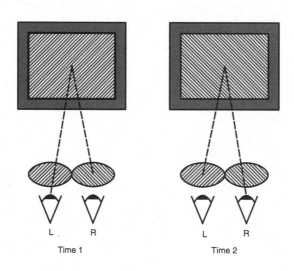

Time 1   Time 2

(c) One Display with Polarizing Filters

Figure 9.16 Stereoscopic display construction.

The second method employs special glasses that have shutters, either mechanical or electronic, built into each eyepiece. Alternating left- and right-eye images are displayed on a CRT in synchronization with the shutters, thereby allowing only the correct eye to see the appropriate image. These systems can be difficult to maintain to ensure correct operation.

A third method employs a polarizing filter placed over the face of the CRT, which alternately polarizes the light vertically or horizontally. The viewer wears glasses with polarizing filters, ensuring that only the appropriate image is seen by each eye.

Liquid Crystal Displays

Only cathode ray tube display technology has been discussed up to this point. Liquid crystal displays (LCDs) have grown more popular in recent years, paralleling their increasing quality and decreasing price. They are used in laptop computers primarily because of their flat profile, but also because of their very low power consumption, light weight, and reduced fragility compared to CRTs. The field is rather crowded with different types of LCDs, but they all operate on the same principle.

Under "normal" conditions there are three states of matter: solid, liquid, and gas. Liquid crystals can be thought of as a fourth state of matter, primarily exhibiting the properties of a liquid, but also taking on some characteristics of solids. Some liquid crystals occur naturally, while others are manufactured. The first liquid crystal was discovered by Freidrich Reinitzer in 1888. An organic material called cholesterol benzoate had the interesting property of melting from a solid to a cloudy liquid at a temperature of 145.5° Celsius, but then "melted" again at 178.5° to become a clear liquid. Reinitzer realized that the change from cloudy to clear was due to the crystalline nature of the material.

Liquid crystals remained merely a scientific curiosity until the late 1950s, when their unique properties found an application. The property of interest here is the ability of the molecules to orient themselves in a common direction over relatively long distances, which is the definition of a crystal. What is more, this alignment can be controlled with an electrical field. The material then becomes either transparent or opaque, which phenomenon provides the basis for pixels of a display.

There are many types of liquid crystals, and they can be classified in different ways. The *thermotropic* class consists of materials that have a liquid crystal phase at certain temperatures. Those in the *lyotropic* class form liquid crystals in the presence of a solvent. Remember mood rings? In those, and in more modern applications such as thermometers, these devices contain thermotropic liquid crystals that form a cholesterics phase: Depending on their temperature, these materials "twist" and, because of their polarizing effect, reflect only a specific frequency of light. Other phases include nematic, smectic, and chiral nematic.

It is not necessary to go into the chemical properties of these materials; the property that is important for using them in computer displays is that they either reflect or transmit light. Figure 9.17 shows how an LCD could be constructed. The actual liquid, which is only a few microns thick, is sandwiched between panels of transparent glass or plastic. Embedded in these panels are electrodes, usually made of indium tin oxide (ITO), which is a good conductor, transparent, cheap to produce, and durable. Layered on either side of the panels are polarizing filters. When no electrical current passes through the liquid, it allows the incoming polarized light to be reflected off the back panel and re-emerge out the front. When it is energized, the liquid becomes opaque to the polarized light and a dark spot is seen.

There are advantages, certainly, to using liquid crystals in computer displays. There are also many drawbacks, especially with regard to digital imaging applications. Early LCDs had limited depth resolution: pixels were either black or white. The speed at which the display could be updated and refreshed was also a limiting factor. These devices also have low contrast and narrow viewing angles. Color LCDs were very dim because red, green, and blue filter masks were placed over the displays to create colored pixels, further attenuating the reflected light.

In recent years there has been much research into new techniques for producing better and more applicable LCDs, and it appears that this trend will continue. Active matrix displays, where current is applied directly to each pixel, produce better contrast and faster update times; these are attributes that the multiplexed passive matrix LCDs lack. The spatial resolution of these displays currently is no better than 640×480 pixels, but this also is changing, with the promise of near-laser printer quality on the horizon.

Color is now commonplace. In just the last few years, color LCDs have completely displaced monochrome displays in all except the very cheapest applications. Instead of light-attenuating filters placed over the display screen, LCDs have red, green, and blue dyes injected

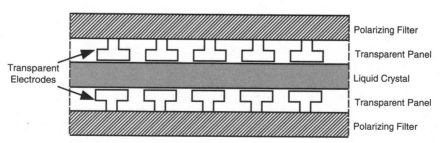

Figure 9.17 LCD display construction.

directly in the liquid to create color. Another development area is the use of polymer-dispersed LCDs. This technology embeds tiny bubbles of liquid crystal into a clear polymer panel; these bubbles can be activated by ITO electrodes to create color pixels. This type of display is very bright because the polarizing filters are not needed, and they also are easy to manufacture, which promises lower cost. While LCD color resolution has risen from 256 possible values to 32,768 or 65,536, they still cannot reproduce the 16 million shades needed for true color imagery. That, too, will surely change.

Three-Dimensional Displays

A new technology, currently in the experimental stage, is that of true three-dimensional displays. Though we can perceive three dimensions on a two-dimensional display screen, we are just fooling our vision systems. But under development are true three-dimensional displays that form an image in a volume, not a plane.

The application of these displays would be for fields that need visualization in three dimensions. Air traffic control is one example, since operators need to know not only the latitudes and longitudes of aircraft, but also their altitudes. Three-dimensional volumetric imaging, for medical or scientific visualization, is also a likely candidate for this technology.

Applications

Almost every day there is a new application area in which digital image processing plays a role. This small offshoot of computer science was at first little more than an endeavor for a few scientists. It has grown into an industry that promises to increase in scale and have ever-greater impact on our lives. This chapter provides an overview of some of the major application areas that use the techniques presented in this book.

Space Exploration and Astronomy

It is difficult to believe that digital image processing came into existence only in the 1960s, especially considering how it has grown into so many areas of interest. Space exploration, led by researchers and technicians at the National Air and Space Administration (NASA), was where it all started. This field, along with the related field of astronomy, today is still one of the most active areas of developing new image processing techniques.

The development of the CCD camera was a great step forward, allowing scientists and astronomers to capture digitally the images of faint, far-away celestial objects. Because of the very weak signals involved, they had to develop better methods for extracting information that was barely detectable. Many of the filtering processes available today came from this need. Image averaging, convolution filters, and FFTs are just a few of the methods involved.

Imaging systems designed for these fields usually are less concerned with color than they are with detail. A good-sized portion of these images are grayscale, but many times they will be pseudocolored to make relevant information stand out. Consider the image of the Eagle Nebula in Fig. 10.1. This is a faint and rather bland-looking celestial object but it can be enhanced with color (not reproducible here) to highlight faint structures that indicate various physical attributes to a trained observer.

Space exploration has taken advantage of other techniques from various application areas. Perspective terrain reconstruction, discussed in a preceding chapter, allows earthbound humans to see the mountains and valleys of distant planets. The Magellan spacecraft was sent to Venus with a radar sensor that could penetrate the thick clouds of the planet and seen details of the surface. But the crowning achievement for digital image processing in this field has been the Hubble Space Telescope. Figure 10.2 is a processed digital image of the Eagle Nebula, taken in 1995 by the HST. There is no denying the increase in spatial resolution that can be achieved with a space-based imaging platform. This wonderful scientific instrument has already changed, and promises to continue to change, the field of stellar exploration.

Military and Intelligence

Digital image processing rapidly became a tool for photo interpreters at the Central Intelligence Agency, Defense Intelligence Agency, and other branches of the intelligence community. The global geopolitical environment of the late 1960s made it necessary to adapt techniques developed for space exploration to a new home in these secret facilities. Early cameras had resolutions of about a meter; the newest space-based telescopes, which are said to be about equal in power to the HST, can see things as small as a grapefruit from over 100 miles above the Earth.

The main function of photo analysts is to identify areas of interest and extract as much information as possible from the image. They may be looking at military installations, research facilities, industrial complex-

Figure 10.1 Eagle Nebula, Earth-based telescope. *(Image courtesy of NASA.)*

Figure 10.2 Eagle Nebula, space-based telescope. *(Image courtesy of NASA.)*

es, or residential structures. What they need most is speed. They need to zoom into small areas of a large picture, or rotate an image to get the proper perspective. The images they acquire might need contrast enhancement or warping to conform to a map. In addition, analysts must annotate the images to provide briefings for strategists and other government personnel.

Figure 10.3 shows examples of how digital images are used in this environment. They were generated by the Mapping Applications Client Server (MACS) System and are provided courtesy of Sterling Software ITD and the United States Air Force. The first shows an area of Baghdad, Iraq, during the Persian Gulf War. For briefings, the image is overlaid with graphics indicating damage to a bridge and the likely route from a military headquarters to an adjacent part of the city. The second image shows a portion of the Persian Gulf coastline of Saudi Arabia. Here an image of the area has been overlaid with graphical map information. There are significant differences between the two products. In this way, the image information can assist not only in better mission planning, but also in making other digital databases more accurate.

There are other military applications for digital imagery in addition to intelligence gathering. While military planners need intelligence to estimate troop strengths and movements, they use digital imagery for other purposes. Digitized paper maps such as that shown in Fig. 10.4

(a) Iraqi Urban Area   (b) Saudi Arabian Coastline

Figure 10.3 Intelligence application. *(Image courtesy of Sterling Software ITD.)*

(also processed by the MACS System) can be combined with satellite imagery to provide a better understanding of what the actual land in a hostile area might be like. Mission planning can be taken one step beyond this by utilizing perspective terrain reconstruction. If reconstructions are then animated, pilots can sit in flight simulators and actually "fly" a simulated mission to acquaint themselves with topographic features they will encounter.

Earth Sciences

Another use of satellite imagery that is less militaristic and more commercially oriented is earth sciences. Geologists can learn much from images of wide areas of land. Faults in the earth's crust can be identified easily, especially when the captured images are multispectral, that is, when many images of the same area are captured in different frequencies of the electromagnetic spectrum.

Figure 10.5 shows an example of this type of remote sensing provided by Sandia National Laboratories. The first image shows the Albuquerque, N.M., airport captured in the visible light spectrum. Many fine details are plainly seen, including writing on the runways and air conditioning units on the roofs of buildings. The second image shows the same area captured in the microwave, or radar, section of the spectrum. Objects that are dark in this image absorb radar energy, while bright areas are those that reflect these wavelengths.

Multispectral images can be used in such endeavors as oil and mineral exploration. Geologists and geophysicists can determine the best places to drill or mine by seeing the macro-structures of where natural gas or precious metals tend to congregate. When pseudocoloring is added to the images they become even more useful and pertinent.

New applications for digital imagery in these fields are becoming more commonplace. With space-based radar sensors, images of the ocean's floor can be captured and mapped. Some sensors are used for charting weather patterns and storm systems, increasing forecasting capabilities that have a direct impact on people's lives.

Government

While earth scientists use digital imagery for resource mapping and exploration, government planners can use the same techniques for other purposes. A large industry has grown up around these capabilities, collectively called Geographic Information Systems, or GIS. The uses of GIS are wide and varied. Government officials can track the progress of construction projects using aerial photography. Maps of population centers can be overlaid with 911 emergency telephone coverage. Hydrographic and watershed information can be combined with digital elevation map (DEM) data to produce terrain perspective views, highlighting potentially flood-prone areas. The infrastructure of an area can be monitored and assessed, as can traffic and land use. Communities even can combine digital imagery with demographic statistics to create promotional videos to attract business and industry. All of these functions require a variety of processing techniques that merge images with graphic and text information.

Consider the images in Fig. 10.6, which were generated by the United States Geological Survey EROS/Ames Research Group. The area shown is the San Francisco Bay and inland portions of California. The images were generated using a combination of topographic maps and Landsat satellite information. Overlaid on this information is the

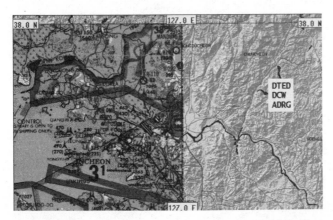

Figure 10.4 Mapping application. *(Image courtesy of Sterling Software ITD.)*

(a) Optical Image   (b) Radar Image

Figure 10.5 Multispectral application. *(Image courtesy of Sandia National Laboratories.)*

human population (as white graphics) over a number of years. At the turn of the century, San Francisco and Oakland were well established; San Jose, Sacramento, and Stockton were small, isolated communities. By 1940 the sprawl of Oakland was obvious, and by the 1960s the entire bay was nearly encircled by people. The last image is from 1990 and shows a burgeoning population in all directions.

This type of analysis can aid governments in estimating urban growth and planning facilities and services. Visual depiction of abstract data sets can offer a much better view of real-world situations than can reams of numbers and statistics.

Scientific Visualization

Research scientists and engineers have a different problem to solve. Most of their work involves computer simulations of existing or potentially real physical systems, using mathematical models. Because of the extremely complex calculations involved, supercomputers are often used. Analysis presents the problem of results that are numerical in form and usually quite voluminous. This is where digital imagery can assist. Humans are visual creatures; some estimates show that 90 percent of the information we gather about our surroundings comes through our eyes, and that over 50 percent of our brain's neurons are dedicated to visual processing. It therefore is reasonable to present this mass of numerical data in a visual fashion.

Many of the processing concepts described in this book can be of use. Scientists often gather results in numerous dimensions. Histograms are a useful tool for analyzing one-dimensional data. Two-dimensional data can be plotted in graphical form or, in some situations, can be expressed as raster information. Pixel location is the result of parametric input and pixel intensity represents magnitude or other results of a calculation. Recall that a 1024×1024 image contains over *one million* pixels. If employed in a visualization context, the results of over a million calculations can be displayed by such an image.

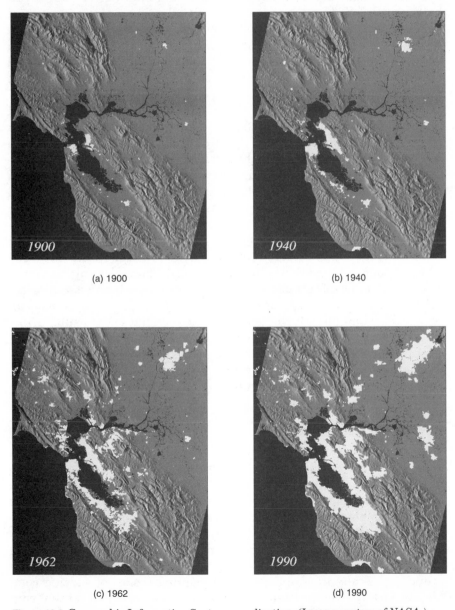

(a) 1900   (b) 1940

(c) 1962   (d) 1990

Figure 10.6 Geographic Information Systems application. *(Image courtesy of NASA.)*

Presented in the proper format, the equivalent of hours of supercomputer processing can be seen at a single glance.

The results are even more staggering in three dimensions, where a cube that has a thousand discrete locations per dimension contains *one billion* voxels! Using three-dimensional volumetrics, where pixel color represents magnitude and pixel transparency represents gradient, or change in magnitude, strikingly beautiful and informative images can be generated. Slicing the three-dimensional volume also can produce useful information for analysis. The volume may be sliced along one of its planar axes, that is, *orthogonally*. This allows for rapid display of a series of two-dimensional images that could exhibit varying behavioral patterns if only one variable were altered. Pseudocoloring can add yet another dimension to the data.

The uses of this sort of scientific visualization are diverse. Virtual wind tunnels now allow researchers to place proposed airfoil designs in a variety of situations to see the lift and turbulence they create — before they are ever constructed. The heat transfer characteristics of materials can be seen easily. Observing seismic phenomena and their effects on proposed structures can make safer buildings in which to live and work. The very small can be probed, now that molecular biologists are able to see how cells and atoms operate based on computer simulation.

Figure 10.7(a) shows such an otherwise unobtainable image. It is a weather model image created by the Environmental Workbench software package from SSESCO in Minneapolis, Minn. Not only are large cloud formations discernible in three dimensions, other meteorological information such as air pressure, temperature, or jet streams also can be visualized. Figure 10.7(b) is a computer simulation of a submarine, created by the Aerospace Engineering and Mechanics Finite Element Group at the Army HPC Research Center, Minneapolis, Minn. Here, displaying the pressure of water flowing around a submerged submarine aids researchers in understanding the fluid dynamics at work.

Computer-Generated Imagery

Computer generated imagery, or CGI, is a large field that continues to grow. While not an application of digital imagery per se, it is noteworthy for several reasons. It has many uses and can take many forms, from simple graphics, such as pie charts and process flow diagrams for business, to photorealism, which strives to make the generated scene look as if it were a photograph taken with a camera.

CGI of this later form has found many uses. Flight simulators, which give pilots the ability to practice various routes while safely on the ground, generally involve computer-generated scenes of varying complexity. Virtual reality systems also provide views of the world that cannot exist in nature. And, of course, most people have seen television

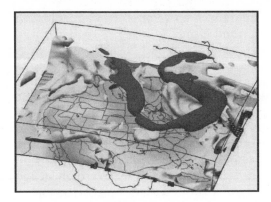

(a) Meteorological Data

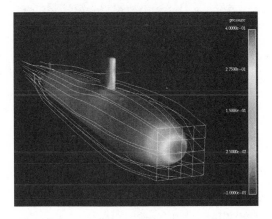

(b) Water Pressure Data

Figure 10.7 Scientific visualization. *(Image "a" courtesy of SSESCO; image "b" courtesy of Army HPC Research Center.)*

programs, commercials, and feature films that employ very lifelike CGI objects and characters. Science fiction programs are a notable example, where CGI is replacing the more expensive modelmaking and motion-control photography for depicting spacecraft and alien starscapes.

As the computer-generated scenes continue to increase in popularity and grow in complexity, they also encounter many of the same problems and requirements as digital imagery. Computer artists might have complete control over shading and lighting of what they create, but they also must contend with image constraints such as resolution, color spaces, and sharpness. In many situations it is necessary to inject artificial grain into a completely clean computer image—just so that it looks as if it had been scanned from film.

Entertainment

The entertainment industry in recent years has become one of the biggest users of digital imagery. Visual effects are not only performed digitally for films and television shows; now even theme park rides and special venues use this technology. In the past, if different objects were to be integrated into the same frame, difficult and tedious film compositing steps were required. This meant that shots either looked very good but were very expensive to produce, or were reasonably priced but of low quality. Using computers to perform these tasks has transformed the industry and opened up new vistas of creativity. One need only watch a recent action- or effects-laden film, compared to one made just a few years ago, to realize how far this art form has come.

The use of digital image processing in the entertainment industry pushes the limits of computers and data storage technology. While most of the application areas discussed here are concerned with a single image, or at most a relatively small number of them, every second of moving footage on television or in the theater translates to 30 or 24 discrete images, respectively. That's several thousand in the course of just minutes—never mind that film images also are quite large and are in true color. For special film venues where 65- or 70-mm film is used, image sizes are larger still.

Digital image use in the entertainment industry also tests the capability of many processing techniques. Blue screen compositing, a mainstay for effects of many types, is but one of the array of methods employed. Intensity mattes are "pulled" from a scene via extreme contrast enhancement; *rotoscoping* produces a hand-generated matte of a particular object for each frame in a sequence. Other techniques include wire and rod removal, color modification, sharpening and blurring, degraining, morphing, and a host of others. Audience appetites for new visual experiences appear insatiable. In addition, most of the elements used in these composites originate on photographic film that must be scanned into a digital form and then output onto new film once the processing is complete.

Perhaps the greatest leap forward that digital image processing has made possible is incorporating computer-generated images into the realm once limited to effects that could be produced with cameras. The traditional method of animation was to meticulously draw each frame of a character on paper or celluloid and then, after many intermediate steps, transfer those images to film. Now characters can be created within the computer, made to walk and talk, be colored and shaded to the point where they are so close to life that no one can be quite sure what is real and what is merely a series of bits and bytes. And finally, these computer-generated elements can be seamlessly merged with true live action, transporting the viewer into new worlds.

Medicine and Dentistry

While the entertainment industry is a hotbed of digital image processing activity today, the medical industry appears to be similarly poised for the same type of growth. Medicine has used digital images for many years; newer techniques promise to promote more use in the future. The processes employed in this field are limited, but they must be performed with the utmost accuracy and reliability, given that human lives might well be at stake.

X-ray photography has long provided physicians with a nonintrusive method of probing into a body. Radiation produced by the X ray source is blocked by certain types of tissue but travels easily through other types, exposing film that then is developed to show very fine detail of internal structures. Doctors use this information for diagnosis, prognosis, and treatment. Over years of use, the combined knowledge of many people has refined this process, increasing doctors' confidence in choosing the proper choice of action based on the results. X-ray film can be digitized easily and displayed on CRTs, or the image can be captured in digital form directly. The result can be greater ease of viewing and powerful integration with databases. The images can be enhanced, scaled, rotated, filtered, pseudocolored, and manipulated in a variety of ways.

But the real question is this: Would you want your doctor making life-and-death decisions about you based on this technological capability? The rational answer is yes, but if and only if there is a proven benefit from doing so. The digital image industry is responding to this challenge, providing very high-resolution display monitors that have the same type of "look and feel" as X-ray film. Only with careful technological progress will these new methods be accepted and lead to better medical treatment.

Other medical imaging technologies are more directly applicable to digital methods than are X-ray photographs. CAT scanners and MRI scanners came into existence in the 1970s and 1980s, and from the beginning the images they produced were tied to computer processing. The physicians and technicians who work with this equipment have already seen how the image processing involved, especially the use of three-dimensional volumetrics, can enhance and extend the data they acquire.

Publishing

The publishing industry represents the most mature and stable of all application areas that use digital imagery. Prepress, the task of assembling and editing all materials prior to printing, has all but completely made the transition to a digital environment. This is evident not only from the online computer resources of any of a number of newspapers and magazines, but also from the infrastructure that has been built to support these endeavors. There are companies that supply services and products to meet the industry's production needs. There are organizations and trade shows that promote and highlight the latest technological advances. And there is a newer generation of people in the industry who have never performed their jobs in any way other than with computers.

Composition and cropping of digital images must be performed in a straightforward and efficient manner. (Imagine what it takes just to produce the layouts for a major newspaper, seven days per week!) Publishing also has the unique requirement of reducing true-color images to just a few bits of information in order to print them on paper. Research into halftoning techniques is ongoing in the search to increase quality.

Document Processing

Related to but different from publishing is the growing industry of document processing. Today's world generates printed words at a phenomenal rate—and most of those words are of little use if they are not read by someone. One of the best examples of document processing is the facsimile machine. It is difficult to image our world without them, but it has been only a relatively few years since they came into existence.

Documents inherently have resolution of one bit per pixel. As such, many specialized techniques have been devised to operate with them. One of the largest areas of research is in compression. ASCII alphanumeric coding is an extremely efficient method to save text—but what if a piece of paper is scanned? If the image of the paper is to be stored for later display on a computer terminal, or if the scanned image is to be transferred via telephone lines for printing at a different facility (which is, of course, what a fax machine does), then CCITT or Huffman coding will minimize the amount of digital data required. A much more intriguing problem is converting the scanned digital image into ASCII characters.

This process is called *optical character recognition,* or OCR. It has made great progress in recent years, and much research continues to be done. Consider the scanned image in Fig. 10.8(a). This is a grayscale representation of a portion of a printed form that has handwritten entries. Using the threshold operator, this image can be transformed to become the binary image shown Fig. 10.8(b). Applying morphological operations, namely skeletonization, can reduce this

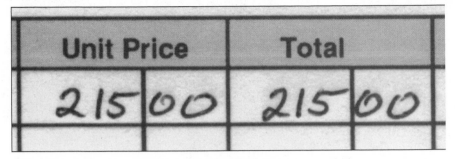

(a) Gray Scale Scan

(b) Binary Image

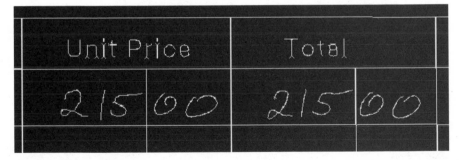

(c) Skeletonized Image

Figure 10.8 Document processing application.

image to its constituent parts, as shown in Fig. 10.8(c). These then can be matched against known patterns to create the proper characters. It obviously is easier to perform OCR on typewritten text, but newer techniques that incorporate "fuzzy" logic are being used to electronically read handwritten material.

Industrial Applications and Machine Vision

Industrial automation is an ongoing process, and for several years the applications of digital imagery have been focused to this end. Just as robots already have taken over many repetitive or dangerous tasks, some of those same machines are now being given the ability to "see" and make decisions based on this input. To do this, many morphological operations are used.

One application for machine vision is sorting and object recognition. Products may be brought via a conveyor belt to an image capture station, where a video or digital camera takes a picture. Using contrast enhancement, thresholding, and a variety of other techniques, individual objects can be isolated and inspected with an expert system or artificial intelligence software. Such characteristics as orientation and correctness of the object are ascertained before the next stage of construction or packaging is performed. Because of the integration of automated inspection imaging systems with larger production operations, the processing of digital information must occur at real-time speeds. This usually means 30 frames per second using 512×512 images. Custom hardware often is constructed to perform an array of very specific tasks in a pipelined fashion to achieve these results.

Machine vision is also becoming more common in robotic systems. Here the key is to provide vision, often stereoscopic vision, to a machine that takes specific action based on its environment. Future exploratory spacecraft may be equipped with independent roving vehicles that will use this type of image processing as "eyes." More down-to-earth applications include robots that can probe objects and areas too dangerous for humans, such as volcanic caldera or unexploded terrorist bombs. The problem of recognition in these applications is complex, since objects no longer are encountered in the controlled setting of an assembly line. In addition, the machines must be able to judge distance and size.

Business

In business, staying competitive and being profitable are absolute requirements. Therefore, businesses always are looking for new ways to provide the edge in their respective fields. In some ways, digital imagery can provide answers. Presentations will continue to be a key to projecting ideas and benefits of services. Simple black-and-white overhead projectors, while still useful, cannot compete with slick graphics and colorful presentations that can be created with digital imagery. Photographic slide scanners and recorders are common fixtures in many corporate offices today, because they can be used to output the powerful graphics and images created by today's desktop computers. Certain display systems allow for the direct projection of digital materials, bypassing the output stage completely.

Newer forms of communication are also streamlining tomorrow's business world. By means of video teleconferencing, cross-country meetings can be held without the participants having to leave their local offices. This requires specialized compression of digital data and display mechanisms, but the results can be financially beneficial.

Household Applications

This application area was saved for last because it promises to be an enormous market that is only now beginning to emerge. As digital cameras (both still and video) move into the mainstream of modern life, they will displace film and videotape as the recording media of choice for our vacations and family get-togethers. It is already possible to snap a digital picture, load it into a home computer, enhance or crop it, annotate it, and then print out as many copies as we wish. We can build an image database of our pictorial history, one that will not deteriorate or get lost over time and will always be at our fingertips for review. All of these functions use ordinary point and neighborhood processes for filtering, color correction, and compositing.

But household use of digital imagery goes beyond merely replacing a box of photographs with a box of computer disks. As with business, perhaps teleconferencing (or the home use equivalent of it) finally will bring the day when video telephones are as common as audio ones, and image compression methods make certain that the images are transferred in the shortest possible time. Scanners already can read fingerprints and identify matches to a database, so why not have keyless locks on our homes and automobiles? All that's needed is some input hardware and various morphological operations. With stored digital images we can shop for a new home without leaving the real estate office, taking virtual "tours" to narrow our choices.

Digital imagery already is ubiquitous on that greatest of communication milestones since the television, the Internet. Nearly every Web page has GIF or JPEG images; it is a simple matter to download them, or even MPEG animation sequences, into our homes. There is a wealth of images on the Net, ranging from NASA spacecraft views to stock photographs of whatever can be imagined. Planning vacations, looking at company's annual reports, and teaching children from online encyclopedias always have been popular household Internet activities. Now those tasks are enhanced with images of remote attractions, corporate facilities, any imaginable products, and pictures of everything from aardvarks to zebras.

Digital imagery is not just for the disconnected scientist or the unconventional artist. It is here among us, in our everyday lives, and will shortly become as common as turning on the television or opening up the daily newspaper. But no matter how complex the algorithms become or how far removed the end user is from the mathematical operations that make it possible, the science of digital image processing will remain rooted in the basic techniques described in this book.

11

Further Reading

This chapter provides some references for further investigation into the field of digital image processing. The first section lists books that should be helpful for anyone wanting to delve into the theory and mathematics of imaging algorithms. The second section lists some periodicals that are devoted primarily to up-to-the minute developments in this field. Last is a listing of some Internet sites that might be of interest.

Books

There are many excellent books in print on digital image processing. It is impossible to review all of them here. Omission of a particular book from this list by no means indicates any lack of merit that it may hold. The intent is to provide an overview of the titles that should be available in any good technical bookstore. I have tried to choose a representative sample of what is available.

Baxes, G.A. *Digital Image Processing: A Practical Primer.* Englewood Cliffs, N.J.: Prentice-Hall, 1984. (Reprinted 1988, Cascade Press, Denver, Colo.)
— — —. *Digital Image Processing: Principles and Applications.* New York: John Wiley & Sons, 1994. The first of these two titles is an excellent introductory book for anyone wanting to gain an overview of the field. It is readable, with very little mathematics required, and provides many simple, real-world examples. Baxes's second book contains much of the same information, but with increased focus on math.
Castleman, K.R. *Digital Image Processing.* Englewood Cliffs, N.J.: Prentice-Hall, 1979. This book was one the first to define digital imaging techniques in a rigorously mathematical sense. It shows how image processing grew out of signal processing and is not for the faint-hearted. In many respects, this book set the standard for all others of its kind to follow.
Pratt, W.K. *Digital Image Processing, 2nd edition.* New York: John Wiley & Sons, 1991. This is one of the best books of processing techniques currently available. It covers almost every conceivable aspect of the field in theoretical and mathematical terms. It does not include pseudocode algorithms or source code, but provides the basis of understanding on which engineers can build.

Kay, D.C., and Levine, J.R. *Graphics File Formats*. Blue Ridge Summit, Pa.: Windcrest/McGraw-Hill, 1992. This book is a must for anyone needing to know about a variety of image and graphics data file formats. It is accurate, concise, and presents the material on a level ideal for programmers and engineers.

Ihrig, S., and Ihrig, E. *Scanning the Professional Way*. Berkeley, Calif.: Osborne/McGraw-Hill, 1995. This book describes scanning and manipulation of digital images from a user's point of view. While there is some technical information, it primarily shows how to use various existing software packages to obtain optimal results. It is geared for individuals working in the publishing industry, but is of value to many other groups.

Foley, J.D., and Van Dam, A. *Fundamentals of Interactive Computer Graphics, 2nd edition*. Reading, Mass.: Addison-Wesley, 1990. This is a classic textbook for the field of computer graphics. It also has large sections relevant to image processing and provides a wealth of information. It is loaded with algorithms and explanations that are both detailed and easy to comprehend.

Hunt, Dr. R.W.G. *The Reproduction of Colour in Photography, Printing and Television, 4th edition*. Tolworth, England: Fountain Press, 1987. Originally published in 1957, this book has been revised and updated to include later technology. While difficult to find, it is the most thorough and beautifully produced text on the subject.

Periodicals

As in any profession, there are many journals and periodicals that provide the latest information on the field. Digital image processing is no different. While there are many more periodicals that have information devoted to image processing, the titles listed below show a cross section of different applications:

Advanced Imaging. This is the primary monthly publication for the image processing marketplace. As any good trade magazine should, it provides insightful articles on the latest developments in the field, as well as the latest products available. It also publishes various buyer's guides that are helpful in finding vendors and equipment suppliers. (PTN Publishing Co., Melville, N.Y.)

CCD Astronomy and *Sky & Telescope*. Long a staple of the astronomy field, *Sky & Telescope* now has a sister magazine devoted to the application of digital image capture and processing. (Sky Publishing Corp., Belmont, Mass.)

Computer Graphics. This is the technical publication of the graphics arm of the ACM. While the primary focus is graphics, imaging and related processing, which play an important role in photorealism, fall under the domain of SIGGRAPH. (ACM SIGGRAPH, New York, N.Y.)

Digital Imaging. This bimonthly trade publication is devoted to products and services for the graphic arts. (Micro Publishing Press, Torrence, Calif.)

Film & Video. This monthly magazine is directed towards the motion picture, television, and entertainment industries and contains articles that describe the latest uses of digital technologies in these applications. (Optic Music, Inc., Los Angeles, Calif.)

Journal of Electronic Imaging. An in-depth journal of the latest theoretical and scholarly developments in imaging science. (Co-published by SPIE, Bellingham, Wash., and IS&T, Springfield, Va.)

NASA Tech Briefs. Sponsored by the National Aeronautics and Space Administration, this monthly publication features articles from scientists and engineers working at the many NASA facilities around the country. Due to the large and diverse nature of NASA, only a small percentage of articles pertain to digital imagery, but those that do provide an insight into the very latest developments of the field. (Associated Business Publications Co., New York, N.Y.)

Photonics Spectra. This monthly publication is directed primarily at the optics, laser, fiber optics, and electro-optics markets, but also contains related information on imaging and optical computing. (Laurin Publishing Co., Pittsfield, Mass.)

Stereo World. This bimonthly magazine is devoted to the history, current applications, and future of stereoscopic photography and imagery. (National Stereoscopic Association, Columbus, Ohio.)

Internet Sites

As with everything else it has touched, the Internet is rapidly changing the face of digital image processing. By using it, an engineer, programmer, or user can find just about anything there is to know about this field. Not only is processing software available, so are a wealth of images. Individuals who are experts in the fields can be located and, most often, are willing to communicate electronically.

The growth potential for imaging on the Internet is boundless and the following list of World Wide Web sites is just a fraction of what is available. They have been categorized as government, organization, education, and commercial sites. Remember that the Net is always changing, so if any of these links are obsolete, enlist the aid of one of the many search engines to locate what you need. I hope this list will provide a basis for more connections. Happy surfing!

Government

Government sites are good sources for many images that are available free of charge.

http://www.nasa.gov/index.html The National Aeronautics and Space Administration (NASA) is a branch of the United States Government that is heavily involved with digital imagery and has a large presence on the Internet. There are many NASA facilities distributed across the country and the net, all of which are accessible through this home page. There is a variety of images available from numerous sites, some of which are highlighted in the following listings.

http://nssdc.gsfc.nasa.gov The National Space Science Data Center (NSSDC) at the Goddard Space Flight Center provides access to a wide variety of astrophysics, space physics, solar physics, lunar, and planetary data from NASA space flight missions. The center is chartered to expand knowledge of the Earth and its environment; many images of weather patterns taken from Earth can be found at this site.

http://www.jpl.nasa.gov The Jet Propulsion Laboratory (JPL) is a NASA center managed by the California Institute of Technology. It maintains an online archive of images ranging from Earth observations taken from space to comets and asteroids. Also available are images captured from planetary missions.

http://www.dfrc.nasa.gov The NASA Dryden Flight Research Center is located in Edwards, Calif. This site contains a large archive of images of experimental aircraft, past and present.

http://www.nih.gov The National Institutes of Health (NIH) maintains the online National Library of Medicine (NLM). Besides sponsoring medical research in various fields, it also makes accessible many medically related digital images. One of the most interesting sites is the Visible Human Project (*http://www.nlm.nih.gov/research/visible*), which is a library of CAT, MRI, and cryosection images of human cadavers.

http://www.sandia.gov The Sandia National Laboratories is one of the premier scientific facilities for research in the fields of energy and remote sensing.

http://www.usgs.gov The United States Geological Survey (USGS) is a primary source for investigating geology, mapping, and water resources. They have a wide variety of products for sale. Satellite images of the Earth are available, as is a wide variety of digitized maps.

http://edcwww.cr.usgs.gov This is the home page for the USGS's EROS Data Center. It provides GIS and remote sensing information and images.

Organizations

Most professional organizations related to digital image processing have Web sites, often containing links to other sites of interest. They help bring order to this youthful, if sometimes chaotic, field. Most of these organizations sponsor trade shows that highlight the latest developments and applications in their areas of interest.

http://www.aas.org American Astronomical Society (AAS). This is the premier organization for professional astronomers in North America.

http://www.acm.org Association of Computing Machines (ACM). The ACM was founded in 1947, only one year after ENIAC, the first digital computer, was created. The association is segmented into various Special Interest Groups, or SIGs. Digital imaging falls under the jurisdiction of the graphics group, SIGGRAPH.

http://www.imaging.org The Society for Imaging Science & Technology (IS&T). With over 2000 members worldwide, this organization's charter is to promote the understanding and application of imaging science and technology.

http://www.iso.ch International Organization for Standardization (ISO). This is a very large worldwide organization that sets standards for just about anything imaginable, including digital imagery.

http://www.smpte.org Society of Motion Picture & Television Engineers (SMPTE). This organization governs the technical aspects of the motion picture and television industry, and has more than 8500 members worldwide.

http://www.spie.org The International Society of Optical Engineering (SPIE). This organization strives for the advancement and application of optics, photonics, imaging, and electronics. There are many diverse groups within SPIE; many specialized conferences are held every year under their sponsorship.

http://www.tisco.com/3d-web/nsa/nsa.htm The National Stereoscopic Association (NSA). The charter of this organization is to study and promote 3D photography — past, present, and future.

Education

The computer science departments of many universities are good locations to look for image processing software and results of the latest research. In addition, larger universities conduct research for government organizations or themilitary and often publish those results on the Web.

http://alcom.kent.edu/ALCOM/ALCOM.html Kent State University is the home of the Liquid Crystal Institute. The Advanced Liquid Crystalline Optical Materials group (ALCOM) conducts basic research that leads to innovations in LCDs for computers.

http://is.arc.umn.edu/html/research The University of Minnesota conducts basic research in mathematics, engineering, and other sciences at the U.S. Army High Performance Computing Research Center (AHPCRC), and produces visualization images of their results.

http://bima.astro.umd.edu The Berkeley Illinois Maryland Association (BIMA) is a three-university consortium for astronomy applications. There are images from radio, millimeter, and visible wavelengths.

http://www.cis.ohio-state.edu The Ohio State University's Computer and Information Sciences Department has online research projects in many subjects related to digital imagery.

http://www.cs.cmu.edu The Computer Science department of the Carnegie-Mellon University has many research projects concerned with machine vision and related image processing.

http://www-video.eecs.berkeley.edu This is the University of California, Berkeley, laboratory for video and image processing.

http://www.eecs.wsu.edu The School of Electrical Engineering and Computer Science at Washington State University is developing image database technology.

http://www.lib.utexas.edu/Libs/PCL/Map_collection/Map_collection.hmtl This online library of the University of Texas contains a collection of scanned maps of virtually every location in the world.

http://sol.med.jhu.edu The Kennedy Krieger Institute in Baltimore, Md., provides a free software package called BrainImage that allows manipulation of 3D image data sets of human brains.

http://www.seds.org Students for the Exploration and Development of Space (SEDS) is a student-based organization that promotes interest is space. There are links to several chapters but the University of Arizona (*http://seds.lpl.arizona.edu*) is a primary site for images of planetary and deep-space objects.

http://www.stsci.edu The Space Telescope Electronic Information Service (STScI) is responsible for the scientific operations of the Hubble Space Telescope (HST). STScI is operated by the Associated Universities for Research in Astronomy (AURA) under contract to NASA and is located on the campus of the Johns Hopkins University in Baltimore, Md. The archives of the HST are available in a range of resolutions.

http://www.tns.lcs.mit.edu This is the Massachusetts Institute of Technology's Laboratory for Computer Science Telemedia, Networks, and Systems Group.

Commercial

The Internet is becoming a direct marketing channel for companies of all kinds. Most digital imaging equipment and software companies have sites on the Web where their products can be browsed (and often demonstrated) without the pressure of a salesperson looking over one's shoulder. Due to obvious constraints, every commercial site related to digital imagery cannot be listed here. I have tried to provide a representative sampling of what is available, but for every site listed below there are hundreds of others that deserve a visit.

http://www.cais.net/arms There are numerous stock photography libraries available on the net, offering just about any type of scenes imaginable. This is a representative example of one such site.

http://www.crd.ge.com The General Electric Corporate Research and Development center investigates many fields, including medical imagery. For an interesting and informative look at the Visible Human Project, go to *http://www.crd.ge.com/esl/cgsp/projects/vm/index.html*.

http://www.disney.com This is Disney's home page. The company offers a full array of its products, including sample images of some favorite movies and programs.

http://www.itd.sterling.com/macs Sterling Software is diversified into many fields. The ITD group generates digital mapping applications, such as the Mapping Application Client Server (MACS) for mission planning and other military uses.

http://www.ingr.com Intergraph has long supplied high-end systems solutions. Their Optronics division also produces scanners, printers, typesetting equipment, and controlling software for the publishing industry.

http://www.kodak.com Eastman Kodak Copmany's home page. Kodak is a primary supplier of cameras, scanners, recorders, CCD chips, processing software, and systems for digital image processing. In addition to telling you just about everything you would want to know about their products, they also provide an extensive library of sample digital images. This is an interesting site that deserves investigation.

http://www.mediacy.com Media Cybernetics is a relatively mature company providing software packages for image processing. Their latest offerings are fully described on the Internet.

http://www.mgi.com Management Graphics, Inc. manufactures CRT film recorders. They sell and support their products worldwide and are the undisputed leaders in this field.

http://www.mteklab.com Microtek is a company that manufactures scanners of all sorts. Their low-priced but good-quality products include flatbed and document scanners that operate on color or grayscale materials. They also provide controlling software that runs on most computer platforms.

http://www.photomet.com Photometrics, Ltd., manufactures CCD cameras that are used in a variety of scientific and commercial applications. The Web site offers examples of digital images scanned with their cameras.

http://www.smartworld.com/imagekit/imagekit.html ImageKit is a digital stock photography library offered by Digital Artists. It is reasonably priced and offers a wide variety of high-quality scenes.

http://www.spot.com SPOT is the French satellite company owned by Centre National d'Etudes Spatiales (CNES). In ten years SPOT has accumulated more that 4 million images of the Earth in its archives. If you are looking for an image of a point on the Earth and SPOT doesn't have it, it probably doesn't exist. And if it doesn't exist, SPOT will reposition one of its satellites and get it for you.

http://www.ssesco.com SSESCO provides software for 3D visualization and for integration of imagery and graphics.

http://www.tek.com Tektronics is a large, diversified company that produces high-quality electronic equipment. For the image processing marketplace they offers printers, X terminals, video equipment, stereoscopic monitors, and a range of other devices.

Index

Illustrations are indicated in **boldface**.

ABOUT THE AUTHOR

Howard E. Burdick has been a software engineer for two decades, and has specialized in digital imagery for the past fifteen years. Widely considered one of the world's leading experts—as well as a pioneer in the field—he is currently employed by Dream Quest Images, an Academy and Emmy Award-winning full-service visual effects company. Brought in to build Dream Quest's digital imaging facility, he has been involved in numerous high-visibility feature film, television, and theme park projects. Previously, he worked with Texas Instruments developing imaging radar software and magnetic anomaly detection systems for naval aircraft. Burdick is a founding engineer of Visual Information Technologies, a company producing chips, hardware, and software for high-speed digital image processing. His background also includes stints with NCR and Harris Corporation.